WE CAN'T RUN AWAY FROM THIS

DAMIAN HALL

Vertebrate Publishing, Sheffield
www.adventurebooks.com

WE CAN'T RUN AWAY FROM THIS

DAMIAN HALL

First published in 2022 by Vertebrate Publishing.

 Vertebrate Publishing
Omega Court, 352 Cemetery Road, Sheffield S11 8FT, United Kingdom.
www.adventurebooks.com

A CIP catalogue record for this book is available from the British Library.

ISBN: 978-1-83981-116-6 (Paperback)
ISBN: 978-1-83981-117-3 (Ebook)
ISBN: 978-1-83981-118-0 (Audiobook)

10 9 8 7 6 5 4 3 2 1

Layout and production by Rosie Edwards, Vertebrate Publishing.
www.adventurebooks.com

Vertebrate Publishing is committed to printing on paper from sustainable sources.

 This book has completed Our Carbon's carbon accounting process in line with the GHG Protocol and ISO 14064:1, the globally recognised standard for carbon accounting. The final emissions total includes scopes 1, 2 and 3 covering the writing, production and distribution of this book. These calculated emissions have been offset to account for this book's carbon impact. For an emissions breakdown, please see *https://profile.ourcarbon.com/wcraft*

Printed and bound in Great Britain by Clays Ltd., Elcograf S.p.A.

CONTENTS

A note from the author v

Foreword by Kilian Jornet vii

1 How bad is running? 1

2 Shoespiracy 16

3 Getting T-shirty 32

4 Industry illusions 58

5 Racing away from net zero 88

6 Great training? 112

7 The planet-based diet 132

8 Fossil fuelling 149

9 Well stuffed 163

10 Little bit activism 173

11 How good is running! 191

Acknowledgements 201

Resources 202

References 207

About the author 215

For details about the carbon accounting process and the carbon impact of this book, see www.adventurebooks.com/WCRAFT-carbon

For Indy and Leif. We tried.

A NOTE FROM THE AUTHOR

In the interest of the full transparency we should expect from companies, the following brands have supported my running in some form (in most cases just product), or I'm an ambassador for them, for some of the time I was researching and writing this book. (And for all long-term agreements, with the exception of those clearly doing their bit already, we've had discussions about improving actions towards greater sustainability.[1])

33Fuel
Garmin
inov-8
Leki
Our Carbon
Outdoor Provisions
Petzl
PHD Designs
Precision Fuel & Hydration
Sungod
Supernatural Fuel
Supersapiens
Trees Not Tees (who my wife works for too)

---

1   Leading to the discontinuation of some relationships, hee hee.

FOREWORD BY KILIAN JORNET

Damian Hall is one of the runners I admire the most. Not only because of all his trail-running achievements – which are pretty cool – but because he stands up for his values. And this is something on everyone's lips when we ask them, but it's often bullshit. Not for Damian. He is one of the runners to have looked most deeply into his environmental footprint to start with, then the footprint of the outdoors sector, and then decided to do something real about it. And this is a lot. It's huge. That's why Damian is a running hero, because he cares and he does.

Since I began running in the mountains a couple of decades ago, I've seen how the trails and mountains I often go to are changing. Glaciers are melting faster than ever, ecosystems are moving to escape warmer temperatures, water is running out in the warmest countries and extreme weather situations are becoming more common. Today, we all know that climate change is real, and that it will lead us to our probable extinction if we don't change some things. Because the planet – the rocks and all this stuff – will do fine without us and some other animals and species on its surface; but as for us, we need the natural resources and biodiversity to exist.

Runners like myself often think that because we run in the outdoors we have a special relation with earth and nature, and that we're more aware of the problems that we're facing, but unfortunately that awareness isn't really that great when we dig deep, and it isn't doing much to solve the issues.

But people like Damian are showing all of us, with actions and wisdom, how we can better understand the complexity of climate change and other environmental problems, and how to go one step further by thinking about what we can do, as runners, to help.

This book is about all this, and Damian is doing excellent work in explaining the different angles, from the industry, our equipment, the races and events we take part in, and how we can influence and be proactive about the systemic changes that are needed. Because miracles don't exist in the real world. As athletes, we know that if we don't train well in the months and weeks prior to an event, during that race we will not perform well; there's only one thing we can do and that is to start training – slower or faster, we have to start. So, if we want to keep running in the mountains, if we want our kids to enjoy the outdoors and, in the end, if we care about the destiny of humans, we shouldn't wait for others to make things happen, but accept that we are part of the problem and understand that we are also part of the solution. And with what Damian has written in this book, we're much closer to seeing where the problems come from and what we can do.

1

HOW BAD IS RUNNING?

The thing we love doing is surprisingly shit for the planet

'Sports such as athletics that are inherently harmless
cause major environmental effects.'
George Monbiot

Stop! Please, for your own sake, put this book down right now. There's a very good chance you'll regret reading it – and not just due to the imminent, criminally bad jokes. You see, you'll probably never think of your running in the same way again.

This book's got some properly depressing stuff in it. There are some productive, positive and hopeful bits as well. But climate change is a right dick. It's really ruining things. Even for us runners. And I was distraught to discover **we are very much part of the problem**.

The issue with climate change is that it can lead to some heated debates. We haven't found a solution to the situation yet, but we're getting warmer. You can't beat a bit of climate-change bantz, eh? Even the Greenland ice sheets are cracking up at that. Sorry (#notsorry). I'll leave apocalyptic mirth for now. But frankly, with this stuff, we need all the frivolity we can get.

You'd think, wouldn't you, that running is a fairly harmless activity environmentally? I mean, sure, it hurts my muscles, tendons and – worst of all – my ego, sometimes. But on the surface, it seems endearingly simple, natural, and indeed it's often done in nature. All we need is a pair of daps (also known as running shoes or trainers), right? In terms of activities that have little impact on the planet, you'd be forgiven for thinking running would be right up there, perhaps even the least environmentally harmful thing we can do. Numerous footprints taken, but with a minuscule carbon footprint, surely? But what if our jogging in beautiful places (and unbeautiful places too, for that matter) was paradoxically contributing to the destruction of those special places? You can probably tell where this is going …

I have some really bad news. My own climate anxiety made me look into this and … **running is surprisingly shit for the planet**.

Anyone who's done a mass-participation road race will remember a sea of discarded plastic cups, plastic bottles and plastic gel wrappers in our wake, plus all those free (plastic) T-shirts in a drawer unused. The global trainer industry creates as much carbon dioxide and equivalent greenhouse gas emissions (CO_2e) as the entire United Kingdom (and, er, some of us have a lot of pairs). Our clothing is *even worse*. Runners tend to consume more animal protein than non-runners, which comes from the second most destructive industry on the planet. It all adds up to a horrifying footprint, and I haven't even mentioned running's biggest negative impact yet.

'From casual joggers to elite athletes, running is the most participated sport in the world,' says climate-change researcher Sean Ross, via @sustainablerunning. 'The benefits of running are well known; however, the environmental impact of the sport is something most people don't think about. From buying a new pair of trainers, travelling for a race or upgrading your running watch, you may be living a healthy life, but you may also be damaging future lives.'

Honestly. You've been warned. Put this book down while you still can.

That said, in amongst all of this, I found some caffeine gels of hope, some rehydrating glugs of inspiration, some easy and genuinely performance-enhancing things we runners can do, towards a fitter planet – though they aren't always the most obvious things.

Plus, you'll be thrilled to know, I found some brill/bad climate-change jokes, which are recycled throughout this book. Please humour me. The feeble mirth and writing this book (and chucking a few cheesy quotes in) are how I'm coping with eco anxiety. Oh, and incessantly retweeting doom-mongering *Guardian* articles …

Who the effing hell am I?

I'm not an expert on any of this. I don't have a science background or even, for most of my life, much enthusiasm for it (I was very much a daydreamy/stoned arts student). But I do now. I'm a forty-six-year-old father of two, a recovering journalist, a midlife-crisis ultramarathon runner, and an accidental climate activist. I got obsessed with running, and more recently I got obsessed with our climate and ecological emergency.

I've done another book about my passion for long-distance bimbles, the award-dodging *In It for the Long Run* (possibly the world's first carbon-negative book, thanks to the wonderful and clever Vertebrate Publishing). But if you've wisely avoided that, just briefly, I ran my first marathon aged thirty-six, dressed as a toilet (and, yes, I did look a bit flushed), and loved it so much – or, more specifically, the realisation this stuff could be done on trails, hills and even bigger lumps and for much longer distances – that I got a bit carried away. I was soon running 100-mile races, completing things like the Spine Race and Dragon's Back Race, flying around Europe to do big mountain races such as Ultra-Trail du Mont-Blanc, getting selected for the GB trail-running team and setting records on UK long-distance trails. It's been life-changing. I ruddy loved it. Still do.

I wrote about most of that for magazines, where I would review shoes and kit too. But as I picked up a little sponsorship (and morphed into a running coach), running became my life. I was obsessed and bought every running book going. Since 2019, though, my personal library has changed markedly. The books by Adharanand Finn, Kilian Jornet and Richard Askwith are being edged out by authors named Michael E. Mann, Mike Berners-Lee and Katharine Hayhoe. Climate scientists.

Growing up with parents who bought organic nosh and voted Green, there was a subtle undercurrent of environmentalism. I was always outdoors, climbing trees, camping and hillwalking, but in my teens that was superseded by Radio 1, football and pubs. I wasn't that interested in the plight of bumblebees. As an alleged adult, when I increasingly saw headlines about hungry polar bears, I assumed those clever scientists and sensible government types would sort all that out. Wouldn't they?

And then you realise a few years later that those polar bears are looking hungrier. And they have less ice to live on. And, er, hasn't this been going on for decades now? David Attenborough seems to have been on the telly a lot lately. Did the BBC just say that was another record-breaking month of weather? Why aren't those Swedish kids in school? And, hold on, why has someone parked a big pink boat at Piccadilly Circus with 'Tell The Truth' written on it?

It was like a weird sort of unhappy party was happening and, not for the first time, I hadn't been invited. Sure, I'd heard of climate change, but we've known about that for yonks. Surely people have sorted that out by now. Haven't they?

The penny dropped: they haven't.

'The scientific evidence is unequivocal: climate change is a threat to human wellbeing and planetary health,' said the Intergovernmental Panel on Climate Change (IPCC) in its Sixth Assessment Report in February 2022.

'What we do over the next three to four years I believe is going to determine the future of humanity,' said Professor Sir David King, former UK Chief Scientific Adviser, a year earlier.

'Anyone who doesn't feel some alarm isn't thinking straight,' says Lancaster University professor Mike Berners-Lee, author of *How Bad Are Bananas?*, the bible for carbon footprints.

'Every disaster movie starts with people ignoring a scientist' was my favourite banner at COP26 in November 2021.

The generations who follow us are going to hate us. We're robbing them of the freedoms we had. We had the chance to right things and it looks like we possibly won't. I want to be able to look my children and their children in the eyes and tell them that, honestly, some of us did try. Although not all hope is lost quite yet …

Realising just how urgent all this climate and ecological emergency lark is, **I felt compelled to *do something*. I just didn't know what.**

In 2019, I was inspired by Dan Lawson and Charlotte Jalley and their incredible work with ReRun Clothing – who sounded the alarm in the running world – and also by Clare Gallagher, Rosie Watson, Finlay Wild and other runners doing great things (more anon). Not least visually impaired double Paralympic gold medallist James Brown, who was sentenced to prison for supergluing himself to a plane in protest. I wish I had 10% of his courage. Inspired by them and family members, I joined in Extinction Rebellion (XR) protests in London, which were great fun and empowering, even though I failed miserably to get arrested.

I read a thought-provoking piece by activist and carbon consultant Rosie Watson, who was running from the UK to Mongolia to raise awareness about climate change. 'We need to face the fact that a lot of our outdoor culture is very destructive, and the athlete and adventurer lifestyle is a massive influencer in that.' She spelt out how damaging some athlete behaviours are and how much influence our actions might have, especially through that glossy, glorifying world of social media.[i]

I was impassioned, but confused too. I started making statements on social media, which were sometimes naive and for which naturally I got called a hypocrite – sometimes fairly, sometimes not. I started to think about my own footprint and decided I was going to race internationally, and certainly fly, much less – which led to being interviewed by popular US website iRunFar.com as a de facto environmentalist alongside mountain legend Kilian Jornet. I felt more eco worrier than warrior. It showed me there was a void to fill. We needed climate activists.

I thought I could definitely be a more sustainable or responsible runner, maybe even a low-carbon or carbon-negative athlete? I attempted a winter record run on the Paddy Buckley Round (a 61-mile, 47-peak challenge in Snowdonia) in January 2020 and decided to use public transport to get there and back (which was fine till I fell asleep on the way home and missed my stop), fuel without animal products (easy) or plastic waste (harder), and unfurl an XR flag my children had made me at the finish. The run was a success and catching a bus seemed to be called activism (but then buses do have history with social change).

I was making it up as I went along. 2020 and 2021 were good years for me running-wise, setting three more national records, on the Pennine Way, South Wales Traverse and Wainwright's Coast to Coast. While the Covid pandemic made public transport a more complicated choice, I stuck with the ethical fuelling method – without forgetting that some people have been vegan for decades – and litter-picked or plogged as I ran (technically, my amazing support runners did 90% of that).

Some of the runs gained national coverage, including television, radio and newspapers, and I was always asked about the litter picking – even the *Daily Mail* were interested in that.

I still didn't know whether collecting occasional crisp packets was actually doing any good (which is worse, a crisp packet stuck in a peatbog or landfill for 200 years, or one that's sent to an incinerator where it'll directly add to global heating?), but it was an effective tool for drawing attention to our climate and ecological emergency. The truth was, each run had led to a load of car journeys that might not have happened otherwise – far more emissions created than saved by any crisp-packet collecting. I felt like an imposter. Somewhere along the line I got myself a silly haircut too, a mohawk. If you care about stuff, you need a silly haircut, right?

I still didn't really understand which aspects of my life had bigger or smaller impacts.

I was increasingly being asked questions about sustainability in interviews or directly via social media, by embryonic races and brands who wanted to do better but, like me, didn't know where to start. Some events had banned single-use plastic but were hawking merchandise. Was that okay? How impactful is fuelling without plastic waste or animal products in a race if you fly or drive there? And what about my kit – how bad was that? Are T-shirts made from recycled plastic bottles and shoes made from mushrooms the answer? Indeed, if I truly cared about our climate and ecological emergency, could I even be an ambassador for a brand without being a massive hypocrite?

With Rosie Watson and Andrew Murray (not that one) I was invited to be part of an ad hoc sustainability committee for a race series. What should races' priority be: reducing emissions from participant flights, eliminating plastic waste or implementing vegan food? I had no idea (luckily Rosie and Andrew knew stuff), but I was fascinated. Andrew is a very experienced sustainability professional and runner, and his Running On Carbon blog (*runningoncarbon.wordpress.com*) helped to illuminate which aspects of running do the most damage.

I devoured books by Andrew Brooks, Jen Gale, Dale Vince and Isabel Losada (I haven't quite got round to Bill Gates's yet), listened voraciously to podcasts (see Resources, page 202), did a Carbon Literacy course and talked – and hopefully listened – to anyone who knew anything, including climate-scientist runner pals.

I was making lifestyle changes, but I wanted some kind of external verification. The carbon-auditing company Our Carbon analysed my family's CO_2e footprint and explained which actions are most impactful. We offset what we couldn't realistically reduce further, which at the time felt like a welcome guilt-reliever but now I know more feels less straightforward. It was enlightening to see which aspects of my lifestyle had the biggest impact (more anon) and where the biggest and/or easiest (regrettably not always the same thing) improvements could be made.

It's complicated

What have I learnt? On one hand, it seems simple. From a non-running perspective, three-quarters of an individual's footprint will usually come from energy, food and travel, and the fourth from the other things we buy, our stuff. Thankfully, energy at home is usually a quick fix. Switching from fossil fuels to a renewable energy supplier takes a few minutes and has a big impact.[2] From a runner's perspective, travel, nutrition and stuff – especially our kit – all loom large and are discussed, probably in too much detail, here.

As my knowledge grew, I became frustrated with some of the sustainability myths being repeated, the top-ten lists mixing reducing flights with turning lights off, without any hierarchy or comparative level of impact – when the differences in emissions saved between those actions could be 50-plus tonnes of CO_2e. Indeed, a 2021 study asked participants to rank the nine most impactful actions to combat climate change and recycling was voted number one, when in fact it was the seventh most effective on the list, while the most impactful action was ranked last.[ii] There are elephants and there are mice.

Most people know some actions that will reduce their impact, but perhaps not whether each is a small squeaky thing or something with satellite-dish-sized ears and a massive grey snake for a nose. Regrettably, Boris Johnson was right about one popular climate-friendly action being something of a red herring. We'll also see how *The A-Team*'s Mr T and Benny Hill were eco-warrior pioneers long before Greta Thunberg was even a twinkle in her parents' eyes.

On the other hand, some aspects are frustratingly complicated. I was confused about **shoe companies making a song and dance about using recycled plastic bottles or sugar cane, or a 'recyclable' shoe**. Is that more 'sustainable' or is it adding to the problem? Is a shoe made from plastic that lasts longer better or worse? I knew a little bit about how bad the fast-fashion industry was for the planet, but how much of that applies to our running kit? ReRun Clothing made me aware of running's T-shirt problem, but otherwise how bad for the environment are running races? And if flying is bad, how much flying is ethically okay and what are the lowest-carbon ways to travel? What impact on a runner's personal footprint does giving up meat and dairy have – and is that healthy or even a performance enhancer?

---

2   Mike Berners-Lee endorses Dale Vince's Ecotricity or Good Energy. Though the UK's 2022 energy crisis has complicated things from a consumer perspective and it could be smarter to delay switching till things have calmed.

Then there's a separate debate to be had about how much we should be analysing and adapting our own behaviour when we're so insignificant in the grand scheme of things.

Ultimately, I wanted to find out how much negative impact I had as a runner, how bad Big Running is for the planet, and what, if anything, we can do about 'It' – and what *should* we do about it (not necessarily the same thing).

This book is my three-year journey from being woken (pun intended) up to our climate and ecological emergency, to trying to understand it and learn *what to do*, and now to spreading the word a bit – mostly from a running perspective. What this book isn't is a 'fifty things you can do to solve climate change'-type thing (although it does have loads of tips – too many, actually, got a bit carried away), for reasons that will be explained. There are several really impactful things we can all do. But it also pays to be a part of the bigger picture.

I had casually assumed running was safe from climate change, an innocent, natural hobby (though it's so much more than a hobby for me). But **our climate and ecological emergency affects everything**: what we eat, what we wear, where we run, even how we use Strava. We pretty much can't move for emitting CO2e.

The solutions can be counterintuitive too: sometimes a plastic bag is better for the environment than a paper one, a flight can be better than a car journey, and a car journey can be better than a train trip (clue: it depends on how many people are in the car). Sometimes wrapping food in plastic is better for the planet. That one blew my tiny little mind a bit.

Indeed, there's a split between the tangible stuff, which tends to be more emotive, more satisfying to act on – but often falsely so – and the stuff you can't see, such as those cursed greenhouse gases, which is what's doing the real harm. Putting your recycling out feels good. We're doing our bit. We can't see CO2e and it's so hard to sense you're making a difference. But it's often the stuff we can't see that's the most urgent problem. Making changes without seeing a clear or immediate outcome is harder and takes some faith. Thankfully, some broad principles apply. And not all solutions are to live like mushroom-foraging hermits.

Some of this is specific to running, but most of it applies to real life too. We are, after all, non-runners sometimes, however reluctantly (I'm told my running tights are NOT appropriate for restaurants). A lot of it also applies almost word for word to other outdoor sports and passions, especially hiking, mountaineering, climbing, cycling, triathlon and adventure sports. There'll be no sport on a dead planet.

Though so much of this is depressing and deeply worrying, happily running can show us some ways out of this Big Kerfufflefuck, and in fact trail/fell/ultra running is already leading the way in some regards. There's plenty we can do, on both an individual footprint level and, importantly, a systemic level. Much of it is empowering, rewarding, easier than might be assumed, and it will make us happier too. Happier than my climate change jokes will, anyway.

One phrase that really struck me is: **if we can't be a part of the solution, at least don't be part of the problem**. We can't fix every climate-change issue as individuals. But in some instances we can at least stop contributing to them – which is a helpful mindset for the more headfucky stuff. That said, to me it's no longer enough to *only* avoid being part of the problem …

The gloomy bit

I'll keep this (very) gloomy bit as brief as possible. You wouldn't have picked up this silly little book if you weren't at least half aware, half concerned, about our climate and ecological emergency – and everyone should be. 'Our house is on fire', warned the incredible Greta Thunberg at Davos in 2019. Indeed, scientists agree the Sixth Mass Extinction (defined as losing 75% of the planet's species relatively rapidly) is underway on Earth, in an era labelled the Anthropocene – meaning humans are, for the first time, the primary agents of change on a planetary scale. Ice sheets melting, floods, wildfires, storms called Colin and Cindy, droughts, crop failures and famine, species extinctions, rising sea levels, mass migrations, wars, pandemics.[3] All these things aren't just predictions, they're happening now.

Antarctica was 40 °C hotter than normal the other day. *Forty degrees.* The UK recorded 40 °C too, in July 2022, its hottest ever day, with the government issuing an unprecedented national emergency red alert. The London fire brigade experienced their busiest day since World War Two, with 2,600 callouts and forty-one properties destroyed. The heatwave, say scientists, was made ten times more likely by climate breakdown. Spain, Portugal, Japan and the US have all had record-breaking heat in the last few weeks; 50,000 people have been evacuated from their homes as floods hit Sydney for the third time this year; large glaciers are breaking off, falling and killing people in the Italian Alps. Oh and thousands of birds are dropping dead from the skies, like some Hitchcock horror. And these apocalyptic things are happening because we're sending too many greenhouse gases (ghg) into the atmosphere. We're wilfully drilling holes in our own submarine.

Only a 'now or never' dash to a low-carbon world will hope to stave off the worst

---

3 In 2020, 30.7 million people were internally displaced by disasters, three times more than by conflict and violence. More than 200 million could migrate over the next three decades because of extreme weather events or disappearance of their homelands, predicts The World Bank. Russia's 2022 invasion of Ukraine was labelled 'a fossil fuel war' by Ukraine's leading climate scientist, Svitlana Krakovska. And pandemics? That's just scaremongering, surely …

ravages of climate breakdown, said scientists on the Intergovernmental Panel on Climate Change (IPCC) in April 2022, in 'a final warning for governments'. Ghg emissions must be nearly halved this decade, according to their sixth report, which took seven years to compile, to give the world a chance of limiting future heating to 1.5 °C above pre-industrial levels – the overshooting of which now looks 'almost inevitable'. The financial costs are minimal (less than 0.1% of global GDP) and the chances are now slim, yet the world is failing to make the changes needed. 'Some government and business leaders are saying one thing – but doing another,' said UN Secretary-General António Guterres. 'Simply put, they are lying. And the results will be catastrophic.' We can no longer continue with business as usual, said Thunberg. 'No more blah, blah, blah.'

This isn't a new thing. Agriculture started the problems and the Industrial Revolution was a massive multiplier, the Big Kerfufflefuck being largely driven by the burning of fossil fuels. And we started it. **French physicist Jean-Baptiste-Joseph Fourier discovered the greenhouse effect in 1824** – almost *200 years ago*. It was first reported in a newspaper in 1912, scientists first warned a US president in 1965, and in 1977 scientist James Black told his employer Exxon (now ExxonMobil) the same thing. The planet is warming with dangerous, destabilising speed, due to man-made emissions.

Despite these warnings and, at the time of writing, *twenty-six* United Nations Conferences of the Parties (COPs), the world has continued regardless, flagrantly ignoring the science, ignoring pleas from scientists and activists, ignoring those in the Global South already suffering catastrophic crop failures, droughts, floods and rising sea levels.

Like Big Tobacco before them, fossil-fuel behemoths, right-wing plutocrats and petrostates have waged a thirty-year disinformation war, which has delayed things considerably, writes Professor Michael E. Mann in *The New Climate War*. We know what's at stake and, largely, what we have to do. Yet almost all major governments and corporations aren't acting quickly enough.[4] The global average temperature is about 1.2 °C hotter than pre-industrial levels and at the current rate of warming, the world will become 1.5 °C warmer within the next five years. We have a 6–10% chance of stalling that rise, and are heading for somewhere between 2.7 and 3.2 °C by the end of this century, which would have numerous devastating and irreversible consequences.[5] If you google them, you won't sleep tonight.

4   Even if all the policies to cut carbon that governments had put in place by the end of 2020 were fully implemented, the world will still warm by 3.2 °C this century.
5   That's the global average, so many places would be far hotter. At 2.5 °C, which is predicted for about 2070, 19% of the planet will be as hot as the Sahara, affecting 3.5 billion people.

We need to get off fossil fuels with an urgency that's beyond, well, urgent, to reduce global emissions by 45% THIS DECADE.

The way we produce food also needs some serious rethinking and most issues boil down to a simple practice: overconsumption. But political will is shamefully lacking. In fact, the UK currently has over forty new fossil-fuel projects in the pipeline and has given the industry £13.6 billion since the Paris agreement in 2015 – even though renewable energies are now cheaper, infinite and quicker to establish and use. Indeed, April 2022's IPCC report stated that the only real obstacles are politics and fossil-fuel interests. Big Oil staffers have been both authors and editors of IPCC reports and unsurprisingly there are plenty of signs of influence at Westminster, with even the current chancellor, Nadhim Zahawi, earning £1.3 million from his second job in the oil industry. In April 2022 scientists said we must get off fossil fuels right away and António Guterres said it's 'moral and economic madness' to fund new projects, adding that campaigners may be regarded as radicals, but the 'truly dangerous radicals' are those countries increasing fossil-fuel production.

Anyhoo, that's probably enough doom and gloom for now. The short version is, things are really bad and urgent, but we have a slim chance of reining in the damage, *if we act NOW*. It's like we're in the last three or four miles of a marathon and this is where we really needed to speed up significantly to grab that PB. But instead, we've bonked badly, we've slowed right down and feel like we're about to puke (or worse). That PB is just about mathematically still possible, but we'll need to run faster than ever and it doesn't look like we realise or even care.

I feel compelled to insert a cheesy but rousing quote about now, if only to try and cheer myself up a little (it's either that or another joke) and here it is: 'He who accepts evil without protesting against it is really cooperating with it,' said Martin Luther King Jr. And he knew stuff.

How climate change is affecting running

What has all of that got to do with running? A surprising amount. The New York City Marathon used to be run in September but now takes place in November, because the earlier month is too hot. (The 2007 Chicago Marathon took place in 31 °C and saw 250 hospitalisations.)

Due to concerns about extreme heat, the 2020 Tokyo Olympics marathon was moved 500 miles north of the Games' host city, to Sapporo. It was the hottest Games ever, with many athletes complaining, suffering bad performances, needing extra medical timeouts and leaving venues in wheelchairs due to heat exhaustion. A study in the scientific journal *The Lancet* prompted speculation that 'climate change might spell the heat death of the Summer Olympics as we currently know them'.[iii] Plus climate change is literally slowing us down,[6] according to a study of 30,000 marathons.[iv] The 2022 Winter Olympics in Beijing was the first Winter Games without any snow. And ironically all the extra energy burnt – and more than 222 million litres of water – to create artificial white stuff added to planet-warming ghg, which in turn reduces the planet's snow yet further. Experts say that rising temperatures threaten the future of the Winter Olympics, with only one of twenty-one former hosts able to host in the future if ghg emissions remain on their current trajectory.[v]

In December 2021 I was en route to an ultramarathon called the Cheviot Goat when I received an SMS message to say it was cancelled because a recent, named storm had caused significant infrastructure damage in Northumberland. In May 2021, twenty-one runners died in a Chinese mountain race, due to a dramatic change in weather, from sunny to freezing temperatures and gale-force winds.[7] Changes in weather and climate have forced disruption to many sports. The competitive ski season has been shortened due to rising temperatures. Australian Open tennis matches have been suspended due to extreme heat, while a football referee made several bad, game-changing, decisions in the 2022 African Cup of Nations, later blaming severe heatstroke. 2019 Rugby World Cup matches were postponed due to a typhoon. There have been calls for popular mountains such as the Matterhorn and Mont Blanc to be closed to mountaineers as warmer conditions make climbing increasingly less safe.

Pollution has stopped play at Indian cricket matches. Indeed, air pollution is the third major factor affecting runners, who naturally breathe in deeply as they run, with mouth-breathing bypassing nasal filters which reduce pollution intake.[8] Londoners were warned to avoid strenuous physical activity on 14 January 2022 due to 'very high' levels of pollution, in a city with over 1,700 asthma hospitalisations due to toxic air between 2017 and 2019. In fact, virtually every home in the UK is subjected to air pollution above World Health Organization guidelines and it was

6 The average runner adds a minute and twenty-five seconds to their marathon finish time for every additional degree Fahrenheit.

7 We can't say with absolute scientific certainty that climate change caused these incidents. However, August 2021's IPCC report said there's 'high confidence' that global increases in extreme weather are linked to human influence. In the UK, warm spells have doubled in length in the last fifty years, according to the Met Office, who forecast an increase in hot days (above 25 °C) for the UK but also 'high-impact rainfall', flooding and warmer, wetter winters.

8 Someone running a marathon inhales the same amount of oxygen as a person would sitting down for two days. It did briefly occur to me that runners may be contributing more CO_2 to the atmosphere than most, what with all that heavy panting. But I looked that up and it doesn't work that way, thankfully. We're in the clear.

responsible for 8.7 million deaths globally in 2018 – one in five of all people who died that year.[vi] The 'invisible killer', caused by the burning of fossil fuels such as coal and oil, is also linked to mental health issues. It's detrimental to running performance too, with up to 11% less oxygen taken in, and at high levels even muscular coordination and perception of time can be impeded.

Many of us run to be in nature. But biodiversity is disappearing rapidly. **We've cut down 3 trillion trees, half the world's total. One million animal and plant species are now threatened with extinction, while global populations of mammals, birds, fish, amphibians and reptiles plunged by 68% between 1970 and 2016.** We've lost 75% of our insects in the last twenty-five years – an insect apocalypse (remember when windscreens used to be splattered with them on summer car journeys?). Insects are food for birds; they pollinate 80% of our trees, 75% of our flowers, 30% of global food crops – the Chinese hand-pollinate crops now because of the decline.

The UK is one of the world's most nature-depleted countries, in the bottom 10% globally and last among G7 nations, with about half of its biodiversity left. No wonder I see so little wildlife when I run in the Brecon Beacons, Lake District, Yorkshire Dales or Scottish Highlands. There are almost no trees or animals. My two children have never seen a hedgehog or a badger in the wild. 'Climate change will decrease access to trails' was one of three conclusions in 'Hot Trail Summer: The Impact of a Warming Climate on Climbing and Trail Sports', a 2022 report by Protect Our Winters. It also warns, 'Climate change will threaten the health and well-being of those who recreate outdoors' and 'Climate change will diminish the experience of getting outdoors'. Cheery stuff, huh?

Climate change is changing running, for the worse. We can see it in extreme weather patterns, extreme heat, air pollution and the biodiversity crisis. And sadly, as we'll see, running is part of the problem. Indeed, outdoor sportspeople may have a 40% greater carbon footprint than practioners of other sports, found a study.[vii]

Some jargon

Climate change has its own language. I knew carbon wasn't a good thing (unless it's in a shoe, apparently), but otherwise it was all new to me. But there are a few key terms to get up to speed on.

CO_2e I found science dull at school, but now I know CO_2 means carbon dioxide, which seems to be in almost everything, but especially fossil fuels, and there's way too much of it in the atmosphere (417.14 parts per million), which is artificially warming the planet. There's much more CO_2 than other gases, but as there are other gases too (which are often staggeringly more potent – such as methane and nitrous oxide), these tend to get called CO_2e (e stands for equivalent greenhouse gases). Or I might just say greenhouses gases, which I've shortened to ghg. Occasionally I might refer to just CO_2 or carbon.

'Good/Bad for the planet' This is a lazy phrase that gets used a lot, including by, er, me. It's incorrect because the scientific consensus seems to be that if the climate continues to heat, our lives will be fucked, but actually the planet will be just fine in time – and likely even more fine without us on it. So really the phrase should be 'good/bad for human existence as we know it on this planet' or perhaps 'a liveable planet'. But that's not as neat, so I've been a bit lazy/convenient with that one. Sorry.

Sustainability Ooof! A toughie. The word has been bandied around so often in the outdoor industry and other places, slapped on so many products and claims, that it's lost its original meaning. So what's the right word? 'Eco-friendly'? Hmmm, also sounds like greenwash (see below). Patagonia prefer 'responsible'. 'Resilience' is the word preferred by Zoë Rom, environmental journalist and editor in chief of America's *Trail Runner* magazine.[9] Some like 'regenerative' (leaving things better off than they were). Others like 'ethical'. I quite like that one. The word we're looking for is currently elusive, so 'sustainable' does slip into the copy here and there, even if it no longer feels quite right.

Greenwash Appearing to be ethical is big business. According to Greenpeace, greenwashing is 'a PR tactic used to make a company or product appear environmentally friendly, without meaningfully reducing its environmental impact'. This happens a lot. It's bad. Because it can make us think that we, and a brand, are doing our bit, when that's not happening. It's manipulative, cashing in and, frankly, in these desperate circumstances, immoral. Generally speaking, lots of finger-pointing may not be helpful. But when it's greenwashing, that's just fine! Point, point, point.

Carbon labelling The simple but ace idea that products have a carbon score, so we know the environmental cost. A few food and shoe brands have started doing this, albeit without independent verification so far.

Life-Cycle Analysis/Assessment (LCA) A study to understand the entire impact of a product, from raw materials to the post-user, 'end of life' phase.

Scopes 1, 2 and 3 When a company footprint is measured, it's split into three areas. Scope 1 is direct ghg emissions from sources owned or controlled by a company, such as offices or vehicles. Scope 2 is emissions from purchased electricity, heat and steam. Scope 3 is the more problematic and often largest – all other

---

9 'Resilience' as in the ability of our human and non-human systems to withstand changes in the climate.

indirect emissions, often from sources not owned or controlled by the company, such as supplier or customer activities.

Net zero   Reaching a state where a company, country or individual is no longer emitting ghg into the atmosphere. For a fuller understanding from a company perspective, I'm told Science Based Targets' Net-Zero Standard is the place to look (*sciencebasedtargets.org*).

Carbon neutral/negative   This usually means some carbon offsetting is involved (a bit more to be carbon negative) and should be seen as an unsatisfactory, halfway measure en route to net zero.

B Corp   A scheme similar to Fairtrade, meaning a company is legally required to consider the impact of their decisions on their workers, customers, suppliers, community and the environment. Science Based Targets, the Higg Index and the UN's Sustainable Development Goals are certifications that offer external audits, but they're all a bit different.

Recycling/Downcycling/Upcycling   Recycling is another term that's been overused and abused. Often products such as shoes and clothes aren't actually recycled into the same product again, but rather downcycled into basketball courts or mattress stuffing – lower-value items. Upcycling is genuinely improving a product and is more likely undertaken by creative individuals, making a new garment out of unwanted materials, for example.

Circular economy/Circularity/Closed loop   A concept much talked about in the clothing industry: the idea of genuinely recyclable apparel. Much talked about. Still mostly a fantasy.

Kerfufflefuck   A word I made up. Good, innit?

Sponbassadencers   And that one. I'll explain!

Climate-emergency hypocrite   Something I call myself. Almost everything we do creates emissions, from our food and clothing to checking our phones. Even if we want all those things to be CO_2e-free, they're not yet, so are we meant to stay quiet until that day, if it ever comes? Things are too urgent. We can't avoid being hypocrites on a minor level. Jonathan Pie said we're either hypocrites or arseholes. Let's embrace that word. Let's be hypocrites rather than arseholes.

The real costs

It's worth having an understanding of the CO_2e costs of a few items as a barometer. For example, in the UK the average person emits 13 tonnes of CO_2e a year; an American emits 21 tonnes a year, a Malawian 0.2 tonnes. These figures come from

Mike Berners-Lee's *How Bad Are Bananas? The Carbon Footprint of Everything*, which I refer to throughout this book (he's also the brother of Tim, inventor of a long-forgotten thing called the internet). Berners-Lee, himself a runner, advocates a 5-tonne lifestyle (5 tonnes of CO_2e per person per year) as 'appropriate and both possible and necessary'.

- A return flight from London to Hong Kong is 4.5 tonnes of CO_2e.
- A return (small, petrol) car journey from London to Glasgow is 237 kilograms of CO_2e.
- A UK steak is 5.8 kilograms of CO_2e, a banana is (thankfully) just 110 grams, while an email can be anything from 0.3 grams up to 17 grams.
- This paperback book you're holding is about 2.48 kilograms of CO_2e.
- A pint of dairy milk costs around 1 kilogram of CO_2e.

Lastly, I've planted a little treat at the end of each chapter, a reward for both the depressing information and the torturous writing. Aren't I good to you? However, the following isn't a joke or even an out-take from *Don't Look Up*.

The word 'cake' was mentioned ten times as often as 'climate change' on UK TV programmes in 2020. 'Scotch egg' received double the mentions of 'biodiversity'; while 'banana bread' beat 'wind power' and 'solar power' put together. Which is a bit disappointing. Cake is good, though.

2

SHOESPIRACY

How bad are our daps?

'Every point of shoe production is an environmental crisis.'
Tansy E. Hoskins

All you need to be a runner is a pair of trainers, right? So let's start there. Hello. My name is Damian and I have twenty-five pairs of daps, also known as trainers, running shoes, kicks, pumps or sneakers. I guess to most non-runners – and, um, maybe most runners – that sounds excessive. But what some struggle to understand is just how many pairs of shoes a person with a midlife-crisis running problem needs.

We need a pair for running on roads, obvs. And we need faster 'flats' for *racing* on roads. We need a pair for trails. We need a hybrid pair for runs which include tarmac *and* trails. A pair for the fells/mountains/rocky terrain (which might need more than one shoe). A pair for long distances on trails (extra comfort, you see). A pair for long distances on fells/mountains/rocky terrain. And roads. We might need another pair of each for shorter races on those terrains. Definitely a pair for winter/mud. Perhaps for snow/ice. A minimal pair, for our connected-to-nature, mindfulness runs. A maximalist pair, for 100-milers. A zero-drop pair, cos Achilles injuries are cool.[10] We'll probably need a waterproof pair. A pair for dossing about in at weekends. A pair for hiking. And what if one day we might go orienteering, or obstacle racing, or do a swimrun? And, look, there's a new version of the trail shoe we bought eighteen months ago but with much acer colours and something tantalisingly newfandangled, called Natural-Hyper-Flex-Carbon-Traction 360. And another brand has brought out something very similar. I wonder which is better? And a friend is raving about the new Super-Speedy-Spidey-Sense X. Plus have you heard about those new 'recovery shoes' (what now?) and the eye-wateringly expensive supershoes with a carbon plate that'll make me as fast as Eliud Kipchoge?

I'm exaggerating. But only a tad. That used to be my mindset. A combination of an insatiable search for The One shoe that would turn me into Kilian Jornet, but also, bad, old-fashioned, naked consumer lust. I wanted All The Shoes.

10 Just kidding. I wear zero drop much of the time.

I'm more informed, conscientious and controlled now. But I still really like running shoes. I like owning and wearing them. I rarely wear anything else. I'm a runner. Daps are my identity.

Until fairly recently, I'd given no thought to what role my running shoes and other kit play in our climate and ecological emergency. So, how damaging are our daps? You sure you want to know?

They're bad. Trainers leave an oversized, er, footprint on the planet.

Horrifying headlines

While we've been polishing our hummus pots for recycling, one hyper-capitalist industry has been allowed to run amok like a fox in a chicken coop. When I started looking into all this stuff, alongside the villainous behaviour of Big Oil (who incidentally make profits of $3 billion a day), what shocked me the most was the actions of the clothing industry. There's so much to take in, I'll try to stick to the headlines …

The clothing and footwear industry is commonly reported to account for up to 10% of global emissions. Its impact is thought to be greater than the aviation and shipping industries combined, and it is considered to be the world's second-largest polluter after Big Oil. That's horrifying. As someone with a greedy collection of daps and drawers full of running clobber, and as an ambassador for a sports brand, that news spiralled me into a gloomy, self-questioning place.

However, while apparel does huge amounts of harm in more ways than I'd even imagined, its CO2e emissions aren't quite that bad. The research by the Ellen MacArthur Foundation which led to these headline-grabbing figures has since been discredited, even if it's still widely reported.[i] 'In general, there is a lack of reputable numbers [for the apparel industry's impact],' says EthicalConsumer.org, a resource endorsed by Mike Berners-Lee, 'but 10% does seem too high.'

Still, according to a 2019 UK government paper, 'Fixing Fashion', the clothing industry has an annual carbon footprint close to that of all twenty-eight EU states (at that point) combined – at 3.3 billion tonnes of CO2e.[ii] The industry also uses *1.5 trillion gallons of water* annually and creates 20% of all the world's waste water and pollution, *5% of all the world's waste*.

Where do shoes fit in amongst all that? Footwear in general has been estimated to be responsible for 1.4% of global CO2e. **As for running shoes, if the trainer industry were a country, it would be the seventeenth-largest polluter in the world.**[iii] That's more than Italy or France and coincidentally about the same as the UK. I might just say that out loud to myself again: **the trainer industry creates as much CO2e as the whole of the UK.** It took me a while to lift my jaw off the floor after learning that one.

Much of the following research and studies concerns the horrifying impact of Fast Fashion, and while a lot of the malpractices apply across the board, Patagonia for example shouldn't always be tarred with the same brush as Boohoo. If those inaccurate 10% headlines have focused attention on the industry, caused some shock, accelerated improvements and raised awareness among consumers, it still feels like a good thing. There's no denying that the clothing industry is taking a wrecking ball to the planet. We may have been tut-tutting at the white fume trails in the skies near airports, but all along, the things on our feet and the things that soak up sweat from our armpits might be bigger problems for the planet. But let's jog back down that hill a little bit …

Some history

The sports footwear industry may date back to sixteenth-century England and rotund, son-wanting King Henry VIII, who also wanted something light and flexible to play tennis in. Later, the black smoke from Britain's Industrial Revolution (around 1760–1900) powered the globalisation of capitalism, and shoes and textiles were two of the first truly global products.

Leather sports shoes gave way to rubber and the development of the plimsoll, also called felonies, brothel creepers or sneakers (because you could sneak around in them) in the US. Germany's Adolf Dassler (later Adi, when his first name became less, er, popular), the founder of adidas, began making shoes in 1920, and would later provide those worn by Jesse Owens at the 1936 Berlin Olympics; while Adi's brother Rudolf, after a feud, founded Puma in 1948. New Balance entered the scene in the 1960s and the international jogging boom of the 1970s triggered a running-shoe explosion, with adidas, Nike, Brooks and Tiger soon producing them too.

Sports footwear is epic business nowadays. America's Nike is ranked the thirteenth most well-known brand – and the biggest apparel brand – in the world. With revenues of $39.1 billion, it hoovers up 27% of the sportswear market. The next biggest brand, Germany's adidas, has a turnover of $22 billion, while Puma, New Balance and Asics are all around the $3- to $4-billion bracket. In 2020 the global sports footwear market revenue was $90 billion and is forecast to reach $102 billion by 2025. That's more than Costa Rica.

In 2018, 66.3 million pairs of shoes (all types) were produced worldwide *every single day*. That's 24.2 billion pairs a year – enough to go around the world 300 times. In sports footwear, Nike sell over 780 million pairs a year and adidas sell over 400 million. Most are made entirely of plastic. Almost none are recyclable.

We just love trainers. Brits are the third-biggest global consumers of sports shoes (after the US and China) and a recent study found that UK teenagers had an average of six pairs each, which is a total of 58 million pairs.[iv] Those 58 million pairs cost the planet 409 million kilograms of CO_2e, the equivalent of circumnavigating the globe in a medium-sized car almost 50,000 times. Oh, and 30% of them – 19 million pairs – hadn't been worn in the last three months. And that's just the teenagers. Those aged twenty-five to thirty-four own *nine pairs each*. If the number of trainers owned in Britain was halved, it would be the equivalent to taking 73,000 cars off the road for a year.

How many pairs of trainers does the average runner own? Shamefully for me and my twenty-five-strong collection (I can explain!), a self-conducted semi-scientific straw poll of fifty committed runners, who've been running for several years and enjoy off-road as well as pavement pounding, suggested an average of eight pairs. Imelda Marcos's legendary collection of 2,700 pairs of shoes, since you ask, had a footprint of around 30 tonnes of CO_2e.

Running costs

A typical pair of running shoes creates between 8 and 16 kilograms of CO_2e over its lifetime. While a pair of jeans by comparison is 32 kilograms, experts say trainers have an unusually high carbon footprint for a product that doesn't use electricity. It's the equivalent of leaving a 100-watt bulb burning for a week.

A synthetic fell shoe made in China and shipped to the UK, like an inov-8 X-Talon, might be as little as 8 kilograms of CO_2e, according to Mike Berners-Lee. Yet when a group of researchers at Massachusetts Institute of Technology (MIT) performed a life-cycle assessment (LCA) of a standard pair of sneakers, they found that a typical pair generated more like 14 kilograms of CO_2e, roughly the same impact as a 50-mile trip in an average petrol car.[v] Industry insiders tell me it might be a little bit more than that. Indeed, while Nike claim that they've created a shoe with a footprint of just 5.3 kilograms of CO_2e (Free RN Flyknit), some of theirs are as much as 16.8 kilograms (Air Force 1).

If we stick with the average CO_2e of a running shoe being 14 kilograms, the cost to the planet of my twenty-five pairs of daps is around 350 kilograms, about the same as a return flight from London to Malaga in southern Spain. As I'd naively assumed flying was bad and running was good, that was upsetting news.

To understand exactly how the humble running shoe creates a disproportionate amount of CO_2e, scientists at MIT divided a trainer's lifecycle into five stages: materials, manufacturing, usage, transportation and end-of-life. Surprisingly, the fact that almost all running shoes are made in Asia and need to be transported, usually by boat to Europe and America, is only a small percentage of their overall CO_2e. Packaging, plastic or otherwise, also isn't a big factor. The vast majority of the CO2e is emitted in the manufacturing process (68% and 9.5 kilograms of CO2e), and secondarily in the processing of the original materials (29% and 4 kilograms of CO2e).

Shoe production is highly labour-intensive, energy-intensive and therefore carbon-intensive. Much of the CO2e impact comes from powering manufacturing plants in Asia, especially China, with some in Vietnam and more recently Cambodia, where coal – the worst type of energy generation – is the dominant source of electricity. The complexity of the shoe only exacerbates its impact. The average pair of kicks is made up of sixty-five parts, requiring 360 processing steps, from sewing and cutting to injection moulding and heating, to pressing the midsole and outsole.

Although a complex mix, trainers are made almost exclusively of synthetic plastics, materials that are cheap to produce and easy to source, good for an industry that wants to mass-produce products quickly. Plastics are of course fossil fuels, the extraction of which causes emissions, including methane, which is *eighty-four times more potent than CO2* over a twenty-year period and has caused about 30% of global heating.

PodiumRunner.com broke it down further (geek alert).[vi] The running shoe's upper is approximately 41% of its CO2e and most commonly made of nylon, polyester and/or polyurethane, the first two being non-biodegradable petro-chemicals, and nylon manufacture produces nitrous oxide, which is over 300 times more potent than carbon dioxide. The upper's flashy colours also need textile dyes, which are toxic chemicals, sometimes dumped in water sources afterwards.

The foamy midsole (the cushiony bit), 30% of a shoe's CO2e, is usually made from EVA, a petroleum-based product that shows no sign of biodeterioration after contact with moist soil for twelve years, and is thought to persist for up to 1,000 years. Popular alternatives polyurethane (PU) and thermoplastic polyurethane (TPU) are also made from fossil fuels. If a carbon plate is involved, as it is in expensive new supershoes, the material is about fourteen times as energy-intensive as producing steel, and emits more CO2e.

The insole (the section of foam the foot sits on inside the shoe) is 13% of a shoe's CO2e. The outsole (the grippy bit underneath) is 10% of CO2e and is usually made from carbon rubber (70% of rubbers are made from petrochemicals). While in use and once discarded, the rubber contributes to the build-up of tiny plastic polymers polluting oceans, lakes and waterways. And 6% of CO2e is taken up by 'other': laces, arch support, other material added for aesthetics and packaging.

Incidentally, running shoes don't tend to have leather in nowadays, but other trainers do. Aside from the animal rights issue, animal agriculture (of which leather is sometimes but not always a co-product) is responsible for even more CO2e.

Leather produces over double the ghg of synthetic leather, while leather tanning can be a highly toxic process that pollutes waterways and environments and harms workers. 'Cattle farming is the number-one cause of deforestation in the Amazon, and 50% of all leather products are shoes,' says Tansy Hoskins, author of *Foot Work: What Your Shoes Are Doing to the World*. 'So there's a direct correlation between chopping down rainforests and the shoes on people's feet.' Leather is something to avoid.

So the creation of the innocent, joyful running shoe causes significant harm to the planet. 'It was a great surprise how inefficient the supply chains and the production processes can be,' an industry insider told me. 'There's quite a lot of waste.' Sometimes 1 kilogram of materials is used to produce a 500-gram component, leaving 500 grams of waste, they explain. Chemicals are used to treat the materials at six to ten stages of production. 'At each of these steps, as well as the chemicals, and materials waste, there's energy usage and all of this can be quite … quite bad. All that was quite surprising to me. There's a lot of room for improvement.'

Tansy Hoskins has stronger views on trainer creation. 'Every point of shoe production is in environmental crisis,' she says. 'The plastic elements of our shoes are made from fossil fuels, and rivers and lakes in the Global South are being destroyed by dye and chemical runoff.'[vii]

I also hadn't considered the deeply unsettling human cost of running shoe production. 'Rampant consumerism shrouds our sense that human beings made all of the objects we buy,' Tansy Hoskins writes. 'Rather than magically appearing out of thin air, every pair of shoes on the planet has been painstakingly made by people, the overwhelming majority of whom are women who have mostly been paid less than they need to survive.'[11]

The footwear industry is at least ten years behind the rest of fashion in terms of human rights and environmental standards, says Hoskins. 'Every day, workers are exposed to toxic chemicals and dangerous materials. Production means poverty wages for millions of people, Syrian refugee children stitching in basements, homeworkers in Pakistan losing their sight from stitching on tiny beads, air filled with glue fumes, fires and factory collapses, and the persecution of people who stand up for their basic rights … The impact of footwear upon the biosphere, upon animals

---

11 Indeed, although the 100-plus processes needed to create a trainer make them one of the most labour-intensive items we own, just 0.4% of retail cost is spent on labour, according to a Consumer International 2009 report. However, that's not true in all cases. My sponsors inov-8 say they spend about 25% of a shoe's cost price at the factory on labour. 'Producing in China is expensive for labour, as they have minimum wages, workers earn enough to live, they own smartphones and eat healthily,' I was told. 'Also, our developers and managers are often female and these are higher-paid roles.'

and the living world remains unconscionable.' Her book details numerous incidents of appalling and unsafe working conditions, incidents of ill health among workers, such as fainting epidemics, and fatal accidents.

For balance, several brands have declarations on their websites about their responsibilities towards human rights, working conditions and codes of conduct. 'However, most codes of conduct comply only with the bare minimum stipulated by International Labour Organisation,' says EthicalConsumer.org.[viii]

This lamentable relationship can be traced back 500 years, to colonial exploitation and the slave trade, argues economic anthropologist Dr Jason Hickel, author of *Less Is More: How Degrowth Will Save the World*. There's a 'deeply exploitative' relationship between the Global North and Global South, he says, with the latter suffering from deforestation and resources depletion. He calculates that 98% of deaths from climate breakdown happen in the Global South, while the Global North is responsible for 92% of that climate breakdown. 'The climate emergency is colonial in nature'.

Learning all this was upsetting on several levels. I used to look at my running-shoe shelf outside the back door and little fireworks of anticipation would go off in my head, an urge to plant my fugly feet into them and prance off across muddy Wiltshire fields. That sight brings as much guilt as happiness now. And there's more bad news …

1,000 years of solitude

Unlike, say, electrical items, during the 'user phase' (i.e. when we're running in them) shoes release almost no emissions – unless you stick them in the washing machine, which is bad for their durability anyway. There is an under-researched issue of wearing down of the outsole cleats, and the seventh-highest source of microplastics in the environment is from the abrasion of shoe soles, found a German study.[ix]

'It's such a tiny fraction compared to car tyres leaving masses on the tarmac, but it still bugs me,' says another industry insider. Dwarfing that, though, is the fact that a shoe's after-, or end-of-use, life is a horrifying problem.

- Globally, 90% of shoes – and more than 85% of trainers – end up being incinerated or in landfill. 300 million pairs of trainers are thrown into landfill each year in the UK alone.
- Only 15% are recycled or redistributed.
- After-life shoe waste in Europe has been estimated at 1.2 million tonnes a year.

Although the MIT study rated a shoe's after-life as only 2.5% and around 0.3 kilograms of their overall CO2e, 90% of 24 billion is a lot of billions. While some natural materials decompose comparatively quickly (cotton takes about six months, leather twenty to forty years), because of their complex construction of different but mostly plastic-based materials, shoes last much, much longer. 'They can take as much as 1,000 years to decompose,' Dr Sahadat Hossain, director of the Solid Waste Institute for Sustainability, told Fashionista.com.[x] In modern landfills, which are lined in plastic and then sealed shut, our shoes sit intact for 'as long as you can imagine'. And while they do, they're leaching plasticisers, heavy metals and other toxic chemicals.

'The dumping of waste in landfill can result in serious environmental pollution of groundwater and rivers and harmful emissions of greenhouse gases (e.g. methane)', according to Loughborough University's Centre for Sustainable Manufacturing and Reuse/Recycling Technologies.[xi] Methane is eighty-four times more powerful in trapping heat than CO2 over a twenty-year period and 18% of the world's – and 22% of the UK's – methane comes from landfill.

The debate about whether incinerating waste or burying it in the ground is better for the environment is a proverbial tennis match. Incineration produces huge amounts of carbon dioxide, nitrous oxides and other ghgs such as dioxins (which are highly toxic, can cause reproductive and developmental problems, damage the immune system, interfere with hormones and cause cancer, according to the World Health Organization). In England, more waste is now burnt than is recycled, with 11.6 million tonnes incinerated in 2019. Electricity can be produced from waste, but it's more carbon-intensive than gas. Ultimately, it's putting more ghgs into the atmosphere than landfill. Both options are terrible.

Trainers are resolutely unrecyclable – from a commercial perspective, anyway. In other words, with the exception of some pioneering new examples (more anon), it's not commercially viable to recycle shoes. 'It costs us too much money and the end product isn't worthwhile,' says an industry source. 'Painstakingly taking all the different materials of a shoe apart is very time-consuming and inefficient, so we can't recycle them without it being a total money-drain.'

The problem lies in shoes' complex construction of multiple materials and huge amounts of strong glue. 'To create a shoe you can fully recycle, that's fully circular, so it goes back into the shoe again – not downcycling like Nike does by grinding shoes up for football courts – you have to make it from one material,' says Bodil Oudshoorn, Footwear Product Manager for Lake-District-based brand inov-8, who has a PhD in sports-shoe grip (and is nicknamed Dr Grip around the office). 'Otherwise the reassembly is just too hard. The additional problem for us, as trail-running shoe makers, is that glues are really difficult to remove. You can't currently make a trail shoe that's truly circular as it needs a rubber outsole for grip and durability. But we're working on it!'

Before I drill down (bad choice of words, sorry) any further, this is a good moment for a disclaimer. I'm currently an ambassador for inov-8. This is something I'm regularly re-evaluating, especially when I learnt of the harm caused by running shoes and kit in general. The relationship goes back seven years and they've helped me break records and win races. It doesn't seem fair to disown them for being imperfect when I'm not perfect either (no one is). Even if I did, I would still need some good daps to run in. inov-8 aren't the best, but nor are they the worst – Ethical Consumer rank them in the top third of sportswear brands. They know they could do more. So could I. I feel like I challenge them regularly, I've definitely adapted my role as an ambassador (to be much less of a salesperson – and there's very little pressure from them to directly promote products), and some of the people who work there are very knowledgeable and really care about the Big Kerfufflefuck. I feel some discomfort representing a brand, but not enough currently to end the relationship. Regardless, because I know their kit best and have easy access to them, they do get disproportionate coverage in the book, both the good and the bad.

The huge post-consumer shoe-waste problem may partly be ignorance. Indeed, I used to unwittingly bung my knackered old pairs in the bin. But most brands play no part in helping runners here. They're pretty coy about how bad for the planet their product is and leave the problem of how best to dispose of their shoes up to us.

ReRun Clothing, a Community Interest Company aiming to prolong the life of running clothes and equipment, is the brainchild of record-breaking GB ultramarathon-runner Dan Lawson, his wife Charlotte Jalley and their daughters Lilly and Ruby, after he was moved to tears by huge piles of plastic waste in India. 'There are no bins in India. So you're really aware when you buy something that you have nowhere to put it,' says Charlotte. They were concerned too with the amount of excess kit Dan was being given as a sponsored athlete, which seemed wasteful. He decided to eschew sponsorship and instead promote the fact you don't need to be buying new stuff all the time: you can run in second-hand clothes and shoes.

The initial idea was to have a second-hand online running-kit shop. They were soon being sent thousands of pairs of shoes. The state of the daps was depressing. 'Never mind 300 miles, some had done nearer 30. So many of the shoes we get have a lot of life still in them,' says Dan. 'It sums up the problem and this lazy, throwaway culture. We clean them up and some of them are literally a month old. If only people understood what went into creating a shoe, maybe they wouldn't do that sort of stuff.'

Billions of pairs of trainers are created each year and consumers are encouraged to buy these products with a relatively high carbon footprint and upsetting human cost, although they often don't need them; then after just a few months (more anon) are told to ditch them, even though they have another 1,000 years of existence ahead of them.

'**Almost every shoe that's ever been made is still on the Earth**,' says Dan, 'and will outlive us ten times over. They just palm the responsibility on to us. The brands need to take responsibility for what happens to those shoes in their after-life. If you add up all these shoes, where are they all? It's unbelievable. I'd love to collect all the shoes we've got from adidas and Nike and bundle them up in a huge lorry, dump them off at their HQ and say, "Here, you deal with this." It should be their responsibility. It's outright irresponsible to make something that lasts for three months but hangs around for another 1,000 years.'

Extending the useful life of a running shoe saves CO_2e.[12] 'We're conditioned to ditch things rather than fix them,' says Dan. 'We've lost the skill in a generation. I'm not sure how much our parents fixed things, but our grandparents did.'

Since chatting to Dan, Tuff Tape and Fantastic Elastic have become my new friends. 'You can repair anything with anything,' he says. 'I'm not a cobbler, but I've added 400 miles to shoes with a bit of tape or glue. If you don't care what they look like, just their function, it's easy to find a fix. Plus it's fun and satisfying; you get a sense of achievement. If it doesn't work, your shoe was broken anyway, so what's the worst that can happen? Just have a go, experiment.'

After we've worn our daps for 1,000 miles or more, with conscious product care and a few repairs along the way to extend life, what should we do with them? a) Keep wearing them for gardening, DIY and dog walks (before being put to rest as a de facto plant pot – the shoes, not the dog); or b) Pass them on for someone else to wear. The worst thing to do is throw them in the bin.

'So many people tell us they put their shoes in the bin when they're finished with them,' says Dan. 'But you don't have to. They can be used by you or another person. Many homeless people, many refugees would be so grateful of them. They might get another year out of them.'

It does seem like the message is belatedly getting out there: 68% of runners say they repurpose their shoes and 11% recycle them, according to research by David Moulding.[xii]

---

12 *Runner's World* suggest that extending shoe use by three months leads to a 30% reduction of CO_2e, but their source is elusive. Extending the life of clothes by nine months of active use reduces carbon, water and waste footprints by around 20–30% per item, according to fashion campaign group New Standard Institute, so it may be feasible.

What exactly charities do with our donations is discussed more from page 47 and there's inevitably some more waste at this stage. Around 5% of donations are passed on to textile traders such as SOEX or just get incinerated because they're too dirty or too worn to resell or, most frustratingly of all, shoes aren't tied together and end up as unmatched odds.

ReRun have stopped accepting donations. 'If you really want to help,' says Dan, 'keep wearing the shoes. We were becoming a cog in the consumption machine. People gave us their stuff and felt good about donating their old shoes and might go and buy new ones. We try to talk people out of buying our stuff unless they really, really need it.'

Unlike with electronic goods, shoe (and clothing) companies are not currently required by UK legislation to take responsibility for end-of-life recovery of the products they sell, known as Extended Producer Responsibility. But doing so in France has nearly trebled the amount of collected clothing, with 60% being reused and 1,400 jobs created.

Nike and adidas have made noises about recycling services, but Nike cancelled their UK offerings after Brexit and while adidas apparently offer it at three London stores, it's downcycling. Blatantly this service should be much more widely available and other brands should be doing more. With billions of running shoes being created and billions of pounds of profits received, surely the creators should take responsibility for clearing up after themselves, especially when they created such un-eco-friendly products. There's almost no recycling in the shoe (or clothing) industry at the moment. 'That's something that we are actively working to find a solution for,' says On Running's Laurent Vandepaer.

Far worse, several UK independent running shops informally report that at least four major brands ask for any faulty returns to be destroyed by the outlets in order to maintain good waste statistics. 'It's appalling,' an insider told me. 'It's quite common and often referred to as fashion's dirty secret.'

The 300-mile myth

Many runners may be adding to the tragic life of the running shoe simply by throwing them away prematurely. Conventional running wisdom has it that a trainer lasts for 300–500 miles. Then, even if it doesn't look worn out, it's about to do an 'Et tu, Brute', turn on us and inflict injury, so we should act pre-emptively and bin it before it hurts us (presumably a little arm comes out with an axe and starts hacking away at our toes?).

On Running are among the more ethical brands (more anon), but similarly to other running company websites, they recommend 310–465 miles for their shoes.

Semi-serious runners will run five to eight times a week, and if we wore the same shoe on every run, 310 miles would be just six to eight weeks. More realistically, runners tend to swap between trainers day to day, meaning a pair lasts four to six months. Strava auto-notifies you after 250 miles in a shoe (though you can tweak the setting up to 800 miles), and repeats the scaremongering: 'replace shoes between 300 and 500 miles to prevent injury'. 'Imagine if Strava had a badge for the person who did the most amount of miles in their trainers,' says Charlotte.

Some shoes aren't even built to endure that long. Perversely, Nike created a dap designed to last just 60 miles. 2003's Mayfly 'race day' trainer was named after the insect which lives for up to forty-eight hours.

Runners are terrified of injury, but with some justification: as many as 80% of recreational runners suffer a niggle of sorts each year and a 2007 US study ranks it a close second to basketball – a contact activity, unlike running, except for competitive dads at parkrun – as the sport most likely to induce injury.[xiii] There are two types of runner, goes the joke: those who are injured and those who are about to be injured. But the evidence that injury comes from your shoes is non-existent.

While studies have failed to show that shoes help us avoid injury, more pertinently, several studies have also failed to find a link between shoes and increased injury risk.[xiv] Even though it's unproven, another study found runners think their shoes may be at fault (I wonder where they got that idea from?), concluding, 'some of the runners' beliefs are not supported by the research literature'.[xv] Between 50% and 75% of running injuries are due to 'previous injury, lack of running experience, running to compete and excessive weekly running distance', according to a study back in 1992.[xvi] A 2011 study found, 'Approximately 65% of chronic injuries in distance runners are related to routine high mileage, rapid increases in mileage, increased intensity, hills or irregular surface running, and surface firmness'.[xvii] Other studies have found body mass index and reoccurrence of previous injury to be the most common causes.[xviii] Most, if not all, studies concern road-running shoes. 'You can keep running in trail-running shoes until they fall apart!' I was told. Even then, stick in a fresh inner sole for another lease of life.

Naturally, a shoe will lose some sturdiness and midsole cushioning may compress as it ages. But there's nothing in peer-reviewed journals on how shoe design affects injury, concluded Craig Richards from the University of Newcastle (Australia) in 2009.[xix] He and his co-authors found that the practice of prescribing cushioned shoes with pronation support, which had been presented as a good idea for more than twenty years, had no evidence to back it up. A 2020 review in the *Journal of Athletic Training* looked at four decades of research on shoes and injury, concluding 'footwear does not cause injury'.[xx]

An ageing shoe may even be doing us some good. Running shoes reduce the spring-like function of the human foot during running, showed a 2016 study; and highly cushioned shoes increase leg stiffness and amplify impact loading, found a 2018 study.[xxi] But, as shoes wear down and their cushioning thins, runners become less wobbly, more stable and gain more foot control, found a 1988 study by the University of Oregon.[xxii]

Indeed, palaeoanthropologist Professor Erik Trinkaus estimated that humans started to wear shoes 40,000 years ago, because he detected that's when our toes began to lose sturdiness. It's reasonable to suppose that shoes have made us weaker. And nowadays, the more shoe there is – and there is a trend for more and more cushioning – the weaker it may be making our feet.

The midsole very slowly degrades and flattens through use, an industry insider explained to me. 'Most people wouldn't notice, since it happens so slowly – the opposite of your kids growing, I guess. The recommendation that shoes only last 300–500 miles came about so people would realise their shoes needed replacing even if they weren't falling apart. That's if – and this is a big if – they rely on that cushioning to be fresh and springy to protect against injury. This is much less true in trail running, because cushioning is less important and trail shoes degrade quicker in the upper and the outsole.'

I'm a big fan of Alex Hutchinson's work, so I asked the former elite runner, renowned sports-science journalist and author of the brilliant *Endure: Mind, Body and the Curiously Elastic Limits of Human Performance* what he thought about the '500-mile rule'.

'Any "rule" is going to be a gross approximation,' he says, 'because everyone's body and running style is different, as are different shoe models. But I think the *general* principle that shoes lose their cushioning over time (and thus, if you think that cushioning does something useful, you should replace them) is probably true.'

Again, that cushioning caveat. So, does cushioning actually help runners? Ultrarunners especially are drawn to highly cushioned, maximalist shoes, imagining they will protect joints from all those big miles. Two studies that addressed cushioning as an injury-prevention strategy did not show a significant decrease of the injury frequency when changing the midsole hardness.[xxiii] In fact, maximalist shoes make runners absorb more impact forces, according to two other studies, which could increase the risk of injury (though a 2022 study suggests a softer cushioning spreads out impact more and may therefore deter injury).[xxiv]

One of the greatest ultrarunners of all time, Arthur Newton, famously saw no reason to change his plimsolls until he'd done at least 4,000 miles in them. With that approach he broke the world record for 100 miles at the age of fifty-one, and won South Africa's very competitive 55-mile Comrades Marathon five times.

'I think it was Ed Whitlock [an English-born Canadian runner and the first person over seventy to run a marathon in less than three hours] who famously ran in the same shoes for years on end,' says Alex Hutchinson. 'For that matter, I have a friend and training partner who runs in the same pair for years and years at a time.'

Indeed, my experience is that most trainers can comfortably do 1,000 miles, a view echoed by runner friends and coached athletes.

'The 500-mile rule is a clever ploy by shoe companies,' says Dan Lawson. 'They frighten you by saying, "Your shoes may cause injury", or they'll try and bribe you by saying, "You'll run better in this new pair". It becomes a self-fulfilling prophecy. People start to throw out their shoes after 300–400 miles, and if they do that, running shoes become not fit for purpose for them, because their feet aren't conditioned for anything other than bouncy new ones. It's like if someone always flies first class, they'll think economy is a nightmare. But it's not. Lots of people travel in economy class and are fine. It's the same with shoes.'

Indeed, a biomechanical study testing 156 models of running shoe concluded that the life cycle of a good-quality trainer is expected to be much higher than even 600 miles.[xxv] Dan only runs in second-hand shoes. 'I get at least 1,000 more miles out of them, often many more. Old shoes don't injure you.' Dan doesn't get injured despite high training volume, winning six-day races, podium finishes at 100-plus-mile races such as Spartathlon and Badwater, and winning the 24-Hour European Championships.

Materials have improved a lot since running-shoe brands started advising the 500-mile mark, an industry insider told me, so they can probably handle more now, 'dependent on the shoe and a person's weight. I always thought shoe brands purposefully made their shoes only last a certain number of miles so you have to keep buying from them. However, I don't believe this any more. Although I'm still suspicious of bigger brands like Nike and adidas.'

Shoes causing injury is probably a big bad myth – one that rather suits the industry, but not the planet (or purse). It's easy to blame your kicks for a niggle. Shoes are tangible – certainly more so than running too many miles too soon, under-fuelling , inadequate sleep, or the strength work we should have done. Plus they look a bit tatty and there's a shiny new version out …

Having shamed myself with my twenty-five-strong dap collection, I feel I need to explain a little. In my feeble defence, I'm very lucky that I get sent daps by my sponsors inov-8. Often they're prototypes for me to test, especially their durability – and yes, they always last 500 miles and usually well beyond 1,000 miles. That does mean I can accidentally amass a bit of a stockpile and this has been a good reminder

I could be better at saying 'no thanks' sometimes, though I regularly pass daps on to local runner pals. I haven't suffered an overuse injury in training for over five years.

Despite a recent cull, I somehow still seem to have fifteen active pairs listed on Strava. That's not perfect. But it is progress. Now that I know what I know, I feel determined to wring every last drop out of my daps, to carry on using them till death do us part. I'm in the habit of sticking them under an outdoor tap after a muddy run, extending their life a little, and I get emotionally attached to pairs, especially if they've got me through a memorable race or run, which again makes me look after them. I think you can love running shoes, in an ethical way.

Anyhoo, time for some mirth.

Hippos seem unconcerned about the effects of climate change on their habitat. That's because they live in de-Nile.

Yeah, but what can we do about it?

1 Read: *Foot Work* by Tansy E. Hoskins.
2 Think: Refuse, Reduce, Reuse, Repair, Recycle
3 Refuse

- Ask yourself, do you really need that new shoe? Overconsumption goes hand in hand with climate and ecological damage. Studies show materialism makes us miserable and, conversely, when we spend less, our wellbeing rises. The best thing we can do is to refuse to buy so many new products and over time reduce the amount of shoes we have (in my case, anyway).

4 Reduce

- 'The most effective way to reduce waste is to not create it in the first place,' writes Sean Ross (@sustainablerunning), a sustainability expert. 'If you don't need it, don't buy it. If it's not broken, don't replace it. If it is broken, repair it. Don't listen to people telling you to change your shoes every 400 miles. Think about whether you need something new and reduce.'
- If you really feel sure you do need new daps, could you buy second-hand? Consider a pre-loved bargain from ReRun Clothing (*rerunclothing.org*), who have all sorts of options in excellent condition. Try Facebook gear exchange groups and the Vinted app too.

5 Reuse

- Does the shoe seem built to last? Durability is more economical too.
- Make 'em last. It's not just up to brands to make shoes durable. The terrain you run on, your build and form will affect wear and tear, so try to run on the surfaces the shoe's designed for, with good technique (think yourself tall and light). Wash them when they get muddy (bogs include shoe-eating bacteria),

but don't put them in the washing machine, which is bad for the shoe and your energy usage. And dry them, but don't put them on radiators (newspaper helps). Undo laces properly before taking them off so as not to damage their structure when forcing them on in a rush.

- Donate for reuse with friends, running clubs, charity shops, running shops, local recycling centres and kerbside recycling. Also try *jogonagain.com*, *oneworldrunning.com*, *shareyoursoles.org* and *shoe4africa.org*
- Even if they lack their former grip, would they still work as hiking, gardening, DIY or weekend doss-about shoes?
- If they've truly served their use as shoes, perhaps they could be given a second life in a new role, plant pots being a popular option. Please. Anywhere but the bin.

6 Repair
- See the ReRun guide in the photo section.
- Buy less, wear more. Use glue, duct tape or a needle and thread to repair your daps. Let's see how many miles you can do with them.
- adidas are launching an app for shoe repair.

7 Recycle
- This should be the final option. As well as ReRun Clothing, the excellently named Jog On (*jogonagain.com*) repairs shoes and works with a network of partners to distribute trainers across eleven hubs around the world.

8 Speak up: email brands about shoe overconsumption and the waste crisis, with a templated letter from ReRun Clothing: *rerunclothing.org/pages/take-action*

9 Ethical consumerism: if you go new, are you buying from an ethical company with a sustainability or environmental policy that seems transparent and has measurable targets (Science Based or similar – more on page 70)? Do they talk about their supply chain? Do they have a code of conduct for suppliers or pledges about workers' rights? Do they offer product care guidelines? Ethical Consumer (subscription) and Good On You (free, but some strange rankings) can help you see which brands are more ethical. Let's support ethical companies where we can. Look for brands endorsed by SMETA, which audits supply chains and ethical working conditions.

3

GETTING T-SHIRTY

How the humble tee hides a shocking litany of harm to people,
animals and the planet

'The journey of a T-shirt is a tragedy.'
Charlotte Jalley

Who doesn't love free stuff? Over my eleven-plus years as a runner, I've been given
a free T-shirt at most races I've done, from my local Corsham 10K to the 105-mile
Ultra-Trail du Mont-Blanc (who've also given me four gilets down the years). Some
tees are cotton. Most are polyester. A handful are tasteful or have special memories
and might get worn. Most are thick and heavy 'tech tees', hurriedly and horribly
designed, garishly coloured, plastered with logos and often ill-fitting.

Female runners complain that race T-shirts are unisex, a 'one size fits all' which
invariably doesn't. 'I honestly cried after I was given my Spine Fusion T-shirt,' says
ultrarunner and SheRACES founder Sophie Power. 'Okay, I'd had eleven hours'
sleep in five nights so was a *bit* emotional. But I put it on to wear home and it
almost came to my knees. I'm not anti a high-quality, sustainable, well-fitting
T-shirt. But when they don't fit at all, they'll get zero wear and crap female-fit ones
are harder to rehome too.'

Seventy-five per cent of runners often or very often receive a post-race T-shirt,
and 60% of UK runners own ten or more.[i] I've certainly been given more. I didn't
need, want or ask for them. I just took the free thing offered at the finish line, in a
tired state without really thinking – and if I did think, it was that I'd already paid for
it with the race entry fee. It usually came with a plastic bottle of water, a medal and
cod liver oil tablets (eh?), all in a plastic, ironically named, goodie bag. Especially at
a road race, that's standard. You do a race. You get some free gubbins.

My gratis garments went into a drawer and most stayed there for years, sweated
in infrequently, if at all. Because race T-shirts are free, usually I simply didn't value
them. They also tend to be too warm, compared to better-made, more breathable
base layers, and therefore pong after a while too. Or maybe that's just me?

A pile of unused luminous tees didn't seem like a big deal. But unfortunately it is.
It was Charlotte and Dan from ReRun who first made me aware of running's XXL

T-shirt problem and how it's a nightmarish burden on the world. The humble tee hides a shocking litany of harm – to people, animals and the planet.

Most of the following endemic problems are part of the wider textile, clothing and fashion industries. Outdoor sportswear is a part of that, but it's different in some ways too. Anyway, most of us runners wear non-running clothes sometimes. Some of running apparel's problems are shared with shoes, but some are very different. And frankly, they're even more depressing. Fasten your seatbelt and tuck your T-shirt in …

Cottoning on

Other than lots of people getting lots of socks and pants to wear, it's difficult to find many positives in the history of global textiles and especially the cotton industry, which has been central to the slave trade, colonialism, industrialisation and globalisation.

The UK's role in global slavery and especially the depressing exploitation of cotton-powerhouse India set us up nicely for the Industrial Revolution (1760–1900), which began with textiles and made the country – or at least the rich people in it – considerably richer. Thousands of children worked in the textile mills, mass slavery helped mushroom the USA's cotton trade and the material continues to be in huge demand today. Both slavery and child labour are still thriving too.

Made from petrochemicals, or 'coal, water, and air', as was announced at the time, nylon was created in America in 1938. The 'miracle fibre' boasted superior durability, versatility and a stable supply of raw materials. Polyester was invented in 1946, made by American chemical company DuPont. A post-war boom caused a shortage of traditional materials and made these alternatives all the more popular. 'The staggering success of nylon and its synthetic counterparts obscures the unlikely alliance of the chemical and fashion industries that underwrote the post-war fashion revolution', says ScienceHistory.org.[ii] In the 1950s, synthetic fabrics helped satisfy the public's huge appetite for new clothes after war and economic depression. Washing-machine sales in the US tripled and the country's GDP almost doubled, in what became known as the Golden Age of American Capitalism.

Capitalism is consumerism. To keep the necessary endless quest for profit going, consumers need to be seduced into perpetually buying stuff – often stuff they don't really need. 'The changes in the new model should be so novel as to create demand … and a certain amount of dissatisfaction with past models,' the president of General Motors, Alfred P. Sloan, famously said, as far back as the 1920s. Planned obsolescence was in full swing by the 1950s. 'We make good products, we induce people to buy them,' echoed an industrial designer three decades later.[iii] 'And then the next year we deliberately introduce something that will make those products old fashioned, out of date, obsolete. We do that for the soundest reason: to make money.'

- After technology and automotive, clothing is the world's third-largest industry, with revenues of $3 trillion and 2% of global GDP.
- 100 million tonnes of textiles are produced each year – enough to provide twenty new items to every person on the planet.
- Clothes use in Europe has the fourth-highest impact on the environment, exceeded only by food, housing and transport, according to the European Environment Agency.
- One in every six people in the world works in the clothing industry.
- Global clothing production doubled between 2000 and 2014. By 2018 the average consumer was buying 60% more items than fifteen years earlier.
- We buy more clothing per person in the UK than any other country in Europe.
- To provide the natural resources needed to sustain current lifestyles, with population growth, by 2050 we will need almost three planets, says the UN.

The clothing industry produces somewhere between 3% and 10% of global CO2e. Clearly we have enough clothes. If growth continues on its current trajectory, by 2050 the textile industry will account for a quarter of the world's total allowable carbon emissions, according to the Ellen MacArthur Foundation (EMF).[iv] Which might be okayish if there was a need for all these T-shirts, but people are keeping clothes for half as long as they did fifteen years ago.

The textile industry is burning through the planet's resources like they're going out of, er, fashion. Once you take into account full life-cycle emissions, the industry could be responsible for as much as 3.3 billion tonnes of CO2e – close to the combined carbon footprint of all twenty-eight members of the EU in 2019. It's worth re-reading that sentence. That really is quite a lot.

What's the environmental cost of an individual item of clothing? A standard pair of cotton jeans emits 33.4 kilograms of CO2e over its lifetime, about the same as driving 69 miles in a fossil-fuel-powered car. A T-shirt? A small, women's, cotton T-shirt that's one colour with a one-colour print, certified organic and manufactured in a low-carbon process, has a life-cycle footprint of 2.34 kilograms of CO2e. However, that's a best-case scenario, a pipe dream rather than standard. Another study estimated average CO2e for the life cycle of a cotton T-shirt at 8.8 kilograms, so like driving 18 miles in a car.[v]

Most runners don't tend to run in cotton much. But I've been given at least a dozen cotton race tees down the years (I still wear three, from Lakes In A Day,

Ultra Tour Monte Rosa and California's Canyons 100K, because they either have ace memories or they're well made and look good). I was curious about the footprint of my race T-shirts. I learnt that cotton production is an epic nightmare ...

Cotton's costs

As with shoes, and indeed our whole climate and ecological emergency, fossil-fuel-powered energy is a big part of the problem. In China (35% of global exports), Vietnam and India, energy comes mostly from coal. (Using renewable energy instead could reduce emissions by 62% or 4 kilograms of CO_2e per T-shirt.) There's material waste at this stage too, as much as 15%, and cotton is a seriously thirsty fabric. Making a T-shirt uses 700 gallons of water – enough for one person for three and a half years.

Textile production usually requires hazardous chemicals (more anon), uses 79 trillion litres of water annually and generates 20% of the world's water wastage. The textile industry is the world's second-largest polluter of water. In fact, a quarter of the chemicals produced in the world are used in textiles, and the dyeing process uses enough water to fill 2 million Olympic-sized swimming pools each year.

Cotton production is increasingly affecting soil degradation and water scarcity. The Aral Sea, formerly the world's fourth-largest lake, has dried up in part as a consequence of cotton farming and is now known as the Aralkum Desert.

More and more land is needed for cotton production, causing more biodiversity loss and deforestation, and the industry is projected to use 35% more land by 2030. (Although it does use more land, organic cotton has about half the emissions of conventional cotton.)

It gets worse. Cotton farming uses 18% of the world's pesticides and 25% of the world's insecticides, more than any other major crop. Pesticides have a devastating effect on wildlife, especially bees when used in the UK, as well as birds, numerous insects, earthworms, hedgehogs, frogs and fish – plus a negative impact on water and soils, plants and fungi, and they threaten food safety.

Insecticides, designed to deliberately kill insects, are also toxic to other animals and humans. 'Huge amounts of insects – a vital part of many ecosystems, including those that enable food production – are destroyed to feed our fashion frenzy,' says Greenpeace.[vi]

The human costs

Those toxic chemicals are seriously hazardous for workers. As cotton isn't a food source, far higher levels can be used, leading to numerous health issues in pickers (which is why 100% organic cotton and Fairtrade cotton are far more ethical choices).

In developing countries, around 20,000 people die of cancer and suffer miscarriages as a result of chemicals sprayed on cotton, according to WHO. In India, 11,772 farmers committed suicide in 2013 alone, according to government data, likely due to financial pressures. That's forty-four deaths every day and the total is thought to be upwards of 40,000 over twenty-five years.

'Agricultural workers in the cotton sector have been treated in an abhorrent way for centuries,' says Andrew Brooks in *Clothing Poverty*, where he cites some horrifying contemporary examples.[vii] Let's not forget the 2013 Rana Plaza disaster in Bangladesh, the clothing industry's darkest hour, where more than 1,130 people were killed and another 2,500 injured when a building collapsed on them.

So much of climate change is caused by the Global North, yet the Global South bears the brunt of it, a distasteful lingering colonialism. Environmental racism is seen too, in how polluting infrastructure such as power plants, landfills, incinerators, uranium mines and factories disproportionately affects low-income and ethnic-minority communities. 'It's hitting Indigenous and vulnerable communities, for whom climate breakdown is the culmination of centuries of colonial and social oppression,' wrote US scientist Peter Kalmus in the *Guardian*.[viii] Oh, and slavery is still a thing.

Seventy-seven per cent of leading UK retailers think there's a likelihood of modern slavery in their supply chains.[ix] EthicalConsumer.org warns that companies should ensure their cotton is not sourced from Uzbekistan, the world's fourth-largest exporter, where the government forcibly mobilised one million citizens to harvest the plant, according to Anti-Slavery International (ASI). There are concerns too about Turkmenistan, while the Chinese government are accused of using forced labour of Uyghur Muslims in the region of Xinjiang, which produces 20% of the world's and 80% of China's cotton. Both Nike and adidas have been linked to Xinjiang cotton.

There are reports of child labour in China and India, Pakistan, Brazil, Uzbekistan, Turkey and even the USA, says World Vision.[x] Some 170 million or 11% of the world's children are engaged in child labour, mostly making textiles and garments for Europe and the US, according to the International Labour Organisation. 'In cotton picking, employers prefer to hire children for their small fingers, which do not damage the crop,' reports Unicef.[xi]

Elsewhere, textile workers, mainly women and girls in developing countries, are paid derisory wages and made to work long hours in terrible conditions which sometimes infringe on human rights, while most Fast Fashion CEOs are well-paid men. 'All the problems that persist across the value chain [are] a huge feminist issue,' says Sarah Ditty, former policy director of Fashion Revolution, the world's largest fashion activism movement.[xii] 'Too many people working in the fashion industry, mostly women, are still underpaid, unsafe and mistreated,' the movement's co-founder Carry Somers told the *Guardian*. 'It's time for change.'[xiii] Galvanised by the Rana Plaza tragedy, Fashion Revolution urged the industry to show greater transparency in supply chains and a recent campaign asked a pointed 'Who made my clothes?'

inov-8 had already given me some reassurance about the working conditions in the factories they use, pointing out they have a higher than average number of women in management roles and their workers are well paid enough to afford smartphones. A coalition of working rights organisations created The Transparency Pledge (*transparencypledge.org*), asking companies to publish on their websites details of all the factories involved in manufacturing their products. Some major sports brands are aligned with the pledge, including adidas, Asics, Nike and Under Armour.

Clothing factories are a complex international web to navigate. A tier-one supplier is the factory you actually speak to, inov-8's Bodil Oudshoorn explained to me. Tier-two suppliers are the material suppliers, the ones that weave the fabrics, supplying it to different factories in different countries. 'You have to ask for their email address, but you might be able to get hold of them. Tier three is who supplies those materials to that tier-two factory, and it's very difficult to find out much about them.' Nevertheless, Know The Origin, while not a sportswear brand, is the one clothing company EthicalConsumer.org hails for showing ultimate transparency in their supply chain.

Nike, meanwhile, have an externally audited Sustainable Manufacturing and Sourcing Index (SMSI) to help monitor their 525 supplier factories in forty-two countries. Their most recent figures (2019), however, show only 10 were rated Silver and 478 rated Bronze, underperforming on working hours, wages and benefits. But at least they're being transparent.

Additional accreditation schemes exist, such as the Fair Wear Foundation, Fairtrade Label Organisations, the Global Organic Textile Standard and the Ethical Trading Initiative. But membership is voluntary and a general lack of transparency doesn't reflect well on an industry that makes A LOT of money.

Fossil fashion

So that's cotton for you. A barrel of laughs, eh? However, most of us runners are jogging round in T-shirts, shorts, socks and jackets made from synthetic fibres, usually polyester. On the surface, polyester is amazing. It's quick and cheap to produce, versatile and lightweight, so transporting it in bulk releases less CO_2e

than cotton, and likewise it takes up less space in a washing machine and absorbs less water, meaning fewer emissions there (more anon). Indeed, it's quick to clean and dry, often more comfortable than cotton, has much better performance overall for runners, and is super durable too.

Partly because of these benefits, global production of polyester has doubled since 2000, overtaking cotton as the world's dominant fibre, and now accounts for up to 69% of all our clothing, with synthetic fibres expected to represent 73% of the world's clothing by 2030 and polyester 85% of that. Polyester production is much kinder to water supplies and land and isn't linked to as much tragedy as cotton – not directly, anyway. However, in terms of global heating, it's worse. The CO_2e of a polyester T-shirt throughout its life cycle could be as much as 20.56 kilograms, the same as travelling from Glasgow to London by coach.

In more bad news, virgin synthetic fibres come from polyethylene terephthalate (PET), which is what plastic bottles are made from. In other words, our T-shirts, shorts, socks, jackets and pretty much everything else we run in are made from plastic – or rather, oil. We joggers are going round in fossil fuels (now known as hydrocarbons, apparently, due to a rebrand). We're wearing fossil fashion. Which is thoroughly depressing, because nothing is worse for the planet, more unsustainable, than extraction and use of fossil fuels. Scientists say we must leave them in the ground to have any chance of averting climate and ecological disaster. And yet the clothing industry has a 'hidden reliance' on and a 'dangerous addiction' to fossil fuels, said a 2021 report by the Changing Markets Foundation (CMF).[xiv]

My wife used to joke that some of my running jackets were 'like plastic bags'. I hadn't realised the irony of her comments till now. Synthetic fibres have 'become the backbone of the prevailing unsustainable fast fashion business model, which is driving runaway consumption,' said the report, which also found a 'striking correlation between the rise of polyester and the explosion of cheap, low-quality clothing that is causing a mounting waste crisis' (more anon).

And the thing is, we runners are being played by these fossil fuel companies. As the huge tasks of decarbonising energy and transport are underway, these companies want to keep those profits up. 'Investing in plastics has therefore become a key strategy', according to an article in *The Conversation*.[xv] Fourteen per cent of petrochemicals are now turned into plastics, mostly packaging and synthetics, with textile production accounting for 1.35% of global oil production and 15% of total plastic use. Which may not sound like much, but it's more than Spain uses in a year.

It's forecast that plastics and other petrochemicals will become the largest driver of oil demand, accounting for almost 50% by 2050, according to the International Energy Agency (IEA). BP reportedly projects 95% of its growth from plastics.

Ironically, as fossil fuels go out of fashion, they increasingly need the clothing industry and are especially well suited to sportswear. 'The oil and gas industry are betting on production of plastic, including plastic-fibres, as a growing share of their revenue,' says the CMF report. In other words, all those free T-shirts at running races suit Big Oil.

- The extraction of oil from the earth and the production of synthetic polymers emits two to three times more CO2e than cotton.
- Polyester production emits 700 million tonnes of carbon into the atmosphere each year, more than the total annual emissions of Mexico.

The chemical problem

I was feeling pretty depressed about the huge environmental and human costs of my running kit and the fact that it's become an outlet for the fossil-fuel empire to keep us dependent on their planet-wrecking wares. But the further I dug into our sportswear, the more bad stuff I found. The production of nylon, for example, which is sometimes used for running kit, emits nitrous oxide (N_2O), which is *300 times* more damaging than CO_2. All these T-shirts of ours need colour, and dye is petroleum-based, energy intensive (requiring temperatures above 100 °C) and uses harmful chemicals such as acids and alkalis. The colours that sell best, bright yellows and reds, are often most harmful, with green, blue and black being more eco-friendly.

'If we'd all accept that we can't have super bright colours, we could all move to nice, environmentally friendly colourings,' an industry insider told me. 'But if one company does it, they just look rubbish compared to the rest!'

I began to repeatedly hear the phrase 'forever chemicals' and fell down another troubling rabbit hole. This nickname is given to PFAS (per- and polyfluoroalkyl substances), a chemical used on outdoor garments to make them water- and stain-resistant. A PFAS-based durable water repellent (DWR) coating is applied to waterproofs, and sometimes to shoes and packaging too (oh, and half of all make-up products). PFAS don't naturally break down, hence 'forever chemicals'. Airborne compounds attach to dust or float freely through indoor environments, making their way into our food and water, and continuously moving through the ground. They're a 'significant source' of pollution in our air and water, found a recent study, contaminating the air in our homes, classrooms and shops at 'alarming levels'.[xvi] The chemical industry dumps PFAS into the ocean, which the study concluded is unsafe. The chemicals have been found in penguin eggs in Antarctica and polar bears in the Arctic, in orcas, in otters in the UK, in US lakes, rivers and rain, in 100% of breastmilk in a study in Washington in the US, and in the blood of 97% of

Americans. Oh, and rainwater isn't safe to drink anywhere on Earth, due to forever chemicals, found another study.[xvii]

These chemicals are linked to cancer, a weaker immune system, increased cholesterol, kidney disease, birth defects, liver problems and a range of other serious diseases. Oh, and are a danger to garment workers, retail workers (transmitting through the air in stores) and potentially us runners too. The production of PFAS also releases the potent ghg HCFC-22, an ozone-depleting chemical with a global warming potential 5,280 times higher than carbon dioxide. Cheery stuff, huh?

The DWR dilemma is industry-wide, with even Patagonia struggling for the most ethical solution (though I like how they are open about it on their website). Scientists have been working on PFAS replacements for DWR for years. 'However, the sticking point quite literally is the other aspects a DWR resists – dirt and stains like grass and mud and anything oil-based, including detritus from the body such as sweat,' says Helen Stuart, head of clothing and equipment at inov-8 and a former Scotland international mountain runner. 'Alternative DWR finishes are easily contaminated and lose performance rapidly, reducing effectiveness and longevity.'

By pure coincidence, I recently tested a potential new waterproof jacket for inov-8 and fed back that it seemed to pick up dirt and stains disappointingly easily. It was of course coated in a PFAS-free DWR. If I'd been a customer I would have sent the item back.

'With so much energy used in the production of a product, durability is critical,' says Helen. 'A jacket with a reduced lifespan is yet another environmental problem. But we are determined to phase PFAS out from our products completely and have tests in progress right now.'

There are other hazardous chemicals too in what's referred to as nanotechnology, which is linked to environmental toxicity and human health problems. Perfluorinated chemicals (PFCs) help textiles repel water; phthalates help soften the plastic; plus starch, paraffin and other harmful pollutants can be used for odour prevention, sun protection and to disperse static charge. All of these are released into the air, water and soil at the production stage. Nanosilver – the most widely used nanoparticle – is shed from clothing in sweat and, while not thought to be particularly toxic to humans, it accumulates in post-washing waste water and could be harmful for aquatic life. It's all a bit alarming.

'For the environmentally conscious athlete, the issue of nanotechnology is particularly troublesome,' reports EthicalConsumer.org, 'due to the release of nanoscale particles without full knowledge of the effects of many chemicals at nanoscale on the human body, animals and the environment.'

'Increases in [chemical] production and releases of novel entities are not consistent with keeping humanity within the safe operating space,'[13] declared scientists recently.[xviii]

Some manufacturers are finally phasing nanotechnology chemicals out, thanks in part to Greenpeace campaigning. inov-8 say they're continuously testing PFC-free alternatives and have succeeded in finding less harmful solutions for 55% of their apparel styles. I've since learnt that runners should look for trusted validations such as the Oeko-Tex Standard 100, which certifies that fabrics have been tested for harmful substances (all of inov-8's main apparel fabrics carry the certification). Sweden has plans for a new tax on toxic chemicals in clothing.

The packaging problem

Talking of chemicals and plastics, I used to find it super-frustrating when a product turned up on my doorstep in non-recyclable plastic packaging. **Packaging represents less than 10% of clothing's CO_2e in most cases**, so it isn't the primary harm caused, as we'll see with food too. That said, on a macro level, the fashion industry uses 180 billion polythene bags every year. They're the clear bags your gear often arrives in, designed to protect it in transit from Asia. They're super-cheap, strong, very light – which keeps transport emissions low – and see-through, which helps retailers and customers. But they're made from petrochemicals and if they make their way into the ocean they do great harm.

That said, plastic isn't always the wrong choice. A paper bag causes more CO_2e in creation and transportation, because it's heavier: if clothes get damaged in transit in a less protective paper bag, that's worse waste than a plastic bag causes.

Nevertheless, inov-8 have made progress here, switching to new Back to Earth Polybags wherever feasible, which are 100% recycled. The magic is in the organic technology. The bag can be kerbside-recycled in most cases, but if it does find its way to landfill it will naturally decompose within a few years, as opposed to the hundreds of years that most plastic takes. As well as being made from waste materials, cleverly the biotechnology attracts naturally occurring microbes which accelerate the biodegradation of plastics. The polybag leaves no microplastics or toxic residue, instead leaving beneficial remnants like biogas and nitrogen-rich compost. 'It's a more closed-loop life cycle,' says Helen Stuart. 'Ideally packaging would be

---

13 This alarming tangent led me to a book called *Killer Clothes: How Seemingly Innocent Clothing Choices Endanger Your Health ... and How to Protect Yourself!* by Anna Maria and Brian R. Clement, which frankly looked too upsetting to read (and a little conspiratorial). In the back cover spiel they link a litany of increasing health problems (all the big ones) that parallel our increasing use of synthetic clothing.

eliminated entirely, but there is a need to keep the garment in good condition on its journey. Damage before use would be an even worse environmental sin.'

So that's something positive. But naturally things get worse again.

A macro micro problem

The biggest difference between CO2e from shoes and clothes is that the largest chunk of emissions from a T-shirt comes not from materials or production, but *during the consumer phase*. **Between a third and half of the emissions from a T-shirt are caused by us runners.** And that's mostly from washing it.

The consumer phase of a cotton tee accounts for 48% of its overall CO2e, caused by automatic washing (24%), tumble drying (45%) and ironing (31%). Pleasingly, avoiding tumble drying and ironing would result in an overall reduction of 37% of a T-shirt's footprint. I've always considered ironing to be a pretty dumb idea and finally feel validated.

And a polyester T-shirt? **The consumer phase accounts for 30% of the CO2e of plastic tees,** up to 6.25 kilograms, caused by washing it, tumble drying and detergent. **Thankfully, we as the T-shirt owner can do something about those emissions** (see the washing tips on page 55). However, before we get too smug about that, something else bad happens when we wash our smelly clobber.

- Up to 35% of microplastics in marine environments are from synthetic clothing.
- Microfibres shed from our clothing account for 85% of the human-made material found along ocean shores.
- A 6-kilogram domestic washing cycle can release 700,000 microfibres.
- Around 1,900 individual fibres can be rinsed off a single synthetic garment.
- Over 9.4 trillion fibres could be released per week in the UK.
- Shedding from polyester contributes to the 14 million tonnes of microplastics on our ocean floors.

Microplastics and microfibres (5 millimetres or smaller) have been found at the highest point on Earth (the summit of Mount Everest), the coldest places on Earth (both poles and the Arctic Ocean), and the deepest point on Earth (the Mariana Trench). They're in our dust, our food (fish, fruit, honey, sugar, shellfish), our beer, in bottled water, in animals, in the air, in our lungs, in our faeces, in UK streams 400 feet underground (in 100% of samples), in 80% of tap water around the world and in the placentas of unborn babies. In March 2022, scientists revealed that they had been found in human blood cells (in 80% of those tested)[xix] – and half of the samples contained PET.[14] Then in April, microplastics were discovered deep in the lungs of living people for the first time (again in almost all samples analysed), the most common particles being polypropylene, used in plastic packaging and pipes, and PET.[xx]

Microfibres leach toxic chemicals such as performance additives, waterproofing and manufacturing chemicals; and they absorb toxic chemicals from waterways, including BPA, PFAS, pesticides, fertilisers and dioxins. Oh, and microplastics are found in nine out of ten cosmetics. It sounds like something from a dystopian novel that doesn't end well. Our world is turning plastic and it's not fantastic.

Microplastics were found in ninety-six of ninety-seven seawater samples from Arctic seas, a huge proportion of which was polyester, 'the same width and colours as those used in clothes'.[xxi] Tiny organisms like plankton mistake microfibres for food; microfibres clog the stomach, starving or poisoning the plankton. There are 5 trillion pieces of plastic in the world's oceans, estimated a 2014 study.[xxii] 'This is the tip of the iceberg,' said the Natural History Museum's Professor Lucy Woodall.[xxiii] 'It's making the oceans into a big plastic soup,' marine scientist Dr Imogen Napper told Kilian Jornet and Huw James's Athlete Climate Academy. And we can't remove it. 'It could persist in the environment for hundreds if not thousands of years.'

When you open your dryer, you are also breathing in toxic fibres; you are literally inhaling your clothing. Another reason not to use driers (at the risk of sounding judgemental, emitting a needless 1.7 kilograms of CO_2e when clothes can be air-dried is a bit iffy).

'This is an urgent wake-up call,' Laura Díaz Sánchez, campaigner at the Plastic Soup Foundation, told the *Independent*. 'We are already eating and breathing what we are wearing.'[xxiv]

And then, deeper sigh, there's nanoplastics. Tiny plastic particles, smaller and more toxic than microplastics, have recently been discovered in polar regions for the first time, but have been present there for fifty years. A quarter of the particles are from vehicle tyres, but in the 'cocktail of chemical pollution', half were polyethylene (PE), used in single-use plastic bags and packaging, and a fifth were PET, used in drinks bottles and our clothing.[xxv]

Fibres in our clothes could be poisoning waterways and food chains on a massive scale and this semi-invisible nightmare isn't just from washing and drying clothes. Dr Imogen Napper was involved in the Everest research, which concluded that the

14 A third contained polystyrene, used for packaging food, and a quarter contained polyethylene, from plastic bags. The scientists' previous work had shown that microplastics were ten times higher in the faeces of babies compared with adults, and that babies fed with plastic bottles are swallowing millions of microplastic particles a day.

microplastics found at the top of the world corresponded with climbers' paths. They weren't related to washing machines, but simply human activity. 'Wherever we go, we're leaving a trail of breadcrumbs of plastic, from our clothing.' So are these tiny little bits of plastic actually harmful?

A common myth is that microfibres are only shed by synthetic garments. But 'natural' materials shed too. In fact, because they're weaker than synthetic fibres, in a laundry there's more breakoff than from polyester.

'Everyone said, "It's fine, because they are biodegradable,"' says design and innovation consultant Anne Prahl. 'But if they end up in the fish or whatever else's stomach they're still loaded with chemicals, colouration and finishes.[15] No one's interviewed the fish and asked if it feels any better off. In Canada, they've found oysters totally stuffed with natural fibres on the inside. And no one knows whether that's okay ... '

Until recently, it was thought maybe it *was* okay. But we now know microplastics cause damage to cell walls in humans, cell death and allergic responses. They can also alter the shape of human lung cells and accumulate in mammal brains, 'resulting in [the death of cells], and alterations in immune responses, and inflammatory responses'.[xxvi] Microplastics can latch on to the outer membranes of red blood cells and may limit their ability to transport oxygen. People with inflammatory bowel disease have 50% more microplastics in their faeces. We're breathing them in, consuming them via food and water. Workers exposed to high levels of microplastics are also known to have developed disease.

Microplastics have turned up in the guts of sea turtles all over the world and been discovered in seal poo. Several studies have shown negative effects on marine life, such as plankton. Small pieces of plastic are more likely to be eaten by wildlife and have been shown to weaken the adhesive abilities of mussels, impair the cognitive ability of hermit crabs, change their behaviour and stunt their growth, cause aneurysms and reproductive changes in fish. They have the potential to bio-accumulate in larger animals, concentrating toxins. Tiny plastic particles in the lungs of pregnant rats pass rapidly into the hearts, brains and other organs of their foetuses, found a 2020 study.[xxvii] Anyone else need a break from this? I do. Cripes.

Anyway ... textiles contribute less plastic to the ocean than car tyres and paint, but they're clearly complicit. So what's being done? Most outdoor brands have signed up to the Microfibre Consortium, which is looking at different ways to stop microfibre shedding, such as filtration in our washing machines and eliminating shedding in the first place. But papers have been published with opposing and

---

15 The fibres become carriers for dodgy chemicals already in the sea, the top five being PCBs, PFCs, DDT, pesticides and herbicides – the latter two extensively used in growing cotton.

complex claims: some argue newer items shed more, others claim it's older garments. Shedding seems to be caused by multiple factors: colouration and finishing, cutting and manufacture, wear and wash-care. 'It's not just the material, it's how it was made,' says Anne Prahl. 'There are so many steps that could make microfibre shedding worse or better. It's a huge, complex issue.'

The slowness to solve the issue is depressing, she says. 'From a design perspective, everyone's been waiting for instructions: when can you tell us what to use or what not to use?' The microplastic problem may even start at the production stage, where they could be released into the air, causing yet another health hazard for workers.

Meanwhile garments carry on polluting: 500,000 tons of microfibres are released into the ocean each year from washing clothes, the equivalent of 50 billion plastic bottles. It seems that the humble fleece jacket is the worst offender, potentially shedding 250,000 microfibres per wash. The 100,000 fleece jackets in use worldwide each year produce enough plastic to make 11,900 shopping bags.

In conversation with Charles Ross, a specialist in performance sportswear and sustainability, I ask whether we should even be making fleeces until the situation is improved, but he points out that no one is talking about banning cotton, clothing or driving.

'Ultimate responsibility for stopping this pollution, however, must lie with the companies making the products that are shedding the fibres,' said the UK government report 'Fixing Fashion'.[xxviii]

So the good news is that us runners can have some impact on plastic microfibre shedding from our T-shirts and kit and have some power in keeping CO2e down. The bad news is … yep, you've guessed it, there's *even more* bad news.

The after-life problem

Polyester T-shirts have advantages, not least durability. In my eleven years as a runner, not one of my synthetic tops has worn out. I don't even know what that would look like. Which is good. Durability means a long lifespan, which reduces the purchase of new items. But that very same petrochemical-based durability becomes a problem if a T-shirt is thrown out before it's worn out. And that happens a lot: **80% of clothing ends up in landfills or incinerators, the equivalent to one rubbish truck every second,** according to the Ellen MacArthur Foundation.[xxix] All those precious human and natural resources, all that harm caused along the way, and what happens to that T-shirt when we decide we're done with it? One in two people throw unwanted clothing straight into the bin, which means incineration or into the ground.

- 32 billion garments are produced each year and 64% of these will end up in landfill.
- The equivalent of one rubbish truck of clothes – 2,625 kilograms – is burnt or dumped into landfill every second, enough to fill 1.5 Empire State Buildings in twenty-four hours.
- 75% of people say they throw away clothes rather than donating or recycling them.
- 13 million items of clothing are thrown into landfill each week in the UK.
- 95% of the textiles that are landfilled each year could be recycled.
- 235 million items – 1 million tonnes (£140 million worth) – of clothing are sent to landfill each year in the UK.
- Less than 1% of used clothing is recycled into new garments.

For all of cotton's ills, it's fundamentally a natural fabric, so it should break down in landfill in around six months.[16] Though we're using so many pesticides, fertilisers and dyes nowadays that 'a natural fibre bears more resemblance to a synthetic fibre', says Charles Ross. And as natural materials biodegrade, they release the dreaded methane. **Plastic or polyester fibres, however, take more than 200 years to decompose, and while doing so release heavy metals, more microfibres and other additives into the soil and water.**

Incineration, on the other hand, 'multiplies the climate impact of the product by generating further emissions and air pollutants that can harm human health,' said the UK parliamentary 'Fixing Fashion' committee report. It may also release even further plastic microfibres into the atmosphere. Some fashion brands were found to be burning unsold stock worth millions of pounds, rather than sell them at a discount, to help maintain brand exclusivity. (France is bringing in a law to ban this.) It's all quite the Kerfufflefuck.

'Our reliance on polyester is one of the reasons why the fashion industry is one of the most polluting industries in the world,' says Greenpeace, 'both in terms of its emissions-heavy production and the non-biodegradable waste it leaves behind.'[xxx]

Clothing companies are not currently required by UK legislation to take responsibility for post-user-phase waste. However, they are in France, which as we learnt earlier has seen a near-trebling of the amount of collected clothing, with 60% being reused. Though some high-street fashion brands such as Marks & Spencer have been proactive in incentivising recycling, it's barely been seen in the running world yet, with Italian brand La Sportiva and Patagonia recently launching limited

---

16 In theory, anyway. A BBC documentary, *The Secret Life of Landfill*, investigated a 1980s tip and found almost fully intact cotton clothing, as well as a legible newspaper.

recycling options, which is a start.[17] It's trickier than it seems, as even an average cotton T-shirt has a label and threads made of different materials, which hampers the process. Enabling unwanted clothes to be reused by someone else is a much better option and it's easy to pass those pre-loved garments on nowadays. They can be collected at the kerbside in some counties, deposited at council recycling centres or clothing banks outside supermarkets, and accepted at charity shops or via collection bags (more on page 56). Even if those clothes may not end up where you were expecting …

Overly loved items are downcycled, for carpet padding, industrial rags, insulation for mattresses, car seats and similar. Of the reusable stuff, charities resell 10–30% of what we donate in UK shops. And they sell the rest to textile recyclers and merchants, who feed a £2.8-billion global trade in second-hand garments. The UK is the second-largest exporter of pre-loved clothes, after the US, sending 351,000 tonnes of clothing primarily to Poland, Ghana and Pakistan. Recycling companies sort rejected items into bales of 40–50 kilograms to be shipped, while at their destinations, these bundles are sold to warehouses, who sell them to local sellers, who sell them at village and market stalls. Sounds like a good thing, right? Dr Andrew Brooks thinks not.

Firstly, the contents of each bale are a lottery, so sometimes a trader will earn enough money to cover rent and food, sometimes not. Secondly, many unwanted clothes flood poorer countries, destabilising their own textile industries, perpetuating poverty and dependency cycles. Ghana's textile and clothing employment fell by 80% from 1975 to 2000, while Nigeria's 200,000-person textile workforce has practically vanished. Thirdly, there's just so much of it. At the Owino market in Kampala, Uganda, there's such a proliferation of second-hand stalls it's become a perverse, postmodern attraction, with local guides taking tourists around it.

Used clothing imports forge a relationship of dependency on the west and

---

17 The 'recycling' is done by SOEX, and an industry insider told me it's actually downcycling. 'They separate shoes into fluff, foam and rubber, very roughly. But they have a really hard job to do, because shoes are made from so many different materials, which are ever-evolving.' But it's a step in the right direction. 'The great thing about their project is that they have their priorities right: first making shoes more durable, then finding ways to repair and reuse, recycling being the last option. Although, if the whole fashion industry recycles like this, there won't be enough places for all the downcycled fluff! If that fluff ends up in landfill anyway, we've lost loads of energy (transport, recycling machines) and not reduced waste. As usual, it's so multi-faceted. It's hard for companies, as you pay per pair of shoes, for shipping, handling and recycling, which can quickly add up and has no return on investment – besides people knowing you're trying to do the right thing. It will mean your shoes will be more expensive to buy. To keep a fair market, it would be much better if that was a legal requirement so every company has the same additional costs.'

prevent Africa from developing, writes Dr Brooks. 'One of the sad ironies of today's globalised economy is that many cotton farmers and ex-factory workers in countries such as Zambia are now too poor to afford any clothes other than imported second-hand ones from the west, whereas thirty or forty years ago they could buy locally produced new clothes.'[xxxi]

'There is greater supply than there is demand,' Liz Ricketts, co-founder of the OR Foundation, a non-profit that researches the second-hand industry in Ghana, told Fashionista.com. Ghana is the second-biggest importer of clothing from the UK, spending $65 million in the process. As much as 40% of clothing imported from the West is directly landfilled or burned in Ghana and Liz suspects the percentage is even higher with footwear.[xxxii] In many cases, we're just passing a first-world problem on to the third world.

Indeed, as I was researching this, emotive images appeared on the internet of huge mountains of clothing waste in Chile's lunar-esque Atacama Desert (a place I've been lucky to visit), with the BBC reporting, 'More than half of the 60,000 tonnes of clothes imported [from the US and Europe] each year ends up in illegal desert landfills, with dire consequences for the environment and the local community.'[xxxiii] A local politician commented, 'Unfortunately, we have transformed our city into the world's largest dump.'

Uganda, Tanzania and Rwanda are all now seeking to prevent second-hand imports to protect domestic industries. Refusing to take waste from the West should force developed nations to adopt better policies, encouraging us to deal with end-of-life clothing more effectively. Waste, some clothing designers now say, is a design flaw.

Sigh. With our running clobber, it's never simple, is it? The message isn't that we shouldn't donate to charity shops, because that's certainly better than landfill or incineration. But it's not quite the ethically clean solution we might have assumed. In most cases, refugees and homeless people have greater need for our excess clothes (somewhere in Calais there are some folk wearing nearly new, GB-branded running kit).

It's clear that we're creating far too much stuff, huge amounts of needless pollution and horrifying waste. It's a crisis of overconsumption. The Fast Fashion ethos is the root of the problem: low-value clothes, mass-produced and sold for as little as £1. *Pile 'em high, sell 'em cheap.* The government know this well. 'The current "fast fashion" business model is encouraging over-consumption and generating excessive waste,' said the 2019 report, 'Fixing Fashion: Clothing Consumption and Sustainability', in which fashion was labelled a 'monstrous disposable industry' by renowned designer Phoebe English: 'We, and the waves of the new generation, will look back on the practices of today's fashion industry in the same way we now look back at Victorian Workhouses, with utter incredulous horror.'[xxxiv]

Why do we feel an urge to keep consuming, to yearn for the newer, shinier version when our current one is just fine? I'll admit that even now that I understand the impact of my running kit, my head is still turned a little when a new shoe or jacket comes out (before I remind myself of the cost to the planet). But why? I don't need it. People experience spikes of pleasure when shopping, a dopamine hit from the anticipation – it floods our system, but wears off and we crave it again. And we're often relatively uninterested in our purchases once we have them, says Kate Fletcher, Professor of Sustainability Design and Fashion at the Centre for Sustainable Fashion.[xxxv] Online shopping increases the dopamine hit because of the anticipatory wait for the product to arrive – studies show we prefer to shop online now.

More materialistic people tend to be less happy and are actually more likely to become depressed, showed a 2006 study.[xxxvi]

Emotional durability is key to ending this restless acquisitiveness, thinks Charles Ross. In outdoor clothing, that means designing to ignore trends, such as smartphone pockets which become obsolete with new releases, fashionable colours and designs that may feel outdated. Brilliantly designed kit should last, along with our affections for it.

The T-shirt problem

When a runner eyes a £250 pair of Nike ZoomX Vaporfly NEXT% wistfully through a shop window, that's not fast fashion. Even though running shoes have their own problems, they're often expensive, designed for a specific purpose and, let's hope, valued, durable and looked after. But that garish, mass-produced race T-shirt very much fits this ugly ethos.

How many are made? Officially a fuckton. Globally, 1.1 million people ran marathons in 2018. Half marathons and 10Ks are even more popular and often also distribute the 'free', planet-costly item. One website lists 226 13.1-mile road races in the UK for 2022. The Great North Run has 57,000 entrants, Great Manchester Run 30,000, Great South Run 24,000, Cardiff Half 27,500 ... Then there are ultramarathons, trail races, 10Ks ... Even my local Corsham 10K has well over 1,000 runners.[18] Race T-shirts are cheaply made en masse, as part of an out-of-date marketing strategy, largely unwanted and unused.

---

18 Though, to their credit, they offer 'no frills' entries, without the free gubbins, as well as wooden medals (with spares recycled), recyclable cups, water refills in the race village, and bike racks to encourage cycling to the event.

Of course, *some* are valued and cherished. That first half marathon, marathon and ultra are big moments and I sure as hell wanted a memento at the time – less so the fifth time I did the Bath Half. I don't remember there being any choice to opt out when I signed up. I was just handed yet another white cotton T-shirt at the finish, which looked very much like all the rest, plastered with logos.

Andrew Murray, a sustainability professional, runner and blogger at Running On Carbon, makes the great point that he'd rather get finisher socks. He has enough T-shirts, but gets through a lot of socks. But, of course, they aren't as good at displaying a sponsor's logo. Though ironically they are, because they might actually get worn.

'Since we set up ReRun, we've become more and more aware of the colossal scale of fast fashion and waste,' says Dan Lawson. ReRun was intended to be a second-hand online running-kit store, but they were so overwhelmed with donated T-shirts that they changed focus. 'It took off really quickly. But 90% of the running kit we get sent is T-shirts.' They're sent by individual runners, often ten at a time. 'We realised they are the biggest problem. We have an entire room full of unwanted race T-shirts. They're in the thousands.'

They started working on changing behaviour, 'raising awareness, coming up with solutions. The biggest way to reduce waste in the running industry at the moment is to stop race T-shirts. That's our first mission,' says Charlotte Jalley. 'They are the most unwanted and unloved items in the running industry.' They've sent upwards of 20,000 T-shirts to various parts of the world.

Charlotte and Dan started talking to events. 'The big races don't want to talk to you,' says Charlotte, 'but the mid-sized and smaller ones will. They were sending most of their stuff off to be recycled, turned into shoddy [i.e. rags], mattress stuffing, basically.'

Charlotte has cared about 'this stuff … since forever. I've always been aware of the end of the world, as long as I can remember. I don't know why.' She's turned down well-paid dancing work and quit jobs on ethical grounds, being unhappy promoting chewing gum or working with cellophane wrappers. Working in a charity shop before ReRun opened her eyes to the scale of clothing waste.

'When you consider the journey of a T-shirt, it's such a waste,' she says. 'They've done this tragic journey, coming from the ground as oil, then all this energy, all this water pollution – and we don't even talk about issues with garment workers – the waste water going into local communities, we've polluted the planet, then we've shipped it somewhere, to several places, then it's given away to someone who didn't even want it in the first place, then it needs to be shipped again, and hopefully it gets to that place where it can be made into shoddy. Maybe it just gets incinerated or chucked in the bin – people still do put clothing in the bin. Or they use it as a rag once. Best case scenario: it becomes mattress stuffing. It's a real tragedy.'

'Race T-shirts are probably the highest impact per wear of all of our clothes,' estimates Andrew Murray. 'The total environmental cost may not be as high as a nice woollen coat, but that coat may be worn hundreds of times over its life.'

Races create T-shirts as marketing tools and sometimes they help with a sponsorship package. 'There's certainly an assumption by many race directors that runners want a T-shirt and a medal,' says Chris Zair from Trees Not Tees (more anon). 'But I think this is changing as we educate people on the impact and the alternatives.' Indeed, hundreds of races in the UK and US now offer runners the option to plant a tree, rather than take home yet another T-shirt they don't want, thanks to Trees Not Tees.

In three years, ReRun has doubled in size and now operates from a 15 x 6-metre building. 'We're bursting at the seams, but we just about manage not to explode.' They've added a shoe bank to their operations, giving away returns and products with minor defects, donated by a handful of brands, to those who can't afford them. I went to visit them and found their HQ both depressing and inspiring. I was inspired by their dedication, but I just couldn't believe the epic and decadent rainbow-plastic piles of unwanted T-shirts (often new) and shoes.

ReRun's unwanted T-shirt mountain isn't formed exclusively of event merchandise, though. 'Half of the Crane (Aldi) and Crivit (Lidl) stuff we get in has never ever been worn – it still has the labels on,' says Dan. 'You can see it was a real impulse purchase. When clothing gets sold so cheaply, people may not ask themselves, "Do I really need this?" It creates a flippant attitude. You think, "Well it only costs a few quid, it doesn't matter if I don't wear it much." But it does.'

Returns are another area of unnecessary waste and CO2e. Because of the huge recent rise in online sales, the average return rate is now 15–30% and about 25% of those items simply get discarded.[19]

ReRun sell some of the donated running kit, but are far busier sending big boxes of T-shirts off around the world to refugees and other charities. However, finding places that actually want our garish T-shirts takes work. Homeless projects are often well served. A Calais refugee camp wanted T-shirts, but not XS, XL or women's versions.

19 In the US, getting an item back into a company's new-product sales stream can be 'logistically prohibitive'. 'Perfectly good stuff gets thrown away all the time, simply because the financial math of doing anything else doesn't work out ... Stores don't want to talk about returns,' said an exposé in *The Atlantic*, in which seven of the eight shops contacted declined to comment. Plus there are emissions from extra transportation.

'We're getting all this shit no one wants and we have to do something with,' says Charlotte. 'There's just so much of it. When you start down this road, and you start seeing it all, you can't go back, because you've seen the damage being caused. **You can't unsee it.** We feel we need to share that message.'

Their business plan is that they want to put themselves out of business. 'Because then there'll be nothing left to repurpose,' says Dan. 'We actively encourage people not to donate stuff to us, and the stuff we have for sale we actively encourage people not to buy.' Indeed, product descriptions on their website include 'It's rubbish' and 'Just a bit of plastic'. **'If you really want to help, don't give us clothes, keep wearing them.'** But if someone buys from ReRun instead of buying new, that's still a win, they say.

How can runners shop more sustainably? 'It's not about foundations and certifications,' says Charlotte. 'The most sustainable kit is the stuff that already exists. Start with yourself: will you wear it and will you look after it? Then that's a sustainable action. That's so important: we must lessen the demand. **We can have a huge, positive impact on climate change just by wearing our clothes for longer.** I have clothes that are fifteen years old.'

Indeed, extending the active life of clothes by three months results in a 5–10% reduction of their CO_2e, water and waste footprints; while extending active life by nine months results in a 20–30% reduction.

Stopping the flow of Fast Fashion, especially race T-shirts, has to come from the top, says Dan. 'The clothing companies, the big sports companies, the races, they all need to change. But **they're only going to change if, from the bottom up, we're telling them we want change.** It's about consumer demand. If you want to make a difference, don't buy new – and say 'no thanks' to free kit if you don't need it. That's the best thing you can do.'

'All roads lead to less,' says Charlotte. 'Which is why we're so focused now on telling people to love the clothes you have. I'd love to see people take pride in putting a little patch on their shoe. I think it gives the trainer or piece of clothing a different feel when you've fixed it. Those loved clothes, you keep them a bit longer. I really love clothing stories. I love the connection you can have with clothes – that makes me really happy. Dan has a pair of shoes that have been to the Gobi Desert and Jordan and I love that they have so many adventures in them.' There's some emotional durability right there.

How can we reconnect with our clothing? 'We've lost that connection, like with food. We don't know what they're made of or who made them. If we can make that connection with the journey, we'll have more of a relationship and be less likely to throw it away or want something new. Instead, we'll care for it, keep hold of it and then pass it on, because it was something really special. I kept a lot of my children's clothes and now we have a granddaughter and I love seeing the clothes on her. There's something really magical about that.' In Japan, items are often repaired with gold. The fix is seen as part of its beauty, something to be proud of.

Brands should have been doing what ReRun are doing a long time ago, says Anne Prahl. 'It's quite funny in a way: companies are always blaming the consumer, saying, "Oh, the consumer doesn't want to pay more for this and that." But they shouldn't wait for the consumer to push us. The brands have responsibility to create their own initiatives. Patagonia are a really good example, supporting grassroots initiatives, helping them financially. That's quite an interesting model for brands, looking at what exists already and how they can support it or offering funds to people who want to run something like ReRun.'

After I first heard Charlotte and Dan talk about ReRun and running's endemic T-shirt problem, I had a clear-out. As well as being a sponsored athlete, I used to review outdoor and running kit for magazines and websites, receiving six new items every month (never long enough in advance to satisfactorily test their durability before deadline). I had a drawer full of redundant T-shirts and a cupboard stuffed with jackets, shoes and running packs. Some kit was being used. But a lot wasn't.

I realised I was kind of hoarding it and other people could be making good use of it. I sold some items very cheaply via a Facebook group, gave several items away to mates, sent some to ReRun and other charities, until I was down to the stuff I was actually using.

I was surprised how good it felt to have less kit. I value it more now too. I wash it more conscientiously (i.e. less – though my shoes more), enjoying making repairs and taking pride in longevity.

With the washing, my wife hasn't noticed that some items no longer go straight into the 'dirty bucket' near our back door. I'm experimenting with how many runs I can get certain garments past her hypersensitive nose and there's no talk of divorce yet . . .

I ask Charlotte what she would say if she had the heads of all the major sports brands sitting round a table in front of her. 'I would say, "You need to work together." It's really sad, this competition between them when we're in a climate crisis. You're being screamed at to change this obsession with growth, with making more, trying to get bigger. What if they could share ideas and work together? You can't think just about your brand. You have to be thinking collectively. If you're being sustainable just within your own little corner, that's not sustainable, because we can't sustain that many sports brands.'

And what about us runners? 'In the end, we can't buy ourselves out of it. Buying a Patagonia jacket won't actually help. If you do buy a jacket, you should keep it for fifteen years. You can't buy a jacket every two years, that's not being sustainable.

'We're past the word "sustainable" now,' Charlotte adds. 'We've already polluted the Earth. We can't use that word any more.'

Phew. Anyone else need cheering up a notch?

What's the difference between Greta Thunberg and Donald Trump? One is an angry, attention-seeking child who yells at foreign leaders on international conferences and never does anything that actually helps. The other one is a Swedish climate activist.

Yeah, but what can we do about it?

1 Read: *Clothing Poverty* by Andrew Brooks and *Cradle to Cradle* by Michael Braungart and William McDonough.
2 Think: Refuse, Reduce, Repair, Reuse, Recycle
3 Refuse
   - Unless you know you're going to wear it plenty, say a polite 'no thanks' to race T-shirts, and medals, either when signing up to a race or at the finish line. Tell the RD about Trees Not Tees (other schemes are available).
   - Susan Paulson, co-author of *The Case for Degrowth*, points out that manipulative fashion-brand marketing keeps us trapped in a cycle of constant consumption. 'They make you feel out of date, dowdy, fat, ugly, not with the cool kids and feeling bad about yourself and that drives you to search on the web or go out and try new clothes.' Join the Fashion Revolution and demand to know who made your clothes. Spending less time on social media helps too.
   - Check ethical standards. Buying certified organic means no slave labour or toxic pesticides. Also look out for the Soil Association, Global Organic Textile Standard (GOTS) label and Better Cotton Initiative (BCI).
4 Reduce
   - Buy less, be happier. 'Pretty much whatever the item, everything has an environmental impact to some degree; the more we buy, the bigger the impact,' says Andrew Murray. 'Relieving the burden of ownership makes people feel better.' A recent study on consumption habits that found those who consumed less scored higher on personal wellbeing and had lower psychological distress, while the higher-consumption group showed none of these benefits (even though they bought 'green' products).
   - Do you really need that new thing? Haven't you already got one that's just fine, or could be just fine with some minor repairs? If you definitely need a new thing, would second-hand do? It'll be better for the wallet and the planet. Practise slow fashion. 'Release yourself from the shackles of trend,'

says fashion campaigner Venetia La Manna. 'Fall in love with second-hand fashion'.

- **Buying used extends a garment's life by about two years, which cuts its combined carbon, waste and water footprint by 82%**, according to thredUP. For second-hand shopping, try ReRun Clothing, Run Again, Depop, eBay, thredUP, Vinted, COS Resell, Clothes Swap or even Facebook.
- Consider spending a little more money on a product that's designed to last. A handful of brands, including Patagonia and Craghoppers, offer lifetime guarantees or at least 'limited' lifetime guarantees.
- Also consider whether it's definitely what you need, whether it'll fit you and whether it's fit for purpose. Especially if you're shopping online. Between 25% and 30% of items get returned, which effectively doubles the emissions from transporting your goods, and if you factor in failed collections and deliveries, that number can grow further.
- Try low-impact washing. 'You don't need to wash clothes as often as you might think,' Fee Gilfeather, a sustainable fashion expert at Oxfam, told the BBC.[xxxvii] She hangs some of her dresses out to air, rather than washing them after each wear. 'Reducing the amount of washing is the best way of making sure that the plastics don't get into the water system.' Consider 'spot washing' too – taking a wet cloth to small marks. Read the washing instructions for specialist kit such as waterproofs, as the wrong wash cycle can speed up their decline.
- Reconsidering clothes-washing habits will cut down CO_2e and microfibres, extend products' lives and save you money. Ask yourself if it really needs washing. Will a cold or colder wash do? (80–90% of the energy used by the washing machine is for heating the water.) Could you create a fuller load? (Half loads are less efficient and delicate wash cycles release more microfibres.) Avoid tumble drying as much as possible. (This uses three times the energy of a wash over a year.)
- 9.4 trillion microfibres could be released every week in the UK through the washing process, and while in France washing machine filters are mandatory, they're not yet in the UK. They're thought to be around 80% effective (some are available from *planetcare.org*). A cheaper option is to wash synthetic fibres inside a pillowcase, which allows them to be cleaned but can prevent some of the fibres being released. Also consider a Guppy Friend bag (via Patagonia) or Cora Ball in your washing machine, claimed to help collect microfibres.
- Consider slow, rather than fast, fashion: *slowfashion.global*

5   Repair

- We need to get back to the 'make do and mend' idea. Using a piece of clothing for nine additional months can reduce that product's associated CO_2 emissions by 27%, its water use by 33% and its waste by 22%, according to UK recycling charity WRAP (Waste and Resources Action Programme).[xxxviii] Fix things early, before a small tear becomes a big rip. Fixing gear helps strengthen your bond to it.
- Try to keep zips clean and replace them when they break, rather than the whole garment.
- Keep an eye out for Patagonia's Worn Wear tour, which travels around the US and Europe every year. You can bring gear from any brand to be repaired.
- Online, websites such as Love Your Clothes (*loveyourclothes.org.uk*), set up by WRAP, offer tips on repairing and extending the life of clothes. iFixit (*ifixit.com*) has good tutorials on how to repair a variety of technical apparel and running gear. Outdoors Magic has some useful repair guides for waterproofs (including re-taping seams), down jackets and sleeping mats: *outdoorsmagic.com/article/kit-care-guide*
- Don't forget to get in touch with the brand who made your kit too. Even if it's out of warranty, they may fix it for you or provide replacement parts.
- See Resources (page 202) for repair service options.
- You can also refer to The British Mountaineering Council's list: *thebmc. co.uk/where-can-I-reuse-repair-recycle-my-outdoor-climbing-hiking-gear*

6   Reuse

- A whole movement has sprung about around decluttering your house/life, and less genuinely can feel like more. Donate, share, gift clothes to friends or resell them. Never put them in the bin, which means landfill or incinerator. Visit *rerunclothing.org/pages/drop-off-locations* for more ideas.
- The North Face's Clothes the Loop programme allows runners to drop off their unwanted clothing and footwear at their stores, regardless of what condition they're in or what brand they are. Alpkit will take unwanted kit from any brand as part of their Continuum Project and find it a new home. Rohan have a Gift Your Gear scheme (*rohan.co.uk/giftyourgear*) which supports various charities, as long as your gear is useable. Kit Collective (*kitcollective. co.uk*) encourage diversity in the outdoors and may want your donations. Preloved Sports will resell your pre-loved kit with money going to charity (*prelovedsports.org.uk*). Run Again (*runagain.uk*) are similar to ReRun.
- Outdoor groups such as Girl Guides, Scouts and Duke of Edinburgh will accept functional kit. Facebook groups such as the Outdoor Gear Exchange

or Outdoor Kit Exchange are great places to buy and sell unwanted outdoor gear. Unwanted kit can also be sold and bought on eBay or Gumtree.

- Also consider donating to local homeless (via *homeless.org.uk*) or refugee charities, or council clothing recycling banks.
- Arrange a swap shop at your running club. Maybe fellow runners would happily adopt your unwanted tops? Also see Swap Box (you'll find them on Instagram @theswapboxcornwall).

7 Recycle
- Upcycle kit at home. Old T-shirts can become good rags (polyester lasts forever), jumpers can transmogrify into cushions, T-shirts into bags. There's plenty of inspiration and advice at *loveyourclothes.org.uk*
- See Resources (page 202) for more options.

4

INDUSTRY ILLUSIONS

So what is the sportswear industry doing about this biblical mess?

'If you want to save the planet, don't buy eco-sneakers.
Try just buying fewer pairs.'
Danny McLoughlin

Sigh. What a Kerfufflefuck. Regardless of how much of Fast Fashion's depressingly unsustainable practices apply to sportswear, I felt crappy for having become unwittingly complicit in this rotten corner of our climate and ecological emergency; in the pollution crisis, the waste crisis, the overconsumption crisis. Once I understood Big Sportswear's harmful relationship with the world, my burning question was, 'Well, what the eff are they doing about it, then?'

The thing is, they *say* they're doing a lot. But it's such a huge, Byzantine, hyper-competitive and squabbly industry, with so many different materials (the more natural-sounding the better, right?) and ideas (the more outlandish the better?), alien processes, jargon and seemingly hundreds of ethical-sounding certifications of varying validity, awash with marketingtalk and infighting (just watch the fisticuffs fly on LinkedIn!). It's really quite confusing, perhaps deliberately so. Though I feel I understood in the end.

At the daps end of things, brands are racing to be the first to bring out eco trainers, and ostensibly some of the concepts sound groundbreakingly amazing. But are they really? Can making new products – adding yet more CO_2e and waste – even be good for the planet? Broadly, there are two approaches to creating more sustainable running shoes: use lower-impact (less CO_2e) or natural materials, or attempt to create genuinely recyclable shoes and circularity in footwear.

In a first-of-its-kind collaboration, behemoths adidas have worked with up-and-comers Allbirds to create the Futurecraft.Footprint, made from 70% recycled polyester and 30% wood pulp (Tencel, which uses 90% less water to produce), with a sugar-cane-based midsole (well, 17% of it). In order to reduce CO_2e, as well as the materials, the production process needs to be improved and they say their tier-one factories will be converted 'towards a renewable model', they'll 'neutralise' shipping emissions and 'reimagine packaging'. As a result, they claim the shoe – the 'lowest ever carbon footprint' for an adidas running shoe – will clock in at a remarkable 2.94 kilograms of CO2e.

The shoe's not out yet and so far it's just marketing prattle, but Allbirds seem credible and it's encouraging to see brands working together, uncharacteristically for an industry quick to litigate at a hint of plagiarism.

It's hard not to fall for Allbirds' stylish kicks made with natural, 'renewable materials' such as merino wool, eucalyptus trees, sugar-cane outsoles, castor-bean oil and even discarded snow-crab shells, plus recycled plastics. They've even made the patent on their sugar-cane SweetFoam material public so other brands can use it. There are plenty of eco proclamations elsewhere, from brands familiar and fresh.

French brand Veja makes shoes which it claims are 'the first post-petroleum running' options, with a vegan model made from 53% recycled materials including plastic bottles, plus bio-based materials such as banana oil and sugar cane, while others include natural Amazonian rubber and rice waste.

Nike's Space Hippie collection is 85–90% recycled content, including plastic bottles, T-shirts and post-industrial scraps. Reebok launched a completely vegan shoe, with a 100% cotton upper, a sole derived from corn and insoles made from castor-bean oil. Elsewhere they've used eucalyptus trees, algae and an outsole made from real rubber trees. Brooks use a biodegradable midsole in their Adrenaline GTS 18 to lessen end-of-life impact (more anon).

Recyclable shoes?

These new products sound fantastical. We'll soon be living in some Peter Pan world, skipping through the fields in trainers made from buttercups and dandelions, more at one with nature than ever before, that exploitative relationship with the planet remedied. Right?

Hmm. While mushrooms sound more eco-sexy, the shoes need to last, plus recycled materials are generally better, it seems, because that means leaving raw materials where they are. However, whether it's plastic bottles or running shoes, recycled and recyclable sound about the same to the half-interested online shopper, but they're very different. 'Recycled' means some materials – usually plastic bottles/ PET – are being reused, but this may only be a small percentage of the shoe and it doesn't mean they can be used again. 'Recyclable', however, would be a pioneering, truly circular shoe that could theoretically be reused and reused again without the need for virgin materials and without creating waste. That's the dream. And it is starting to happen.

The Swiss brand On Running has potentially come up with the biggest idea yet: the '100% recyclable' running shoe you will never own. The Cyclon is made from just six components and two materials, including castor beans and without plastic in the upper, dyes, bleaches or other harmful chemicals. The runner pays a monthly subscription and simply returns the shoes to be recycled when they are worn out, getting a fresh pair in return.

On Running pledge the trainer will be 'zero waste', as 100% of the material will be reused (though they admit 10% of virgin materials may need to be added), allowing the shoe to be recycled up to ten times, with pairs expected to last 373 miles, slashing overall waste by 90%, energy use by 70% and CO_2e by around 50%.

It's potentially a huge leap forward, effectively a 90% reduction of CO_2e for a new shoe. The Cyclon won Product of the Year at the outdoor industry's largest trade show, ISPO, in 2021.

'Even without the circular end of life of the Cyclon, the footprint of the shoe is already better than a regular shoe, by carefully choosing the suppliers and raw materials,' says Laurent Vandepaer, who conducted the Cyclon's life-cycle analysis (LCA), following ISO guidelines. 'We started from the raw materials and we have a pretty short supply chain, and all the steps are very efficient. So you have a really good improvement. There's less wastage.'

Vandepaer, who's been passionate about the environment ever since making an early-2000s trip to Tasmania (much like this writer), is convinced by this new approach. 'Not only by the project's end of life, but when you can control the entire supply chain and which partners you choose, you can have major change, decreasing your impact by almost 50%. That's something we need to replicate with other products.'

Teaming up with environmental initiative Parley for the Oceans, adidas have created something similar, the Futurecraft.Loop; and French ski brand Salomon claim a similar shoe, the Index.01; while Hylo Athletics have pulled off the impressive double by making a shoe from natural materials that's *also* recyclable. Hylo pay you to send them back daps, made from corn, natural rubber, organic cotton, algae and water-based glue, turning the fabrics into compost and grinding up the soles to be used in new ones. Impressively, they accept shoes from any brand.

Too good to be true?

However, if this new eco-trainer craze sounds too good to be true, that's because it is.

'How much do these "eco-sneakers" actually reduce carbon emissions by?' asks RunRepeat.com's Research Director Danny McLoughlin. In an exceptional piece of analysis, McLoughlin conducted LCAs of the adidas Ultraboost Parley and Brooks Adrenaline GTS 18. The former uses recycled plastic bottles rescued from landfill and plastic bags from the ocean in its upper – pushing all the right emotive buttons – while the Brooks boasts a biodegradable midsole.

However, plastic bottles still need to go through a processing stage, which emits significant CO_2e. Plus the idea of recycled plastics is so popular in sportswear – both footwear and clothing, as we'll see anon – that we're facing a global shortage. That both drives up the price and means more plastic bottles and bags which could have been made from old items are made from virgin materials instead. 'By buying up this plastic and putting it into shoes, we're taking it out of a circular process and destine the plastic for landfill,' sustainability design expert Anne Prahl tells me. 'This is *only* a problem if too many businesses want to use recycled plastic. Which is our current situation.'

Also, while Brooks's biodegradable midsole is a lovely idea, it's not so effective if the rest of the shoe isn't biodegradable.

The reduction of impact of the two shoes is estimated at a decidedly underwhelming 1.34 kilograms (9.6%) of CO_2e for adidas, and 0.34 kilograms (2.5%) of CO_2e for Brooks. Indeed, McLoughlin's analysis of eighty-nine eco shoes found that the maximum reduction in CO_2e from any shoe currently on the market is … *less than 13%.*

Even if a shoe is made from 100% recycled materials, it will still emit around 10.64 kilograms of CO_2e, a moderate saving of 24% (though On Running claim they've managed a 50% reduction with the Cyclon).

Indeed, if each runner buys eco trainers rather than standard daps, their carbon emissions will fall to 38.31 kilograms per year rather than 42 kilograms, a reduction of 8.8%.[20] **But it's the buying of shoes that's the problem. It doesn't really matter what they're made of.**

'Eco-sneakers are not going to save the planet,' McLoughlin concludes (also noting that of the RunRepeat database of 2,556 shoes, only eighty-nine are 'eco-friendly'). 'In fact, all they'll do is kill it a little more slowly … Nike and adidas don't really care that much about the environment. They just want you to think they do so that you'll buy more sneakers … If companies were really serious … they would make their sneakers more durable, release fewer variations, and work to change buying behaviour … [but] Nike is never going to tell customers to buy fewer pairs.' It's tempting to add, 'Don't buy trainers for their snazzy new colours and bold performance claims. Just buy ones that will last.'[i]

'One speciality product is no match for the ecological impact of a global brand,' weighs in Tansy Hoskins. 'It also begs the question of why, if brands have the

20 Based on the average American buying seven pairs of shoes per year, of which three are 'athletic shoes'.

capacity to produce less harmful shoes, they don't apply these planet-friendly methods to everything they do.'[ii]

McLoughlin concludes: 'If you want to save the planet, don't buy eco-sneakers. Try just buying fewer pairs.'

Some optimism

'These innovations/experimentations will not disrupt how sports shoes are made, worn and disposed of,' agrees Anne Prahl, an independent design consultant who's worked with Nike, Puma, Karrimor, Rohan, inov-8, Speedo and Topshop, earning the nickname 'the Sustainability Police'.

'Consumers are sold concepts of recyclable/biodegradable or carbon-neutral/positive shoes that are not yet achievable. But the eco-shoes are small steps to test and develop more impactful and complete solutions in the long run. At least these brands are "at it" and pushing their suppliers for solutions. It's a start.'[21]

I was learning that this stuff is almost never as simple as it sounds from the outside. Frustratingly, a shoe made from one material, such as On Running's Cyclon, is unlikely to be as durable as current models. 'Also, you add all of the sending back and forth, because you are replacing your shoes more frequently, and how sustainable is that in terms of emissions? It may be better overall, but it's not nothing. We won't be able to just buy and throw away shoes guilt-free.'

However, circularity is the only true solution, thinks inov-8's Bodil Oudshoorn, 'just like we have cans at home that we recycle into cans again. We just need to make the model and process feasible in terms of the shoe's performance. We still need grip on trail-running shoes and we still need durability.'

So unless a brand is reinventing its whole supply chain and applying it across their range, let's not be fooled by eco trainers. In many cases, it's pretty much greenwashing. Circular shoes, however, have the potential to be a game changer. If they work. Ultimately, all of these new eco shoes need to feel good to run in – and, let's be honest, look good too – or runners won't buy them. And they need to last.

Performance metrics

Never mind mushrooms and algae, I was beginning to understand that **if a brand is sincere about our climate and ecological emergency it will have conducted**

---

21 Several brands boast various levels of recycled and recyclable packaging and On Running estimate they've saved 160 tonnes of CO_2e by reducing packaging for the Cyclon. Shoes are light compared to, say, bikes and furniture anyway, so space is more of an issue when shipping, and Allbirds redesigned the shape of the shoe box into a cone to maximise shipping space. A 40% reduction in total packaging enables 30% more pairs of shoes to be carried in each carton.

a LCA on its supply chain, know its CO2e and be working measurably towards net zero with external auditing and transparency. Reducing a company's CO2e will have far greater impact – as in, less – on the planet than creating fake-news daps.

A few brands do publish sustainability reports and/or emissions-reduction targets. But again here, it's easy to be hoodwinked. For starters, the shop-front operation of a company represents a minor share of overall impact. It's their supply chain, usually in Asia, that will have by far the highest emissions. A credible sustainability report calculates scope 1 to 3 emissions (see page 13), and in this industry scope 3 will be around 80–90% of overall CO2e.

On Running has joined Science Based Targets (SBT), is transparent about its suppliers and has published a sustainability report aiming to reduce scope 3 emissions by 55% by 2030, reduce scope 1 and 2 emissions by 46% by 2030, as well as reduce water use, support workers' rights and more.

Alongside them, a handful of small, progressive brands stand out. Allbirds are B-Corp certified, have been carbon neutral since 2019, aim to halve their CO2e by 2025 and be close to net zero by 2030, carbon label their products, and espouse regenerative agriculture (healthy soil removes CO2 from the atmosphere), renewable materials (replacing petroleum-based ones with natural ones 'and inventing alternatives that don't yet exist') and responsible energy (cleaner fuel and electricity, and using less).[22]

Icebug, the 'small independent Swedish brand in a dirty business', became the **first 'climate positive' outdoor footwear brand** in 2019, following the United Nations Climate Change Climate Neutral Now guidelines. They aim to cut CO2e by 50% for 2030. 'You can't save the planet by buying Icebug shoes,' they warn. 'Consumption consumes resources.' It's their small print that impresses most: 'One of our basic principles for being sustainable is to have models that carry over from year to year.' In other words, unlike most brands, they're not constantly 'revamping' shoe models to encourage that pathological 'need the new one' desire in consumers.

With only one product, Hylo's LCA will have been quicker than most brands'. They have reduced their carbon footprint to 7.83 kilograms of CO2e per shoe and offset all CO2e to be carbon negative.

---

22 Carbon labelling feels inevitable and important, like nutritional information on food. But it's problematic as, so far, the figures are self-calculated. 'Brands are not applying the same methodology, so it's almost impossible to compare the results from Allbirds to adidas or Nike,' says On's Laurent Vandepaer. 'But it is a good initiative, they are the first to do it and it's forced the sector to have a conversation.' Even if 'some players make methodological choices that lead to low environmental "scores" which aren't necessarily the reality. What is urgently needed are stricter sectoral standards helping brands to apply the LCA methodology in the same way.'

Unusually, Veja 'work directly with the producers' they source from, requiring farmers to practise agroecology (the philosophy behind regenerative agriculture) and they have a shoe bearing the logo of Sea Shepherd, the controversial Greenpeace offshoot known for its direct approach to confronting illegal fishing, with all profits going to the NGO.

What these guys are doing seems really admirable. Even if they haven't yet rolled out the impressive CO_2e reduction gains from the Cyclon across their range, On Running also belong in the disappointingly small pantheon of running-shoe brands doing the right thing. Sadly, however, I haven't yet actually seen anyone running in Allbirds, Icebug or Hylo daps, and on a screen they don't look as durable as my trail shoes. But let's hope this approach becomes the norm.

Vivobarefoot boast a B-Corp certification, but – most impressively yet – they pledge to **simply make fewer products**. 'We can't just keep on pumping shoes into the environment,' Head of Sustainability Emma Hamilton-Foster told *Runner's World*. 'We're trying to consolidate the product range, to focus on six or so shoes … And then offer repairability, recyclability and compostability as standard.'

Vivobarefoot, Veja, La Sportiva and Scarpa all offer repair options too. While most brands have product care tips on their websites, I couldn't find any on the big five brands' pages – with the exception of Nike, though you have to dig around to find it. Presumably seeing consumers coming back a little more slowly doesn't interest them so much.

Brands behaving badly?

Like On Running, Nike have signed up for SBT and aim to reduce scope 1 and 2 emissions by 65%, and scope 3 by 30% across their supply chain. They must also make a 70% absolute reduction of emissions in their owned or operated facilities. Which sounds pretty good. Asics, Under Armour and Brooks have all also set 1.5 °C-compatible goals approved by SBT.

adidas have committed to SBT too, and for the last couple of years have achieved a B rating, notes Andrew Murray. 'Scoring a B is OK but others score higher, with Nike and Asics both achieving an A- last year.' Their business target is to have their own operation carbon neutral by 2025 (only a 15% reduction per item from 2017 levels) and full value chain carbon neutrality by 2050. 'This all sounds good but technically is quite weak,' says Andrew. 'It's a crap target; with no set requirements to reduce emissions.'

Andrew estimates only 10% of companies with net-zero ambitions are credible.

All these different schemes, initiatives and approaches make it confusing for a runner to understand which brands are genuinely trying to make a difference.

So much of the terminology is new and esoteric. Indeed the Competition and Markets Authority found 40% of firms' green claims could be misleading, with other polls putting the figure even higher.[iii]

Buzzwords and bunkum

Helpfully, RunRepeat.com's Danny McLoughlin conducted a forensic analysis of both Nike and adidas's sustainability goals and is withering about some of them. For example, Nike, easily the biggest sportswear brand in the world, lest we forget, aims to implement 100% renewable energy at owned and operated factories, offices and shops (scope 1), but not at contracted factories (scope 3), which would have so much more impact. 'It's easy to play fast and loose with words … **This is simply a case of using sustainable as a buzzword. It's meaningless** … The level of carbon emissions in the footwear market is unsustainable and requires radical action.'

McLoughlin is also unimpressed by adidas, not least their definition of sustainability, which tellingly includes the phrase 'shareholder expectations'.

If we want to change things, we have to pressure the factories into using sustainable energy resources, says Bodil Oudshoorn. The way the supply chains are organised makes real progress really difficult, both she and Laurent Vandepaer assure me. 'You have like 30 to 100 components coming from different suppliers, so everything's super exploded,' he says. 'It's quite difficult to go into the supply chain and have an influence, because sometimes you're only a small client for these suppliers.' The further you go down the chain, the more complicated it becomes, because there's no direct commercial relationship. So the supplier has little incentive to make big changes. It's changing and we managed it with the Cyclon. But it's hard to have a major influence.'

To make progress, you would have to do it as a collective of brands who are manufacturing in a certain factory, explains Bodil. 'The same is true with things like dyeing strategies,' she says. 'Basically, it's about encouraging factories to take up new technologies, which would often be a wider investment. But that's where you can make the biggest headway.' For a company like inov-8, there's little control over dyeing, or the materials extraction process, because a factory will have hundreds of tier-two and -three suppliers.

'The biggest brands with the biggest budgets and teams can actually investigate these things,' says Bodil. 'They're the ones with the leverage to make a change. Whenever Nike starts inventing a new dyeing process, I get excited because it means we'll be able to use it in a year's time. That's the way it works for the smaller brands.'

Nike do some things well. But the thing that really pisses people in the industry off is their naked hypocrisy. **Nike are open about their ambition to halve the** company's environmental impact – *while aiming to double their business.*[iv] Creating loads more products for a planet already saturated with trainers doesn't scream sustainability to me.

'Isn't Nike already big enough?' says an impassioned industry insider. 'How could you possibly have a better environmental impact while doubling your sales? **That's actually selling shoes that people don't need. That's just plain greedy.** The bigger brands are the worst for making false and dishonest claims.'

Two more people interviewed in this book who would rather not be quoted are equally outraged by Nike's stance. McLoughlin isn't so shy. 'If Nike's aim is to double the size of their business, then surely its grand objective is simply to continue polluting at the same rate? Both Nike and adidas are dipping their toes in the water, but they don't want to get wet.'

Ethical consumption

I felt like I was learning some important things about the running footwear industry, both depressing and occasionally hopeful. But some aspects were still pretty confusing, such as all the different schemes brands sign up to. For a final word on this, I found the amazing resource that is EthicalConsumer.org (EC). In a comprehensive guide to ethical trainers, EC investigated, scored and ranked the ethical and environmental record of fifty brands, for vegan credentials, carbon footprints, recycling, forced labour, supply chains, with bonus mark-ups for product sustainability and company ethos.[v]

Again, it's the smaller, newer brands who get the kudos, with Veja (13) commended for using only organic cotton and wild rubber. Allbirds (11.5) and On Running (10.5) are right up there too, while Vivobarefoot (10.5) and inov-8 (10 – phew!) are singled out for plaudits for their vegan stance and aims to improve product durability.

Next up are La Sportiva (9), Asics and Scarpa (8.5), Sketchers (8), Mizuno (7.5), Hoka (7), Arc'Teryx (6.5), Salomon (6), Puma (5.5), Nike (5), Altra (4.5), Under Armour (4), adidas and Merrell (3.5), Reebok and Saucony (3.5) and Karrimor (1.5), with Brooks scoring a big fat 0 (for unethical investments).

A boycott of Puma is encouraged (for issues regarding Israel and Palestine) and brands belonging to Frasers Group plc (Sports Direct), Lonsdale, Karrimor and Slazenger are given large black marks because of numerous issues with working conditions, even in the UK. Indeed, Sports Direct are the epitome of the Fast Fashion ethos of 'make 'em cheap, pile 'em high' that has allowed the fashion industry to reap such chaos on our planet.

Reviewing the running-shoe industry as a whole, EC highlight the regrettable use of coal to power factories and point out how simpler designs would cut CO2e from both manufacture and materials.[23]

'Let's make some simple, comfortable, durable shoes, which maybe we can even disassemble and would be easier to repair!' says Bodil.

'While a number of companies have either adopted, or begun work on, science-based carbon-reduction targets, and might claim notable carbon reductions for certain lines,' EC say, 'there are no signs of them cancelling their more damaging products.'

The report notes the irony of brands speaking out about the need for circularity while most recycled materials are PET from plastic bottles rather than shoes, and 'recycled' trainers tend to go towards AstroTurf, racetracks and basketball courts instead of back to the shoe factory.

Getting a grip

That seemed a good summation and left me feeling glum. But what has given me hope above all else as I've researched the environmental impact of daps, is the people. Everyone I spoke to for these mostly depressing chapters is either a brilliant actor, or they really care. There is a genuine willingness in the industry to be more sustainable, insists Laurent Vandepaer. Collaboration, especially between brands who share factories, is the way forward, he thinks, as does Bodil. And it is happening. 'There are round tables where brands are trying to work together,' says Laurent. 'But it's quite challenging,' he caveats, 'because often they want to be the first to announce they're using a new fibre that's very sustainable or the first to implement a recycling programme, so there's an incentive for the brands to retain some information. From a sustainability point of view it's really stupid. You do not win alone.'

To try to cheer myself up, I had a longer chat with inov-8's 'Dr Grip', Bodil Oudshoorn. Like me, she battles with the conflict of caring about our climate and ecological emergency while being deep into an industry that's a big part of the problem. How does Bodil, who's taken about the biggest planet-friendly sacrifice she can, rationalise her conscience with her work? 'Walking away from something that's not great isn't the way to solve it,' she says. 'Yes, I know inov-8 is currently not great – yet. But if I left the footwear industry, I wouldn't have any influence on it. In a small company you can make a change.'

As a company, inov-8 take sustainability seriously, she insists. 'They do genuinely care. Though it's when things are easy to marry together that they get acted on.

---

23 'This makes it sound like factories have a coal mine next to them and they choose to use it,' said an insider. 'In Asia, most electricity is government owned/controlled, so you have very little influence over it unless you set up your own solar panel field.'

Reducing waste usually means reducing cost and that's something everyone's keen on! But when an idea is more expensive, that's a much harder conversation.'

Their sustainability strategy is focused almost exclusively on durability. 'If you make more durable shoes, you use less virgin materials, you create less waste, there's less end-of-life products and there's usually less carbon because you haven't produced another shoe.'

Indeed, inov-8 made headlines when the company became the first to add graphene to their shoes. It's a material apparently 200 times stronger than steel, and does make a shoe's outsole, from personal experience, significantly more durable (even if it's the upper that usually wears out first on trail shoes).

Recycled materials – usually PET – are very fashionable in the industry, but often less durable. 'We have experimented with these a lot,' says Bodil. 'But it's still a very energy-intensive process. You have to take the outsole off and the midsole and there's lots of glue and the quality of the material, once you've separated the components, is very low, because of the wide mix of materials. And they'll be the first thing that deteriorates. When recycled materials match virgin materials for performance standards, inov-8 use them. But usually, they simply aren't as durable.'

Repair schemes aren't viable for inov-8 at the moment; a carbon audit and creating a sustainable supply chain are both huge and complex jobs that are 'really easy for a big company to do and really hard for a small company to do' (because of the cost, time and their respective relationships with factories).

'Sustainability is also about how we treat our people, our own staff, our factory workers; paying minimum wages, enough money, workers can send their kids to school,' Bodil says. There's a community aspect too. 'Volunteering locally is a big thing for us [working with food banks, and fundraising towards peatbog restoration].'

How about the idea that if a company really cared, it would simply make, market and sell less? 'It's a really hard one,' she says. 'But that's where being in a small company is amazing. We can say, "We want you to buy fewer shoes", because if more people choose inov-8, we will still sell more. If they would all buy two [pairs of trainers] instead of three and those last longer, we have a great business model.'

She thinks government regulation would really help to standardise products. 'Otherwise it becomes a marketing race. Marketing wins.'

She hates the idea that consumers are being manipulated into thinking that buying products made with recycled materials is good for the planet. 'That's not true. **In the end, the most sustainable product is the one you've already got.**' How can the industry lessen overconsumption? 'By letting you know one pair of running shoes is fine. How often do we think trail shoes aren't suitable for running on a road? And we think we need fell shoes, ultra shoes, scrambling shoes, walking shoes, the list goes on. Product development and marketing can have an influence here: make one versatile, durable shoe that can do anything.'

Our climate and ecological emergency makes her angry. 'Because **almost all of it is not our fault as individuals and yet we're the ones often feeling bad about it**. You know, you make so many sacrifices yourself and like most people don't care. It's frustrating. In the past **I've gone into this massive overdrive of basically feeling guilty for existing**.'

That said, Bodil feels 'really optimistic' about the running industry and the role it can play.

Laurent feels optimistic too. 'I'd quit my job otherwise!' he says. 'Sustainability is challenging work, so it takes time. But slowly, if you persevere, you can achieve some good outcomes. There are so many inefficiencies, but if you take the time to go into the supply chain, you can really make some easy pickings.'

'It's important for the customer to continue to put the pressure on brands,' says an industry insider. 'Every time there's a sustainability-related email it reaches us. **At the moment, we are not overflowing with sustainability emails.** It can have an impact.'

Indeed, we can take the initiative on several fronts. Let's not forget, no one is forcing us to buy shoes. How many pairs do we really need? (Certainly not, ahem, twenty-five.) There are a few – but not nearly enough – reasons to be cheerful in the running-shoe industry. But while this whole thing can seem unbearably complex, it's actually simple: we need to make and buy less stuff. The most sustainable kit isn't made of algae, it's the kit we already own. Let's cherish it, make it last, then pass it on thoughtfully.

But brands, even more than us, have a part to play. Just make fewer shoes and make them last longer and sort out recycling and lower your footprints and be kinder to your workers. **Making more is killing the planet. Making less, but better, is the solution.**

So that's shoes for now. Maybe I'm naive, but I feel a little bit encouraged overall. Some people and some brands are working hard to improve, even if it's the smaller, braver ones doing the pioneering.

Clothicide

I ruddy love running and I used to love running kit. The anticipatory thrill of sliding a light, bright T-shirt over my head, breakfast in my shorts, the subtle crackle of my socks as I pull them up, their reassuring tightness against tired tendons, lacing up my daps, still decorated with splashes of mud from yesterday (I'll clean them today, promise!).

Those actions for me were far more meaningful than simply getting dressed. They meant escapism, me time in nature, feeling alive. I thought running was the best thing in the world. But that's all a bit tainted now.

I feel guilty and conflicted about my shorts and T-shirt and a bit weird about running. I've been contributing far more than I realised to our climate and ecological crisis. I'm a cog in this huge, ugly cycle of overconsumption – and a bigger cog than some, as a brand ambassador.

This is an industry I love – or at least it makes kit I love. It's enabled me to do so much, have some life-changing experiences. But once you see the damage caused, like a burnt corpse in a horror film, you can't simply unsee it. I feel a combination of shame for having my head in the sand, and some level of betrayal too.

I want to know that the outdoor sportswear industry cares, that it's making *real and urgent* **efforts to atone and improve. Not just adding a bit of algae to a shoelace.**

How is it unfucking itself? What, if any, are the main differences between the eco crimes of the Fast Fashion world and outdoor sportswear? And what should I be wearing to be more ethical? (It feels like naked might be the only solution, and in my case no one wants that.)

Certification fatigue

Initially, I found some positive signs. The clothing industry has a bunch of ethical-sounding accreditations, certifications, schemes and programmes, and bigger brands are quick to sign up to them.

And most of the main sportswear brands are working with external carbon auditors to reduce their CO_2e – even if there's some confusion because of the lack of standardisation (and the caveats about Nike and adidas on page 65) – the main ones being Science Based Targets (whose clients include Nike, adidas, Brooks, Puma and Asics), B Corp (Patagonia, Vivobarefoot, Allbirds, Alpkit and Finisterre) and the Higg Index (Salomon, Allbirds, Asics, Brooks, Mammut, New Balance, Nike and Puma).

The UN's 17 Sustainable Development Goals is the ultimate brand audit, says performance sportswear and sustainability expert Charles Ross. And there are loads more. Which, frustratingly, is part of the problem. You can't directly compare brands' ethical performance because they have different standards and are often measuring different things. 'It creates audit fatigue and audit confusion for customers,' says Charles.

Nike, as usual, are a case in point. Due to a Carbon Disclosure Project (CDP) loophole, they've been able to claim emissions are reducing when they're actually increasing, because technically they're getting smaller as a proportion of overall revenue.[24]

Plus almost all of these schemes are voluntary. 'There is an abundance of certifications and standards and, in some ways, it'd be good if government stepped in with a more accountable framework and one-stop approach,' says inov-8's Helen Stuart.

In fact, the multiplying 'eco-friendly' labels and initiatives have become part of the problem, said a March 2022 Changing Markets Foundation report which upturned the apple cart. Analysis of ten sustainability certification schemes and initiatives found 'compromised independence', 'lack of transparency' and little evidence of success, as well as being 'silent on critical issues' such as over-production, microfibre pollution and fossil-fuel dependency. They are 'sustain-ability decoys for brands, enabling greenwashing on a massive scale', with membership giving an illusion of progress while fashion's impact worsens.[vi]

I sense I'm gonna need a bigger mug of tea . . .

Decarbonising clothing

Encouragingly, however, **the clothing industry is one of the cheapest sectors to decarbonise**, according to the World Economic Forum. At least 90% of clothing's footprint is in its manufacturing supply chain and industry emissions could be halved in ten years.

How? Firstly, switching to renewable electricity could reduce CO_2e by 45%, with another 20% saved by using renewable sources for heat, and another 15% by machinery upgrades. Nike is apparently the only brand taking real action in this area so far, by helping its footwear suppliers to electrify their boilers. adidas, meanwhile, have released a guidebook for factories seeking to reduce their energy usage, water usage and waste.

The second idea is moving away from the addiction to fossil-fuel fabrics (more anon).

The third move would be shipping products across the world on boats using clean fuel (inov-8 tell me it's just one container amongst thousands, so influence is thin), with hydrogen showing promise. The fourth pillar is the simplest, potentially most impactful, the one I find myself increasingly wanting to scream, yet ideologically it's so challenging that it feels like the least likely: *just make less stuff!*

---

24 Nike's 2020 climate change report claims a 5% drop in emissions, despite and perversely because of a 7% year-on-year revenue growth [in 2019]. In fact, Nike's scope-1 emissions have increased every year since 2016, and somehow the company's business travel isn't included in its sustainability targets.

The bad news? **'There's no correlation between bold climate commitments and actual carbon reductions'**, found a 2021 study by The Climate Board.[vii] And industry decarbonisation clearly isn't happening fast enough. 'Nearly all of this [decarbonisation] would have to happen at the other end of the supply chain from the glittery brand logos and slick annual reports,' say Ethical Consumer. 'And for many companies, what is happening down that end is murky.'[viii]

The biggest sticking point is the relationship between brands and factories. There are trust issues. Remember, brands don't own the factories, who in turn fulfil orders for multiple companies (Patagonia share with Rab, for example, inov-8 with La Sportiva). It's common practice for apparel companies to hop from factory to factory in search of cost savings, which keeps brands hooked on fossil fuels. Why would a factory agree to expensive energy upgrades to renewables when the brand demanding them may not be around for long?

From what I'm told, the prospect of factories converting to renewables is, as ever, not that simple. Factories tend to be 'very power-hungry' and unable to generate enough solar power from their own roofs to power all their machines.

China is 'an odd country', an industry insider told me, where these types of things are arranged at government level – 'so for electricity you get some hydro/wind energy but also lots of coal. Even in Vietnam, if a factory converted to renewables without government support it would need to invest in modern machinery that uses less electricity to begin with, in order to be able to generate the power sustainably.' Nevertheless, it seems the industry's biggest CO2e savings can be made if brands and factories – and possibly Asian governments – can simply work together better.

Making the manufacturing process less impactful is avoiding the issue of churn, argues Charles Ross. The bigger problem, he believes, is that factories are making a product for as low a price as possible so it can be sold competitively. 'Currently the lowest price wins – that's what makes the consumer second-happiest, after aesthetics. But if there was a standard that said renewable energy must power the factory, the industry would work to it.'

Regardless, garments should be designed with high Emotional Durability (ED), Charles says, 'so that you hold on to the items for so long that the biggest footprint comes during ownership, from laundering'.

I suggest brands bringing out new versions of kit that's already fit for purpose is a problem that overrides whether it's designed for longevity. It feels like most products are updated every two to three years regardless of technological or design breakthroughs, and many 'upgrades' are usually not much more than a new colourway. Marketing (that word again) breaks the Emotional Durability concept,

Charles agrees, but adds: 'If brands don't rush to associate themselves with the latest technology, a rival brand will steal the lead.'

But isn't that the same issue of churn, the overarching problem? Newer, better, buy it quick!

Ten plastic bottles sitting on a wall …

I felt frustrated again. But if the whole model of churning out more and more, regardless of need, is infuriatingly irresponsible verging on criminal, at least there seems to be progress in more sustainable sportswear materials. adidas and Reebok have pledged to replace all virgin polyester with recycled polyester by 2024, with Asics, Nike and Puma making similar commitments.

Polyester is made from PET, the same as plastic bottles. Recycled polyester, or rPET, is more sustainable to some degree, as production uses just a quarter of the emissions, which *sounds* good. However, as ever, it's not that simple. Those bottles were already part of a closed-loop system where they could be recycled up to ten times, as bottles. They're being removed from that loop and placed in a new process, where it's unlikely they can be recycled again, and if that rPET becomes a race T-shirt it's probably destined for landfill sooner. Also, recycled polyester is still a drop in the ocean compared to virgin polyester use, so the footprint reduction is minuscule, an average of 4% (across four major fashion brands). Furthermore, demand for recycled bottles will soon outstrip supply, which is causing soaring prices.

'Making fashion from plastic bottles is just another greenwashing tactic by brands to encourage people to buy more of what they don't need and the planet can't afford,' says environmental organisation City To Sea.[ix] The fashion industry was accused of 'free riding' on PET bottles' circular system by EU environment commissioner Virginijus Sinkevičius. Plus it's all still fossil fuels.

Also, recycled clothing isn't the same and doesn't sound as good to me as *recyclable* clothing. But recycled yarns are far better than recyclable yarns, argues Charles.[25] 'The former is on its second life, while there is no guarantee the latter will be used again.' Which is a fair point, because all the running T-shirts I own are still going strong.

I am confused. Though my polyester tee will get many more years' use than if it was currently a plastic bottle, is recycled polyester a good or a bad thing? Either way, it's de rigueur in sportswear.

25 'Recycled cellulose is much weaker than virgin, so a recycled cotton garment will wear out much faster – which is not the same in performance as the back-to-virgin performance levels of rPET.'

Greenwashing

The sportswear industry went 'sustainability crazy' during lockdown, says design and innovation consultant Anne Prahl. 'Now everyone's talking about it. If you're putting it nicely, it's misinformation or misunderstanding. Everyone jumped on the term "circularity" because it was easier to understand than sustainability. But a lot of people in the industry initially misunderstood and thought, "Oh, as long as we can recycle things, it's fine to keep on churning them out." That's why everyone's changing to recycled polyester, which is better than virgin polyester from a carbon footprint perspective. But there are so many issues around it. Not just environmentally, it could be health issues too [related to toxic chemicals in some plastic bottles, such as BPA]. Everyone's saying, "We're a sustainable brand right now!" But it's not circular to use recycled polyester made from plastic bottles in a product you can't recycle. There's nothing circular about it. **It's so frustrating that people are calling themselves something they're not.** It's the absolute minimum a brand should do, the first step in improving their use of polyester.'

Nike, incidentally, label apparel with over 50% recycled content or shoes with over 20% recycled content (by weight) as 'sustainable materials', meaning a shoe made of 80% oil-based materials is claimed to be a sustainable product. A growing number of brands seem to be making up statements that just aren't true, Anne says. 'Everyone's designing information to make the consumer think they care. Judging by brands' social media **you'd think every one of them is really, really sustainable and really, really cares. But it's greenwash.** It's just being a little bit more sustainable, versus actually having a proper impact. That's really what I'm struggling with. I'm quite fed up with it.'

This isn't a rogue view. As much as 59% of green claims are unsubstantiated, misleading or 'rampant greenwashing', found a Changing Markets Foundation report.[x]

'We need regulation, regulation, regulation,' said George Harding-Rolls, the Changing Markets Foundation campaigns adviser, on the *Planet Pod* podcast. 'The fashion industry is one of the most lightly regulated in the world, yet one of the most environmentally damaging. It's mind-boggling that we're regulating transport, plastics and agriculture, but we're not regulating this behemoth, hugely destructive and divisive industry.'

It's hard to disagree. Ironically, Fast Fashion moves remarkably slowly on sustainability, on advancing from the disastrous 'take, make and dispose' model. Greenwashing is dangerous because it allows a sense of moral licensing: if someone feels like they've made an environmentally conscious effort with their shopping, a study found they feel less inclined to make further efforts elsewhere.[xi] When in fact, by adding to the wrecking ball of overconsumption, they've had a negative impact.

I'm no expert, but it seems that being left largely unregulated has demonstrated spectacularly that the industry isn't ethically mature enough to solve the biblical problem it's created without external policing. Maddeningly, the government rejected every single one of the Fixing Fashion paper's wide-ranging recommendations. Although the Competition and Markets Authority (CMA) watchdog is openly targeting greenwashing and brands could face court action and the Advertising Standards Authority is clamping down, that won't lead to the urgent system changes we need.

However, in March 2022 the European Commission announced a vast expansion of eco-design rules for textiles (and later other products), on durability, recyclability, a curb on hard-to-recycle materials, disclosure of how much unsold stock goes to landfill, banning the phrases 'environmentally friendly' or 'eco' without substantiation, and demanding consumers be given more information on how to reuse, repair and recycle clothes. Which to my ears sounded very promising indeed. The industry has escaped the 'polluter pays principle' for too long, said Nusa Urbancic, the director of the Changing Markets Foundation.[26]

Is all my running kit evil?

So some of that is encouraging. But I'm still confused. If both polyester and recycled polyester are bad, and cotton is bad in different ways, when they really do need new kit, **what is the planet-conscious runner meant to wear? Is there such a thing as a genuinely ethical material?**

Ultimately, recycled polyester is the lesser of two evils, while organic cotton is better than standard cotton. Both wool (epic CO2e, not to mention methane from sheep) and bamboo (usually rayon, which is 'chemically intensive, environmentally polluting and human hazardous'; lyocell, Tencel and Monocel are all better) are championed, but are far from perfect.[xii] Ethical Consumer are happiest with recycled wool, recycled cotton, organic hemp and organic linen. However, that doesn't mean those materials have good running performance and will be bought. (Some biomaterials also show promise but haven't yet been adopted en masse.)

Unsurprisingly – because it's largely the same companies – we're seeing the same pattern in clothing as in footwear. More effort is going into headline-grabbing,

26 Imminent UK government greenwashing legislation 'will just make lawyers rich,' thinks
Charles Ross, 'as it does not address the level that Anne would like. If a shoe used 20%
recycled materials, it will have a lesser impact than a 100% virgin-ingredients shoe –
hence it's hard to argue that the former is not better for the environment.'

often distracting ideas, rather than simply making things last longer, repair and rental schemes, reducing a company's scope 1 to 3 emissions, or the big one almost all brands are avoiding: just making less.

'Brands are focusing on what magical material they can create, rather than doing the less sexy work of improving energy efficiency in textile mills,' Maxine Bédat, executive director of the non-profit New Standard Institute, told the *Guardian*. 'I don't want to pooh-pooh progress, but we really do have to start prioritising where we're going to be able to move the needle the most.'[xiii]

'The most effective solutions for reducing the environmental impacts from the production and consumption of clothing most likely lie within reducing consumption and making fewer and better clothes,' found a 2018 study.[xiv] **We need to simply buy less, mend, rent and share more,'** concluded the government's 'Fixing Fashion' paper.[xv]

Is circularity a myth?

While clearly the industry needs radical change, we runners probably need to change our expectations and behaviours too. A recent outdoor-industry consumer-trend report included the phrases 'pursuit of pre-loved', 'thrifting is trending' and the suggestion that consumers are moving from an 'owning' to an 'experiencing' mindset. The industry is said to be designing for longevity and grappling with **the concept of circularity, meaning rental, repair, resale and (proper) recycling**.

Less than 1% of clothes are currently recycled into new fibres, and while it might make sense that shoes are difficult to recycle because they're made from so many different parts, *a T-shirt?*

What about recycling clothing that's already out there, for that circular-economy approach the industry loves to bang on about? As ever, it's not that simple. Even labels and threads on T-shirts add prohibitive complexity to the recycling process. Fabrics such as polyester are almost impossible to recycle, while mixed fibres cannot be recycled at all.[27] Everyone needs to invest in circular recycling, says Anne, meaning 'textiles to textiles recycling'.

Mechanical and chemical recycling are the two current options. Mechanical recycling is a harsh manual process where fabrics are shredded and pulled, then turned into fibres of shorter length. The new material lacks some of its previous qualities (but retains colour) and can't be used for new clothing, though it can be downcycled for things like carpets. It can, though, be used for synthetic apparel yarns and has big footprint savings over chemical recycling.

27 According to a report by Greens in the EU and European Parliament.

Some, however, believe chemical recycling is the only way to achieve textile-to-textile circularity. This process breaks down plastic waste into a chemical or oil-like solution, rather like its original virgin form, providing raw materials for future plastics. But it's expensive and can't currently be done at scale.

However, there is progress among outdoor brands. Helly Hansen are close to producing genuine textile-to-textile recycling with polypropylene. After realising that its climbing ropes, made from polyamides, caused the highest CO2e, Mammut now make T-shirts with discarded ropes collected at fifty recycle points.[28] Similarly, Berg Outdoor have made an insulated jacket using surplus parachute fabric and recycled zips (which have long been a problem, but are finally recyclable). Rab are making waterproof jackets designed to be recycled at end of use. Presca, who claim to be 'the world's first climate positive sportswear company', are making attire from post-consumer waste and have stripped away trimmings on newer garments so they can be recycled (plus their factories use renewable energy). Teko, meanwhile, are making socks from 'regenerated' fishing nets. Houdini are one of very few brands that can say all of their fabrics are recycled and recyclable, as well as being renewable, biodegradable and/or Bluesign-certified.

There are advancements in **biodegradability**, durable materials that quickly degrade when the product is discarded. (Though that still requires virgin materials and the biodegrading circumstances are very specific at the moment.) B-Corp-certified British outdoor brand Finisterre specialises in recycled and responsibly sourced clothing with a transparent supply chain and has recently made a bio-degradable smock. PrimaLoft and CiClo have produced biodegradable garments that are made from recycled fibres in the first place.

The world's greenest football club, Forest Green Rovers (from my hometown of Nailsworth and for whose youth team I made two, bordering on disastrous, substitute appearances), have been playing in shirts made of '100% biodegradable bamboo', while running brand BAM use it as a fibre additive.[29] More recently Forest Green have been playing in a kit made from coffee beans – something also used by running brand Sundried.

In mainstream fashion, H&M and Levi's collect pre-loved clothing and footwear in their stores for reuse and recycling, while Asda sell second-hand clothes and Unilever are bringing in carbon labelling. A range of other brands are experimenting with rental options, something market research shows runners might

---

28 At end-of-life, the T-shirts can be recycled again and again, while the use of recycled nylon compared to virgin raw materials reduces CO2 emissions by 67%.

29 Though there are question marks about whether bamboo will biodegrade if synthetically dyed.

happily go for – presumably with specific kit, such as packs, poles and head torches, rather than well-stained shorts. In Tokyo you can rent running shoes.

'Sports apparel brands need to offer these kinds of things,' says Anne Prahl. Indeed, rental clothes are proving popular in the fashion world and Rab now offer backpacks, waterproof jackets and sleeping bags for hire. Quality waterproof jackets cost hundreds of pounds, but Rab charge £21 (at time of writing). Not only environmentally better, but helping make the outdoors more accessible too. Arc'teryx and Houdini offer similar.

The fourth 'R' of circularity, the 'right to **repair**' concept, pioneered by Patagonia, is slowly gaining traction over here. In fact, in 2021 a right-to-repair law came in for electrical appliances in the UK, meaning producers legally have to help them be fixed at home. 'When someone purchases a piece of outdoor equipment, they shouldn't be tied in to paying more for that equipment to be repaired,' says Switchback Clothing (*switchbackclothing.co*), an online shop for reused outdoor clothing, founded by science communicator Huw James. 'We're asking for outdoor manufacturers to make their fabrics and threads available to the public so their customers have the right to repair.'

Runners clearly need more repair options, which go foot-in-shoe with the idea of celebrating the longevity of kit and the idea that scars tell the story. In the UK, Rab, Finisterre, Alpkit and a few others have started offering them, sometimes adding contrasting coloured patches. 'People want to show off battle-scar garments that they've had for decades,' says Charles Ross, who cites Prince Charles appearing on *Countryfile* with thirty-seven patches on his jacket. 'If it's good enough for His Royal Highness, it's good enough for me!' Like Charlotte Jalley, he thinks we need to help people love their garments for longer, take pride in the clothes they have.

Anne has worked with sports and fashion companies such as inov-8 on simply making their products more durable, extending the active lifespan of clothing and footwear. 'That is the first step of circularity,' she says. 'Durability has been kind of retrofitted into circularity. **Circular design principles should include first creating something durable, so it can have a long life, or several lives.** It should also be designed for eventual disassembly and recycling. But really, only when the product has been used so much that it is beyond repair should it be recycled. Durability, and quality, should be at the forefront, especially for running.'

Brands shouldn't try to do everything, Anne advises. They should think about what matters to them most. 'I think the brands who have an obvious message – like Icebreaker saying they're eliminating plastic and only using natural materials by 2023 – that's a really big statement, a clear message and a consumer can really identify with it. Rather than saying, "Oh, we are sustainable, we're doing this, we're doing that", doing lots of random little things that probably didn't have any major results. **Unfortunately, the difference between being a bit more sustainable and really having specific or significant impact is not there.** There's a huge gap there. Brands are just going for the "little bit better" option at the moment.'

Are most of these companies simply in it for the money and nothing more, willing to make easy statements about sustainability and recycle a few plastic bottles, all for the sake of perpetual profiteering over the health of the planet? It's hard to shake that idea sometimes. Does any running brand impress Charlotte Jalley? 'I'll be impressed when one says, "Right, we're putting a cap on, we're not intending to grow any more this year." Because most of the damage to the environment is done in production. **We have to cut down on production.** I will personally start listening when they are talking about that, and repair, and longevity.'

Fashion-industry icon Dame Vivienne Westwood puts it even more succinctly: '**Buy less. Choose well. Make it last.**' When you put it like that, things don't seem so complicated.

Fast Fashion vs outdoor sportswear

'The fashion world is simply full of ****s!' said author and 'reluctant futurist' Mark Stevenson on the excellent *Jon Richardson and the Futurenauts* podcast. It's difficult to prise runningwear away from Fast Fashion and see a clear ethical gap between them. But I could at least see outdoor sportswear companies showing some planet-friendly leadership. Unless of course they too are doing the bare minimum to appear 'eco-friendly' while secretly plotting world decimation one T-shirt at a time?

An unregulated outdoor sportswear industry has seen quite a few projects well in advance of where regulation would put them, argues Charles Ross, citing Patagonia's Worn Wear, Rohan's Gift Your Gear (donating pre-loved gear), Finisterre's repair stations, Project Plan B (circular textile solutions) and similar efforts by Rab and Páramo. He points to an 'explosion' of outdoor brands showing ethical leadership. Houdini and Isbjorn offering **rental models,** Fjällräven's help-to-**repair** scheme, while Vaude now have 'better [ethical] products than Patagonia' and are a climate-neutral business. In the UK, Rab are committed to becoming climate neutral. Mountain Equipment are also on that journey; while Alpkit have their Continuum project and repair centres.

'It makes me proud to go through the list of these brands,' Charles says. 'There's no outdoor company not trying to make progress in this area. **The outdoor industry is the early adopter and high-street fashion follows.**'

Outdoor sportswear has pioneered several concepts. Patagonia introduced organic cotton. After The North Face introduced it, Ventura are investing in regenerative cotton and wool, and Timberland are following suit with ReGen leather. Plus there's the strong concept of Regeneration.

'**ReGenAg [regenerative agriculture] can produce carbon-negative textiles, apparel that does more good for the planet in terms of carbon impact,**' says Charles. 'It could flip the reputation of the textile industry, from being a negative industry to an impactful one, for the positive health of the planet.'

I turned to Ethical Consumer for an objective verdict and they weren't so impressed (they never are).[xvi] 'Despite promoting a healthier lifestyle, it would seem brands don't value the environment's health,' it says in an in-depth guide to the most ethical sportswear, 'with over half of the companies rated receiving the worst Ethical Consumer rating for environmental reporting.'

EC ranked twenty-nine sportswear companies (oddly not including Patagonia) on Environment, People, Product Sustainability and Company Ethos. Of the popular running brands, surprisingly Asics ranked highest, albeit with just eight out of twenty (inov-8 didn't feature).

Avoid Nike, adidas, Puma, Under Armour and Sweaty Betty – as well as retailer Sports Direct – EC concluded, as they are all 'facing multiple criticisms over poverty wages', while Columbia and Lululemon 'had workers' rights criticisms'. Nike were also marked down on their footprint, said to use 10 million gallons of oil a year to produce their clothes. Under Armour were criticised for having a 'particularly bad' chemical footprint.

It gets worse. Late-2021 research found that adidas, Nike, Asics, Columbia, Under Armour, Puma, Salomon, Hoka, Saucony and New Balance are among **fifty brands with multiple connections to Amazon deforestation,**[30] via links to the largest Brazilian leather (and beef) exporter, JBS.[xvii] Sigh. My headache's returning …

In Patagonia

However … ask anyone to name an environmentally friendly clothing company and Patagonia will be their answer. If you're wearing Patagonia, you care about the planet – even if creating and buying that hoodie added to the problem. Being an environmentally friendly business is an oxymoron, but if one company could balance out the contradiction, it's them. Indeed, Patagonia have hundreds of stores around the world and factories in sixteen countries, are represented on five continents and make upwards of $800 million a year. They've launched a food line

---

30 For clarity, the analysis didn't prove a direct link between each brand and deforestation; rather 'connections that increase the probability' of any individual garment coming from cattle ranching in the Amazon, 'an industry described as the number-one culprit of deforestation in the area'.

and, more recently, wine. They're not exactly doing less. 'Patagonia is in business to save our home planet,' they proclaim. But if they really cared about the planet, they could sell the company, start a foundation and give away a lot more money that way. So are we being played?

Patagonia have been a certified B Corp since 2012 and aim to be carbon neutral by 2025. They have consistently been ahead of the conscientiousness curve, pioneering the use of organic and reclaimed cotton, recycled polyester, nylon and down products, 100% traceable down (to ensure birds aren't force-fed or live-plucked) and ethical wool. They switched to organic cotton decades ago after employees were routinely calling in sick and they realised formaldehyde (widely used in preservation of natural materials) from clothing was the cause. Patagonia have committed to fair trade in their supply chain, which has seen them split from some suppliers.

Their campus in Nevada houses one of the largest garment-repair facilities in North America. They have a scheme where clothing can be returned for credits for new kit, have resold more than 120,000 repaired items, and have created and sold clothing made from scraps of fabric from used gear. Many of these changes have been counterintuitive from a commercial perspective and indeed usually reduced profits for years at a time.

The company claims to be close to being free of fossil fuels in its materials and is aiming to be 'regenerative', using regenerative agriculture, meaning returning to traditional, more sustainable, farming methods for growing cotton and other crops.[31]

On Black Friday 2011, Patagonia famously ran an advert which read, 'Don't buy this jacket'. It invited customers to reduce consumption, repair and recycle, but, intended or otherwise, had the opposite effect: sales increased by 30%.

'The paradox is that by presenting themselves [as eco-friendly], they are selling a lot more jackets,' writes Marisa Meltzer in a *Guardian* piece titled 'Saving the world – one puffer jacket at a time'.[xviii] 'The entire ethos of growth and profit and consumption is unsustainable for humanity and the health of the planet ... You might call this the authenticity problem.'

'Patagonia will never be completely socially responsible,' founder Yvon Chouinard has written. 'It will never make a totally sustainable non-damaging product. But it is committed to trying.'

---

31 There's an important difference between regenerative fibres (essentially recycled) and regenerative agriculture fibres (being discussed here). The approach has four principles: soil health, irrigation, carbon sequestration and restoring biodiversity. ReGenAg improves carbon absorption too, and healthy soil dramatically slows the potential of floods. There have been entire films made about climate change and soil health, a huge subject in its own right, so I won't go worming into it here.

'Everywhere we work, we try to reduce environmental harm,' says Vincent Stanley, who holds the unique job title of Company Philosopher, as he explains why the brand prefers the word 'responsible' to 'sustainable'. 'Sustainability implies that you can keep going indefinitely. Ultimately, **we're taking back from the planet more than we're giving back. That's unsustainable** … We acknowledge our impacts. Where we can make changes, we make changes. Responsible implies agency, and everybody's got agency to do what they can.'[xix]

Patagonia are an activist company. '**The climate crisis is our business**', declares their website. Yvon Chouinard also co-founded 1% for the Planet (a global network of business and individuals supporting environmental solutions). Patagonia have funded microfibre research, contributed 100% of Black Friday sales ($10 million) to environmental organisations, did the same with $10 million they received from tax cuts, have twice taken up legal proceedings to protect federal land, and much more.

By coincidence, as I was researching this I took part in a Black Trail Runners event at Patagonia's Bristol store and went along, partly to snoop around a bit and see if they really are as authentic and ethical as they seem. Slightly annoyingly, but thankfully, it seems they might be. The walls hosted photos of climate activism, including Extinction Rebellion. The staff were very well informed about fabrics and had intelligent views on the contradictions of ethical business. The shop closes so staff can join in the Fridays for Future protests. Even if there's a cultish feel about the brand, it's a cult you want to join.

'The educational role Patagonia plays to influence bigger changes of behaviours has a far bigger role than the produce they sell,' says Charles Ross. It's hard to be cynical when they're doing more than every other outdoor brand. They're not perfect. But they're honest about that. Quite frankly, the world needs more Patagonias. A lot more. It clearly works from a profit perspective too, so why don't more sports and outdoor brands follow suit? Maybe they don't want to be seen to be copying? Or perhaps they just don't care enough? 'The other brands [don't encourage repairing kit] because they didn't know how to make money from it,' says Anne Prahl. 'They think, if we repair stuff, we're not going to sell so much.'

New NNormal

So, a few brands are stepping up. But not many, really, and not quickly enough. From the outside, progress in the running kit industry seems slow. 'Not all of [the running brands] are succeeding by a long shot,' says Sina Horsthemke, reporting from the 2020 ISPO.[xx] Of nineteen brands surveyed, only 1.6 brands on average can be described as 'producing at least partially sustainably'.

However, most of them were mindful of sustainability, with 'only 35%' not yet paying it any attention (though that sounds like a lot to me).

'We've known for a long time what we need to do to save the climate, because scientists have been telling us for years,' mountain-running demigod Kilian Jornet told the same ISPO. 'Not knowing what to do can no longer be an excuse today. We don't have much time left.'

Talking of Jornet, in early 2022 he announced a new outdoor brand, NNormal. My gut reaction was that we simply don't need any more outdoor brands – that's adding to the problem. But Jornet's announcement touched all the right sustainability buttons. He said all products 'should be' reusable, repairable or recyclable, and mentioned a transparent supply chain, durability, repairability, a goal of 'real, circular products' and 'having the lowest emissions possible'. In the interest of less waste and more timeless products, NNormal will use unisex colour schemes, emphasise multifunctionality of products and – this is the bit that impressed me most – have limited new releases, 'creating new designs only if better materials or strategies are identified, rather than releasing revamped editions each year'. Let's see …

Textiles is like food, says Charles Ross. 'As food has become cheaper over the decades, we waste more and eat worse. The Sunday roast used to be respected and made to last for half of the week, while we used to mend and pass down our clothing. Now we don't value our clothes or food as much.' We seem to want everything Fast.

He agrees that outdoor folk recognise environmental change more and want to work towards solving it. 'Gear that has made our lives better – kept us protected in several storms, enabled us to run faster because it doesn't irritate so much – is respected. The outdoor and sportswear industries have always presented themselves as having technically superior products as their main theme for progress. Would you as an athlete choose to have a second-best product: especially if that is the difference between you getting back or suffering on the hill? **The challenge is having good gear but with a lesser impact, which doesn't always mean having the most eco materials. To me, longevity is sustainability.**'

Huzzah! At last, some real optimism. It does feel like this side of the industry is leading the way, but we're primarily talking about outdoor rather than running brands per se – who have a more nature-loving clientele. It's less easy to discern that running sportswear brands are moving in the right direction fast enough. Which is the polite way of saying, they're not.

Degrowth?

The bigger problem is that the system we're entrenched in revels in overconsumption. The day a brand says they're reducing what they put out into the world is the day Charlotte Jalley will take them seriously on sustainability. '**Cap the growth.**

Give the Earth a break. Haven't you got enough money? Stop this. I really struggle with the amount of money these CEOs make. You've got enough now, so just leave it there. **Stop growing. The solution is less. All roads lead to less.**'

We clearly don't need this many T-shirts, clothes or other stuff. And yet, at great expense to the planet, they're being churned out by the second, because companies want to make profit. Not just profit, but more profit than last year. Ideally millions of pounds more.

Capitalism demands constant consumption, which is devastating the living world, says Dr Jason Hickel, economic anthropologist and author of *Less Is More: How Degrowth Will Save the World*. 'The ecological crisis is ultimately being driven by our economic system, which is predicated on perpetual expansion.' There is only one solution, he says: degrowth. 'A planned reduction of excess resource and energy use in high-income nations, designed to bring the economy back into balance with the living world, while at the same time allowing flourishing lives for all.'

It's all a bit dramatic. But these are dramatic times.

Indeed, 'Growth for the sake of growth is the ideology of the cancer cell', as environmentalist Edward Abbey famously said.

'All the needless production irrelevant to human well-being,' says Jason, 'it's not only a profound ecological waste but a profound waste of human lives. The fashion industry needs to degrow.'

Is everything our fault?

This whole look into running apparel has been thoroughly depressing. I've had to listen to some Joy Division B-sides to cheer myself up. In summary, our running kit is responsible for big emissions in production, huge water waste, water, air and soil pollution, huge toxic chemical use, child labour, slave labour, female exploitation and other human costs, ravaged biodiversity, microplastics … Then, especially if it's a race T-shirt, we runners don't even want or value the kit, so it gets chucked away, causing a waste catastrophe. All along we're being played by the fossil-fuel industry, who know their time will be up, so they're diversifying into clothing. Sportswear companies have seen that sustainability is trending. Their response to our climate and ecological emergency? Most of them have continued with business as usual but also claimed their clothing is sustainable by adding a bit of recycled plastic or algae.

With polyester, it's ironic that something so damaging is so pervasive in a nature-loving industry. It's snuck into most areas of our lives and made us all accidentally part of the fossil-fuel problem. We can't recycle our way out of the big pile of steaming manure that's been dumped on us. We have a waste problem because companies are overproducing, prioritising growth and profit over planetary health.

Buying second-hand, buying durable and repairing, but, above all that, buying less, is a good start. But not enough. We need to make changes to our behaviour to stop contributing to the devastating consequences of overconsumption. We're killing the things we love. It's mostly accidental and it's not really our fault. But we are.

Like Big Oil and Big Ag (as we'll see), Big (Fossil) Fashion's success depends on us upholding the fib that it's our responsibility to fix their problems. But even when we know that, there's a moral imperative on us to do so anyway. Think systemic, rather than individual, urges Heather Higinbotham in the *Independent*. 'Pressure your government to push for supply chain transparency, non-toxic circularity, and Extended Producer Responsibility legislation, placing accountability for textile waste on producers [i.e. the polluters], rather than consumers … Voting with your dollars makes a difference [too]. Sadly, taking your recycling out probably doesn't.'[xxi]

We can pressure brands too. The Outdoor Industry Compass (*oicompass.com*) conducts a 'state of industry' survey and in the most recent, the most popular answer to the question, 'What are the main reasons for your pursuit of sustainability improvements?' was 'Consumers are demanding it' (74%). So we *can* make a real difference.

'We support the systems that enslave us,' says Charlotte Jalley. 'Individuals must challenge the system. If we're pissed off with money going to fossil fuels, then we change our bank. I would like runners to **hold brands more accountable** and I think consumers should change their behaviour as much as they can.' Mass consumer mobilisation is another way in which clothing brands could be forced to catch up with the urgent ethics of our time.

However, at the same time, we shouldn't think it's all on us. 'So much of the blame gets shifted to us as individuals and it really frustrates me,' says Charlotte, 'because these systems are set up in a way that it's really difficult for us to make change. We're told our consumer behaviour is the problem, that our behaviour directs the brand's, they're giving us what we want. But at the same time, they're spending billions of pounds on telling us what we want. And we're really susceptible. We've constantly got this messaging that we need to buy this to run better, look better or feel better. They know what's going to push our buttons.'

Consumers should learn to develop their own lens, says Anne Prahl, 'their own take on sustainability and what they really care about. If they're vegan or vegetarian, that could be your lens. It goes back to having a specific mission as a consumer, whether you care most about microfibres or plastic pollution. Pick something you really care about and try to find the brands that cater for that.'

The idea of degrowth is hopeful, but would clearly be met with resistance. However, we as consumers can kick-start things. **We can just spend less, consider** how many things we really need, shop more carefully, looking for second-hand and more durable products, make things last longer, share and swap, connect with and treasure items, create memories and stories with them, and tell brands we won't support bad practices any more. We do have some power. More so if we act en masse.

Anyway … how many climate change deniers does it take to change a lightbulb? What are you talking about? The lightbulb is fine.

Yeah, but what can we do about it?

1 Read
- *Less Is More* by Jason Hickel, *Let My People Go Surfing* by Yvon Chouinard, *Consumed* by Aja Barber and *Killer Clothes* by Anna Maria and Brian R. Clement.
- The Changing Markets Foundation's 'Fossil Fashion' and 'Synthetics Anonymous' reports.

2 Shop ethically: brands. Look for …
- Science Based Targets, B Corp, SMETA, 'Fair Trade' and 'Fair Trade Certified sewn', Fair Wear Foundation, 1% for the Planet.
- Ethical Consumer's key indicators of an ethical brand:
  - » Fair wages and working conditions for all working in a supply chain
  - » Transparency and traceability
  - » Environmental practices are embedded into how they work
  - » Timeless clothing that lasts
  - » Moving toward circularity?
  - » Animal rights policies

3 Shop ethically: items. Look for …
- Oeko-Tex Standard 100, which proves that an item has been tested for harmful substances and is compliant with European REACH guidelines. REACH (Registration, Evaluation, Authorisation and Restriction of Chemicals) is the legislative framework for chemicals in the EU.
- GRS (Global Recycled Standard) for verifying the recycled content in a product.
- GOTS (Global Organic Textiles Standard) defining environmental and social criteria for textiles made from organic fibres, and B Corp covering social and environmental aspects.
- The Higg Index, a holistic assessment tool covering sustainability throughout a product's entire life cycle, from materials to end of life.
- Fair Wear Foundation for social conditions.

- GOTS for cellulose.
- Bluesign for chemicals used.
- Soil Association, Better Cotton Initiative (BCI), NSF International's Global Traceable Down Standard (TDS), Responsible Down Standard (RDS), Sustainable Down Standards, Responsible Wool Standard (RWS), Leather Working Group (LWG), Ecological and Recycled Textile Standard, Global Recycle Standard or Fair Trade, Cradle to Cradle, ZDHC and Afirm, also PFC-free and PTFE-free.

4 Be alert to greenwashing/wishing.
- Look out for vague claims made loudly, such as 'made from sustainable materials' or 'made from recycled content'. Look for substantiation behind vague buzzwords such as 'green', 'sustainable' or 'eco-friendly'.
- Check the Changing Markets Foundation's *greenwash.com*

5 Become an anti-greenwash activist.
- 'If you're feeling particularly activist-y and you have time and bandwidth,' says Ashlee Piper, sustainability expert and author of *Give a Sh*t: Do Good. Live Better. Save the Planet*, 'it's worth writing a succinct letter or email to the company's director of sustainability or corporate social responsibility on LinkedIn.' Or use social media.
- There are bodies that campaign against misinformation and greenwashing, such as US-based Clean Creatives, the Campaign Against Climate Change, Two Sides and ClientEarth.
- If you feel a company's marketing claims are misleading, you can contact the Advertising Standards Authority (ASA). The government's new Green Claims Code also aims to help businesses comply with the law.

6 Consumer actions
- Go minimalist – Project 333 encourages people to wear thirty-three items for three months, while the Capsule Wardrobe Challenge limits you to thirty-seven items. Pledge to buy no new clothes: *remake.world/stories/style/nonewclothes*
- Buy quality clothing that will last. And repair stuff: *loveyourclothes.org* and *ifixit.com* are great resources.
- Get involved, learn more, join in campaigns and pledges. Lobby the government for regulation. Join the Fashion Revolution: *fashionrevolution.org*. Commit to leave no trace: *leavenotraceireland.org/love-this-place-leave-no-trace/pledge*
- On Instagram follow: @rerun.clothing, @fash_rev, @goodonyou_app, @ethical_consumer_magazine

5

RACING AWAY FROM NET ZERO

For running events, neither T-shirts nor plastic waste
is the elephant in the room

*'It is hard to think of a better formula than a global sporting event for causing
maximum environmental damage.'*
George Monbiot

I ruddy love races, me. That intoxicatingly supportive atmosphere, the fizzing lightsabres of ambition and vulnerability clashing in the air. Lathering your bathing-suit area with copious amounts of Vaseline seeming almost socially acceptable. All those jelly babies ...

The 2011 Bath Half Marathon got me hooked on this running lark. I signed up on a whim, to get fit again after a book project had got in the way of a healthy lifestyle (groan, so little has changed). I loved the struggle within, the supportive crowds with their signs saying 'You know you don't have to do this, right?', the euphoric finish-line feel and addictive post-race bliss. I signed up again as soon as I could. That first running race was a life-changing moment, for me and numerous others.

Though now I understand the lamentable environmental cost behind them, I took pride in those first few finisher T-shirts and medals. I was more uncomfortable with the fields of plastic bottles and gel wrappers scattered down the road in my wake. Stacks of bottled water were generously distributed. I wasn't sure I was thirsty but felt obliged to take one from the eager young volunteers. Runners around me had a few sips, then chucked the two-thirds-full bottles across the street. I sheepishly copied, assuming they knew of some physiological performance benefit I didn't.

As I did more road races, that was the normal if regrettable behaviour. Running's guilty secret. It all gets collected for recycling by the lovely volunteers later, right?

Overhydrated

The average attendee at a sporting event generates a footprint *seven times greater* than someone going about a normal, everyday activity, a Cardiff University study found.[i]

'Major sporting events generate significant unforeseen – or at least unaccounted for – environmental consequences,' notes Gina S. Warren, Associate Professor at the University of Houston Law Center. 'It is time to more holistically address the pollution, waste, greenhouse gases and other negative consequences.'

After travel, the consumption of food and drink, and the energy and resources required to produce it, makes up the next largest part of the footprint. The Cardiff University study was about sporting events in general, however, and we can safely presume more burgers and beer are consumed at football matches than at marathons, where there isn't usually a large venue to power either (unless there's an expo). However, there's probably more waste.

As well as creating some 40,000 medals and 40,000 T-shirts, **the 2018 London Marathon used 920,000 plastic bottles**. When it comes to our climate and ecological emergency, some of the big numbers can flash past the eye without really registering. But please read that number again out loud. That's not far off *1 million plastic bottles*. For just 40,000 runners.

Post-race that year, the City of Westminster collected 5,200 kilograms of rubbish and 3,500 kilograms of recycling from the streets, including 47,000 plastic bottles – hopefully the other 873,000 were collected by race staff? US marathons are similarly wasteful, with a study of nineteen events showing an average of 7.11 tonnes of rubbish, most of it plastic. The 2019 London Marathon acknowledged a stunning 118.86 tonnes of waste – far more than those US marathons (though they tell me that's very likely due to less comprehensive data collection in the US). 'All those discarded bottles, half-eaten bananas and cheap T-shirts ... Are running events an environmental disaster?' asked Kate Carter in the *Guardian*.[ii]

Incidentally, while I haven't found a life-cycle analysis for metal medals, they're almost exclusively made in China and as they're usually made from raw materials, they're likely to have a significant footprint. Wooden medals are far better from a CO_2e perspective, are a sustainable material and are theoretically recyclable. No medals, better still. And then what do we do with them all? Now my children have regrettably realised mine weren't in fact from the Olympics or even from being on a race podium, my collection is in a couple of shoe boxes somewhere in a shed.

We know plastic is generally bad if discarded, and *10 million tonnes of plastic ends up in the oceans* each year in what Sir David Attenborough has described as an 'unfolding catastrophe'. Water in plastic bottles has an impact (in terms of resource extraction) on natural resources up to *3,500 times higher* than tap water. In the US, 17 million barrels of oil per year go towards creating plastic bottles for something that falls naturally from the sky. Race numbers or bibs are often plastic as well, because they need to endure water, sweat and gel smearings, but often lack recycling information, if indeed they can be recycled. Timing-chip paraphernalia too. And then there are those goodie bags. They're not good. It's rare they hold anything useful. Anachronistic marketing (that word again). More stuff no one wants. More waste. More CO2e sent skywards.

Medals, T-shirts, plastic bottles and other food- and drink-related waste initially seemed to me to be running races' obvious negative impact. As it felt right to scrutinise Nike and adidas, the big guns in sportswear, it now feels appropriate to look closely at the UK's, and one of the world's, most pre-eminent running events, the London Marathon. It'll likely have the biggest event footprint, but also the resources to work on it.

It is making progress. In 2019 London used 215,000 fewer plastic bottles than the previous year: by reducing the amount of drinks stations, using paper cups and edible pouches made from seaweed, and trialling 'bottle belts' made from recycled plastic. It now aims to recycle every plastic bottle used. However – and I didn't know this – they can only be recycled if the bottle is empty, 'so please remember to #DrinkDrainDrop', went its campaign.

Along with hundreds of UK and US races, London Marathon Events (LME) has started working with Trees Not Tees (more anon), offering runners the option to plant a tree instead of taking a T-shirt or a medal, at The Big Half anyway. The plan for the 2023 London Marathon is to have an 'opt-in' during registration, where runners can decide if they want T-shirts and medals. As there's a sponsorship deal with New Balance to supply the T-shirts, that's not so straightforward and would be a significant development.

London reduces waste elsewhere by issuing digital rather than printed race instructions and using goodie bags made from sugar cane. Silver blankets are recycled, and clothes discarded by runners at the start – another potentially very wasteful race tradition – are collected for charity and recycling.

'The first things to tackle at events are usually better waste management and just trying to reduce the amount of stuff given out,' says Kate Chapman, a sports sustainability consultant who's worked at the London 2012 Olympics and Paralympics, RideLondon, the Nitto ATP Finals, the London Marathon and many other mass-participation events. 'It's often just *so much stuff* and a lot of that stuff isn't needed. Things like leaving the date off a product if the event will happen again the next year. If you give out less stuff, you create less waste. Things have gotten a bit better. Not across the board, but we're getting there.'

LME does more than that, though. It's a member of the UN Sports for Climate Action Framework and follows the UN's 17 Sustainable Development Goals (SDG) across its twelve sporting events, plus its website includes a brief but sturdy Environmental Policy and Environmental Impact Reports. The reports are thorough and transparent, with measurable reduction goals and ambitious targets.

The event's scope-1 emissions for 2019 (most recent figures for a normal year) were 20.42 tonnes, mostly from energy generators and vehicles. It's aiming for those emissions to be carbon neutral and switching 100% of scope-2 energy to renewables, reducing or eliminating waste and plastic, encouraging better practice with suppliers and taking other actions.[32] More on scope 3 in a moment.

To me, that all sounded pretty encouraging. And it's not the only UK running race acting on sustainability, albeit all a little late in the day. The Bath Half, which provided that life-changing moment for me back in 2011, is the first running event in the world to win an AGF Run Award, from the sustainability team at A Greener Festival.[33]

Similarly, the popular Cardiff Half Marathon has some 27,500 runners pounding the streets of the Welsh capital and has been working with Cardiff University for some time to reduce its impact.[34] Again, encouraging stuff.

As was *Runner's World* magazine's celebration of UK races making efforts to reduce their environmental footprints.[iii] The Oxford Half, for example, went plastic-free in 2019, its 25,000 plastic kit bags replaced by reusable ones and runners 'encouraged' to attend by public transport or cycling. Royal Parks Half Marathon is also plastic-bottle-free, its T-shirts are made from recycled materials and its medals from FSC-certified wood. Organisers 'encourage' suppliers and catering partners to avoid single-use plastics, all cutlery is biodegradable, food waste is composted and wildlife-harming balloons are banned. Royal Parks Half also 'encourages' staff to take public transport or use electric or hybrid vehicles.

The Ashtead 10K prints race bibs on recyclable paper with vegetable-based inks, gives out UK-made wooden medals that double as coasters, uses biodegradable

---

32 Its carbon-neutral ambition involves switching generators from red diesel to hydrotreated vegetable oil fuel (HVO) and using electric vehicles (EVs).

33 Actions included banning sales of single-use plastics by partners and traders; hiring and reuse of materials, equipment and signage; salvage operations for surplus food and T-shirts (which were given to charities); 'enhanced provision and location for maximum public transport usage'; and encouraging runners to bring refillable bottles. The 2020 Bath Half was the first time a UK water company had worked in this way with a mass-participation running event, as the race aims to eliminate single-use plastic by providing water-refill points and compostable cups. The AGF process includes a detailed evidence-based assessment throughout the event process, including 'self-assessment', site visits, post-event proof, a detailed CO_2 analysis – including travel – and a sustainability report. Though it doesn't seem to have been published.

34 Its Environmental Policy aims for no waste to be sent to landfill, reduced dependency on plastic and damaging materials such as signage and tape, a carbon-offsetting initiative for 'unavoidable emissions', and achieving the ISO 20121 Environmental Standard. It's phasing out plastic goodie bags (instead using bags made from compostable corn starch), its medals are made from recycled zinc and its 'Run, Refuel, Recycle' campaign seems to have gained resonance.

cups and awards locally sourced prizes. It also 'encourages' people to arrive by foot, bike or public transport or to car-pool. The Hathersage Hurtle uses biodegradable tape to mark the course, provides environmentally friendly loo roll, has reusable wooden signs, and separates out all waste for recycling. Other races offer water in recyclable pouches (though all such moves need proper waste management or it all ends up in landfill/incineration) or ask runners to bring their own cups – which is normal in the trail-running world.

Uncomfortable with the wastage of over 100 kilograms of leftover T-shirts at their 2018 event, the Manchester Half Marathon has taken the bold move of doing away with them altogether. Centurion Running, who organise numerous, popular ultramarathons in the south-east, have long since removed dates from their T-shirts (and finisher buckles) and use Trees Not Tees, as do hundreds of UK and US races. Looking into running events was feeling like a breath of fresh air compared to the deeply unsavoury world of running kit and shoes.

Trees not tees

Trees Not Tees (TNT) are addressing running's T-shirt problem head-on. 'I was getting fed up of the same thing at every race,' says Jim Mann, record-breaking fell runner and ecologist. 'You'd always get a plastic bag with your bib number, full of single-use plastic items and a cheap, brightly coloured T-shirt, whether you wanted it or not. Most of these T-shirts end up in a bottom drawer never worn or, worse, in landfill, all of those precious resources wasted.' Jim had co-founded The Future Forest Company (TFFC) with biologist Jade Rein, which was already planting trees to combat our climate and ecological emergency, so TNT represented 'a logical solution to bring about change in the event space'.

Conveniently, a sapling and a low-quality T-shirt cost about the same – £2 to £3 – and TNT offer race directors (RDs) an irresistibly simple concept: when runners register for an event online, they can choose between a race T-shirt or planting a tree instead, or both. It's free to the race and each runner receives a personalised e-certificate with a photo of their tree and a what3words geolocation.

TFFC reforestation experts ensure trees are the right species in each forest, with the right mix and density. 'We want to be able to guarantee the tree will be there for its whole lifetime and it's not going to be cut down,' says Jim, so they only plant on land they own. The idea's taken off like, er, wildfire and the company is expanding fast, buying land in Scotland and the US. The aim is to plant 50 million trees by 2025.

In 2014 Chris Zair, now a TNT director, did a marathon a month around Europe. 'It embarrasses me to talk about it now,' he says. 'I had no consciousness of the impact of my carbon footprint back then. I'm definitely not a lifetime environ-mentalist, quite the opposite.' He's making up for that now, though.

Chris heard Jim on a podcast and dropped him a line offering to work for TNT for free. Now he spends most of his working day talking directly to RDs, offering them TNT's tree-planting services. 'It's very, very rare people say they don't want to join us,' says Chris. 'If they don't, it's usually because the race is already working in local partnerships, which is brilliant.'

Initially, some RDs insist that runners love their race T-shirts. But TNT see a minimum of 20% choose to plant a tree instead, and often much higher, sometimes more than 50%. Some races have subsequently abandoned T-shirts altogether, with every entrant planting a tree. For larger events, though, such as the London Marathon or UTMB, often the sponsor gives the race hundreds of their T-shirts for free. But there's not much sponsor coverage in the bottom of a drawer, Chris argues. 'And even worse coverage if it's in landfill. We've been contacted directly from a race whose sponsor said, "We need to be doing something; we don't want these waste T-shirts." We're launching a race this year where adding the TNT option is actually sponsor-led, and it's a big sponsor, which is a pleasant surprise.'

However, some RDs see that tee as part of their event marketing. 'It's easy to get carried away and think every single person is going to wear your T-shirt,' says Chris. 'We're saying, if everybody loves your T-shirts, put the option there, and if no one takes it, it's no skin off our nose. But please give it a go.'

TNT also encourage higher-quality T-shirts. 'Let's not make it a race to the bottom. If you give everyone a tee included in the fee, naturally you're going to choose the cheapest, which is going to come from a part of the world where there's less focus on the environment. Instead, how about a high-quality T-shirt for those who want one? It might be £10 to £15, but make it a really cool one that people will actually wear. If someone's spending their own money on it, it's much more likely to get worn.'

TNT are also developing a 'Meadows, Wildflowers & Peatland' option, while new parent company UNDO is pioneering groundbreaking (pun unintended) carbon-removal technology known as enhanced weathering, breaking down basalt rocks into small pieces and spreading them widely over land to increase the rock's surface area and its ability to absorb CO_2.

Chris feels optimistic about the UK's race scene. 'There's lots of other activities RDs are doing, around water reduction, recyclable race numbers and so on.' However, there isn't a central portal that makes it easy for them to make simple green decisions, he laments. 'Most races are organised by people in second jobs, with decisions made in the back room of a pub, so it has to be simple. In the US, the Council for Responsible Sport or Athletes For a Fit Planet are making big strides. We're missing a central portal here where RDs can go and see what the best water supply is, or the most ethical T-shirt supplier.'

What else could RDs be doing to lower their events' footprint? Energy is an obvious one, easily fixed by switching to a renewable supplier, with plastic and water waste the next two pinch points. 'Water is a challenge. I don't know the solution at the moment,' says Chris. 'Trying to find one that doesn't mean tens of thousands of plastic water bottles – which are not recyclable, as much as they say they are. Look at every element of your race and try to understand what could be done better.'

The elephant in the room

Of course, it's great to cut down on waste, which is tangible and emotive. But in sportswear production, scope 1 and 2 emissions were usually only small percentages of overall CO_2e, and it's the same with running events. Plastic bottles, T-shirts and medals are just a tiny, almost irrelevant, fraction of the overall CO_2e. It's often the things we can't see which are causing the greatest damage.

'Running events are tracking the same trends in society, focusing on things that people believe are material and important, but missing the actual big things,' says Andrew Murray. 'There's a lot of focus on litter and plastic waste and reuse of bowls versus disposables and things like this. When, really, that is now the tiniest part of the problem.'

Regrettably, the real harm comes from us. We, the runners, do by far the most damage.

At running races, food, beverages, waste, merchandise, generators and staff trips – everything that isn't travel – all together amount to *less than 2% of event emissions*, according to 2022 analysis of twenty-nine US mass-participation running events by the Council For Responsible Sport.[iv] 'Participant travel is the elephant in the room,' says the report. 'It's necessary to get to events, but it's also the largest source by far of climate-changing emissions.'

'We look at all mass-participation events and the thing we find has the biggest impact is the way people travel to them,' echoes Dr Andrea Collins, Cardiff University environmental impact researcher.

In the limited number of studies we have, most show that well over 90% of a running event's CO_2e emissions come from participant travel.[35] For example,

---

35 The only outlier I've found is Texas's Cowtown Marathon, which estimated emissions from participant travel at 76%, likely lower because it's a more local affair.

97% of emissions generated by the Cape Town Marathon came from runners' air and road transport to and from the location, found a Climate Neutral Group study, while the Paris Marathon was estimated at 95%.[v]

Several of the world's big city marathons have up to 50,000 participants, not to mention thousands of event workers, volunteers and spectators hugely inflating that number and therefore emissions. The New York City Marathon hosts participants from 150 countries, with 37% of runners coming from overseas. Such a huge volume of people travelling to a city may be great economically, but it's terrible environmentally.

In the US research, the average per-capita emissions are 190 kilograms per runner and the average for an event is 639 tonnes of CO_2e – though it is a bigger country than the UK with different travel patterns.

'Even sports such as football and athletics that are inherently harmless cause major environmental effects, thanks to the transport of spectators,' wrote George Monbiot in the *Guardian*.[vi] 'The organisers of the Sydney Olympics did more or less all they could to make the Games as green as possible ... But Sydney is on the other side of the world. Just one return journey from the UK to Australia uses twice a person's sustainable emission of carbon dioxide for an entire year.' Yet few events seem to be aware of this, publicly at least, let alone combatting the fact that CO_2e emissions caused by participant travel is by far their biggest impact.

The Cardiff Half is aware of this. It knows the average runner comes from 76 miles away, travelling a total of 1.45 million miles, and 70% do so by car, creating 346 tonnes of CO_2e.[vii] Importantly, it aims to 'educate and change the behaviour of participants'. There's a lot of 'encouraging' (use of public transport), 'promoting' (GoCarShare car sharing app) and 'reducing' (fees for pre-bookable parking for minibus travel) in its Environment Policy, which initially sounds a bit vague and wishy-washy. But it's actually one of the most advanced out there, because the event knows, measures and is working to reduce its participant travel emissions. The 2018 event raced ahead of London, Bath and others, with an impressive 49% decrease in travel-related CO_2e.[36]

Why aren't more races acting on the elephant in the room, participant travel? Maybe they just don't realise. But also, 'It's a control and influence thing,' says Kate Chapman. 'Medals, T-shirts and bottles are all the event organisers' control, while participant travel is largely out of their control, unless you are laying on buses and putting a bit of infrastructure in place. I think that's why the focus till now has been

---

36 It's done so, it says, via improving messaging on its website and information packs, cutting fees for those travelling in groups to reduce vehicles on the road, and partnering with Cardiff's Nextbike cycle rental scheme to offer free and discounted bike hire.

on those minor plays.' Most races are tidying up the 5% and ignoring the 95%.

I was curious to know what the overall CO2e impact of a Big Running event is. And it's way bigger than I expected. **The Paris Marathon, with some 57,000 runners, is independently audited at a whopping 26,500 tonnes of CO2e. That's the equivalent of harmful ghg caused by the entire lifetimes of thirty-four people**, or driving around the Earth 2,600 times.[37] The London Marathon has had its figures audited, but at the time of writing, after several requests, it wasn't willing to share them with me. So we can only assume they're in a similar ballpark.[38]

Ninety-five per cent of these emissions are caused by air travel. 'Marathon event organisers must reconsider the dynamics surrounding attracting international participants if they genuinely want to lower the carbon footprint of their events,' concluded a 2021 study, 'The Carbon Footprint of Marathon Runners: Training and Racing'.[viii]

London is in a more advantageous position than Paris, because public transport is better. Indeed, when I did the race in 2017 it was easy to use the Underground, as many thousands did, and the city is easy to access via public transport, which is usually but not always much better environmentally than a car journey (more anon). And yet the event still has such huge emissions from participant travel. In a normal year, some *3,500 runners come from overseas.*

London has partnered with a carbon-offsetting provider and a levy goes on some of the international participant entry fees. 'But offsetting isn't a long-term solution. It's a really difficult one,' sighs Kate Chapman.

Megan Hunt, LME's Head of Procurement and Sustainability, said London would be 'talking to transport partners about sustainable aviation fuel' [more anon], but 'we are a bit at the whim of the airline providers ... Runner travel is outside of our control as such. We do mention on our entry system that [their travel] is the biggest contributor to our footprint, but that's as much as it is. Educating runners is, to be brutally honest, something we can improve on. We can definitely do more in terms of educating. But it's doing it in a way that people understand.'

There are two further issues for London. To conform to the UN Sport for Climate Action Framework, it needs to cut a third of its scope-3 emissions. 'That's a lot,'

---

37 Paris is into offsetting and electrifying its vehicles, aiming for carbon neutrality, which is laudable. But all those emissions still happened and are still heating the planet. According to *How Bad Are Bananas?*, the average person born in the UK with our current carbon footprint causes about 775 tonnes of CO2e throughout their lifetime.

38 Figures from the 2020 London Marathon (an elites-only race, due to the Covid pandemic) showed that about 100 elite international runners caused nearly the same CO2e emissions (316 tonnes at 2.9 tonnes each) as 27,500 largely recreational domestic runners at the Cardiff Half, with flights being the likely difference-maker.

a mass-participation event insider told me. 'There is an issue with people coming from overseas. At some point it's going to mean having conversations about participant travel and what the event does there.' And London is part of the World Marathon Majors. 'People love doing them. I wouldn't want to comment on how you should solve that one. Discouraging people from participating isn't really on the cards at the moment. Will we see quotas for international runners at some races? I think it's probably gonna to have to be. But who makes that call and how is that implemented? I don't know.'

The fact that runners are the problem was a horrifying realisation. The act of saying 'no thanks' to a medal and T-shirt and carrying your own water round the course is hugely overshadowed if you fly or drive to the event. Global sporting events, including big-city marathons, are carbon-emitting juggernauts. **The 2016 Olympics generated 3.6 million tonnes of CO_2 and 17,000 tonnes of waste.** I'll leave you to think about whether these mass-participation running events are even justifiable ethically in our climate and ecological emergency ...

Going public

Helping to inform, but also incentivising and enabling low-carbon travel, is the number-one thing RDs can do to lower their event's emissions. It's fairly common for races in Switzerland to offer free public transport as part of race registration. The popular Swiss City Marathon offers free transport within the whole country – and a free shuttle boat to the start and finish areas for runners and spectators. In the UK, other than Cardiff and London, the big events don't talk about participant travel on their websites, let alone genuinely 'encourage' lower-carbon travel. I'm told that, in contrast, many non-running events do.

Indeed, among UK races with sustainability policies, the word 'encourage' is used a lot and can sound weak. It's not necessarily, such as with the Cardiff Half. But there's a huge difference between saying 'we encourage car-pooling', as one running event I went to in 2021 did, by simply suggesting we use the GoCarShare app. They could have gone further and made the ticket cheaper for those arriving on public transport, and/or financed a vehicle to collect us from a station by charging people who arrived by car more (unless there were four in it).

I found a couple of UK trail races taking a lead by enabling low-carbon travel. As well as having their own ecologist (who conducts impact-assessment reports and offers advice on good route choices to reduce the trampling of vegetation) and sourcing food, beer and other supplies locally, the Original Mountain Marathon encourages all competitors to use public transport – but with real action: *it provides coach travel from railway stations to the event*, which is often fairly remote.

As well as being single-use plastic free, Rathfinny Half Marathon & 10K uses recycled slate medals by Zero Waste Medals with 'pre-loved' trainer laces rather than ribbons. Runners get a pack of Beebombs instead of a T-shirt, trophies made by a local carpenter out of reclaimed wood, Nurhu energy bars in edible wrappers and an 'old kit zone' collecting for ReRun. More crucially, the organisers arrange free shuttle-bus pick-ups from two local train stations and start the races at public-transport-friendly times, saving fifty-four car journeys (they also charge for car parking, except if there are three or more runners per car, in which case it's free, and they offer secure bike storage). Most other races should take note. Though, of course, they need – we all need – runners to buy into it.

Race start times being prohibitive to public transport use is an issue I hadn't considered till recently. But many trail ultramarathons I've done would be impossible to get to in time via a train, if it even gets close to the event location, which they often don't in trail or fell races. Many races simply haven't considered that runners might use public transport – though unfortunately Sunday is both traditionally a popular day for races and for reduced buses and trains – and only have travel details for car journeys on their website. I emailed an RD (see template on page 129) asking how I could get to a race via trains and though he kindly offered to collect me from the station, that missed the point. In some circumstances, a race simply changing the start time could reduce emissions far more radically than going plastic-free or cancelling their T-shirt order.

The question I kept coming back to is: does the moral responsibility for low-carbon travel lie with the event, or with the runner? People wouldn't be travelling to a place if the event didn't exist, but ultimately they're the ones making the decisions: not only to travel there, but *how they travel there*.

For the Lake District's Dunnerdale Fell Race, cars with one or two people in pay £5 to park, vehicles with four or more park free and get a free beer, while, brilliantly, cyclists and walkers are paid £5. That's the sort of cultural change we're looking for and which races can take such a pivotal role in.

Some races have started taking the decisions out of participants' hands. The Paris Marathon, which claims to be the world's first carbon-neutral 26-mile race, can claim so because it carbon-offsets (discussed anon) all CO_2e from travel. The Cape Town Marathon has also declared itself carbon neutral since 2014, by offsetting and investing in local projects.

The US Trail Running Conference, a multi-day event attended by over 200 people, has become something of a, er, trail-blazer. Inspired and certified by America's Council for Responsible Sport, conference director Terry Chiplin analysed the event's waste, energy, travel and diversity, and made it carbon negative, by working with B-Corp-certified Native to offset 12.9 tonnes of CO_2. 'It was a tonne of work,' he told me, 'but the rewards have been incredible. It's been a business-changing experience and a life-changing experience for me.'

Offsetting costs just $5 per person and the conference is part of a consortium with the Council for Responsible Sport, Athletes for a Fit Planet, UltraSignUp, Runners for Public Lands and the American Trail Running Association. 'There's no reason why we can't have the majority of races also doing it. I'm thinking two years is probably a realistic proposition to have the majority of races here be carbon negative,' says Terry.

This approach goes a step further than merely incentivising runners and simply does the decision-making and financial work for them. But in doing so it misses a vital step: education. It's a great chance to sow ethical seeds that may well spread out much, much further. Plus we can't just pay for the problem to go away. The emissions do still happen. So that's not sustainable.

'It's not about just carrying on with life as we have done and offsetting it,' insists Terry. 'This is also about communicating with runners, to get them thinking about their own personal responsibility. And if we can get everybody involved, there's something like 9 million trail runners in the US. I know it's a big dream, but why not?'

'**A lot of people think there's going to be some superhero who comes in and solves all our problems,**' he says. '**But no one person can do everything. However, each of us can do something.** That's a really empowering perspective in terms of climate change. It's an overwhelming subject for a lot of people and they think, you know, "What difference can I make as an individual?" Well, between us, we can make a huge difference. Because **if everybody takes some action, we create a movement that has real power and can make huge changes.**'

I like Terry. I was sceptical about his offsetting plans at first. But our climate and ecological emergency needs more Terrys.

Trails on trial

'The trail- and ultra-running community is ahead of the mass-participation, big-city events,' says Kate Chapman. 'Because of where those events are mostly run, there's a lot more respect for the environment generally. That self-sufficiency aspect is much more common than in road-running too. It's a bit of a mantra for us with sustainability: "What does the ultra community do?"' But it's not always so clear-cut.

While trail-running events have fewer participants, and therefore you might hope lower footprints, they're inevitably further away from populous areas, which requires more participant travel to places not served by public transport, plus logistical support (vehicles transporting kit and sustenance between sometimes remote checkpoints, for example). And some are in exotic places, which dramatically bumps up scope-3 emissions.

If ultra-distance trail-running is a niche, there's a niche within it that I've greatly enjoyed over the years, but which now seems forlornly out of place: international multi-stage races. I've completed the Marathon des Sables in the Sahara Desert, the Ice Ultra in Lapland and The Coastal Challenge in Costa Rica, all events that feel more like travel experiences or well-managed adventures than they do running races. But I look back on them with a sense of guilt because they all require flights for almost all participants – usually long-haul ones.

Companies such as Beyond The Ultimate (BTU; disclaimer: I consider some of the staff friends) and Ultra X (disclaimer: they seem a swell bunch too and invited me to be part of an informal sustainability panel), find themselves in a really difficult position. The former targets UK runners for events in Kenya and Japan, the latter for races in Mexico and the Azores, and both are hugely reliant on participants taking long-haul flights.

In mitigation, BTU tell me they have spent over £1 million on local infrastructure development, recruitment and donations to conservation projects; raised over £250,000 directly for anti-poaching rangers and rhino welfare on their For Rangers Ultra in partnership with Save the Rhino; have five-year conservation projects set up on each race location, working on rewilding, natural woodland restoration or path and trail repair; are well on their way to making all races single-use-plastic-free by 2024; and have a two-part sustainability with two tenets: 'Leave no mark' and 'Build a legacy'.

'At BTU we believe that if people do fly, it should not only be offset [which they say they do for all flights], but worth something', says company director Kris King. 'By limiting our entrants and employing locally, we know we can offset carbon use wherever possible. More importantly, though, **our races are at the sharp end of global warming; our runners meet the people most affected by it, from the Sami reindeer herder struggling with the warmer climates to the local Peruvian biologist studying biodiversity loss in the Amazon.**'

Their races work in partnership with local people and they profit-share with eco lodges, non-profits and conservation bodies to ensure that all local spend goes into protecting the exciting terrain the clients go through. 'Our aim is to fully immerse the runner in the environment and make them want to protect it forever.' As most of their races are in UNESCO World Heritage Sites, continued permissions rely on accountable and industry-leading sustainability plans, Kris says. Maybe I'm easily won over, having massively enjoyed my experience in snowy Lapland on their Ice Ultra, but that seems a reasonable justification to me.

Ultra X are a younger company, in both senses of the phrase, in a similarly unenviable position. As well as a Diversity and Inclusion Policy, they claim to be carbon neutral, certified by Mossy Earth. That inevitably involves offsetting (so far, only in the pandemic era), but Ultra X seem committed to reducing their scope 1 to 3 emissions and encouraging stakeholders to do likewise. In fact, they have aspirations of becoming 'the most sustainable, environmentally responsible, and ethically minded ultramarathon organiser in the world', which isn't easy with their race locations. However, they have a sustainability policy and conduct impact reports and, as well as reductions in plastic, waste, race merch and providing plant-based food during races, they promote a Travel Carbon Calculator at online registration and offer discounts to incentivise offsetting. They also give a 'green ribbon' award to the runner who has 'displayed exceptional commitment to having a positive environmental impact', which is a nice touch.

If multi-stage races in exotic places seem to belong to a different age, the Impact Marathon, meanwhile, *is* a symptom of our times. It offers experiences in Malawi, Guatemala, Nepal and similar and, as well as fundraising, participants spend a week living locally and working on community projects such as building water pipelines, improving agriculture or supporting women's empowerment, all before running a marathon. Of course, significant impact occurs from the flights to these places, but the organisers offset them and again there's a feeling that the experience, for all parties, might be worth it. They've recently started arranging races predominantly for local people, and one on Mull in Scotland, where they've teamed up with Trees Not Tees and runners will get their hands dirty as well as their feet.

In the UK I crewed for a friend on a 100-mile race in early 2022, which introduced me to another ethically awkward practice. The race only has four major aid stations, so each runner tends to be supported by a crew in a vehicle. I probably drove upwards of 150 miles supporting the runner, on top of getting to and from the race, and most of the 250 runners had similar assistance. That would have to be quite a footprint too. When I voiced my concerns, the RD pointed out they wanted the race to feel like an adventure and that it would be difficult to set up an aid station in more remote areas. I'm not sure what the answer is there.

A dragon's footprint

Doing the Dragon's Back Race (some 300 kilometres along the mountains of Wales) in 2015 was the first time I considered running in a context of wider ethics. I noticed that Ourea Events were signed up to 1% for the Planet and the event catering was all vegan. The nosh was delicious and I hardly realised something of my then-usual diet was missing. I wanted to understand a bit more about the dilemmas facing RDs, so I had a chat with Chief Executive Officer Shane Ohly.

As well as being an elite mountain runner and orienteer (and, perhaps unsurprisingly, good friends with Jim Mann), Shane is vegan, no longer flies to destinations in Europe and has joined Extinction Rebellion (XR) protests (sometimes with this writer). He is 'very concerned' about our climate and ecological emergency. 'I think anyone who is clear-thinking should be concerned,' he says. 'If you're not, you're not really understanding the situation. **We've got to a tipping point where people, and society at large, need to be more proactive. I have a responsibility to take action now. Not just saying things. Actually doing things.**'

Hearing Greta Thunberg talking about politicians doing marketing rather than leadership got Shane questioning himself. 'As a business, it's very easy to stick a 1% for the Planet logo on your website and say, "Hey, I'm doing my bit." And while that's better than most, it's not proactively looking in the mirror and going, "Wait a minute, how do we do something meaningful here?" Perhaps I was guilty of outsourcing that responsibility, paying money to appease my conscience a little bit.'

During the 2020 Covid lockdown, Ourea, who operate several running events including the remote Cape Wrath Ultra, upped their sustainability game. As well as joining both Kilian Jornet's Outdoor Friendly and the Vision: 2025 pledges, they were audited by Our Carbon, and started publishing an annual environmental report and operating as a carbon-neutral business – all of which is still very rare for running events, especially outside the mass-participation sphere.

Naturally, the carbon audit spelt out the impact of participant travel to the events. Shane says, 'The realisation of our huge scope-3 emissions, it just became really apparent. Some of our events in some years have had 50% international participants. So when you model out the scope-3 impact of their travel, it's pretty significant.'

The 2021 Dragon's Back Race, which attracts an above average number of overseas runners, emitted 83 tonnes of CO_2e, according to Our Carbon's calculations, with 67% from participant travel, 10% from event team travel, 10% from vehicle mileage and 7% from food – but those emissions were reduced by 82% by not offering meat or fish (discussed more from page 132). The majority of those emissions fell into the scope-3 category.[39]

The big question is: 'who does responsibility for those travel emissions fall on, participant or event?' Shane believes that fundamentally it's on the individual who

39 'Many businesses don't even look at scope 3, but this approach from some businesses cuts out the majority of their footprint,' says Lucy Scrase, Ourea's Chief Operations Officer. 'Obviously this is becoming widely debated!'

is travelling. *However*, 'if you **make it easy for the participants to make the right decision**, a surprising number will do so, in our experience.'[40]

With Shane's urging, UK race-entry website SiEntries is building a calculator into the shopping cart, asking runners, 'You live in X, do you intend to travel by plane, car or public transport?', then estimating their carbon footprint and asking if they want to offset it. 'Every other event organiser gets the benefit of it, but we're the ones driving the innovation. For better or worse, we have a bit of a leadership position in the UK as a sort of gold-standard event organiser and I want us to use that for good.' Run 4 Wales does similar and the London Marathon is considering the same.

Shane freely admits that leading the way ethically makes good commercial sense too. He thinks runners will increasingly make more ethical choices. 'It's a bit like Patagonia having the most sustainable business, which makes commercial sense for them, because it's a point of difference and people make choices to buy their products because of their credentials. I think a race can have a similar reputation within the events industry. You're a runner in France who likes to do a big race somewhere in Europe and you're making choices of where to have an ethical adventure and our events make a lot of sense because they've got great sustainability credentials. As a consumer myself, **every day I make decisions about buying products and services based on the environmental credentials and sustainability of that product or service.'**

However, Ourea Events create tonnes of CO_2e that a non-running puritan might argue are unnecessary. How does Shane justify that to himself? 'Whilst going running and going to events is not an essential part of life, it is an incredibly life-affirming opportunity and experience for many people. And whilst there is a looming environmental crisis, we're not at the point yet where everybody needs to put aside any sense of a pleasurable and self-fulfilling life. I think it's getting the balance right. **I would hope that over the next ten years runners will make more conservative decisions about how often they travel.** When they do travel, then make sure they go to really great races where they can be assured of an incredible experience, which is run as sustainably as it can be.'

How does he think the rest of the running events industry is doing? 'I see a reflection of society at large: there's a lot of indifference, there's a lot of papering over. There are some notable exceptions, but you don't see too many people making

---

40 For example, for their Skyline Scotland race, they asked entrants if they would make a voluntary donation to the local Mountain Rescue team, and soon raised £5,000. Similarly, when they gave entrants the choice to have a T-shirt, plant a tree, or both, 80% went for a tee *and* a tree.

obvious and significant steps to run sustainable events.' He cites the UK's music-festival industry as being further down that road, with their Vision:2025 pledge of running sustainable or carbon-neutral events.[41] Indeed, the sports industry could learn a lot from the green initiatives of the music industry, such as Green Gathering, Green Man, Shambala and even Reading Festival.

'It wouldn't be hard for running events to pick up the slack,' says Shane. 'As an industry we could do better. We're behind.' Ironic, really, as you'd hope the running industry would be good in a race.

That said, getting to the industry-leading stage Ourea are at hasn't been easy, even with a more professional set-up than most running-event companies. 'For the very first time, in 2021 we put an entry in the budget for sustainability costs. The sustainability cost is extra we're going to spend specifically to be more sustainable. It's stuff like buying reusable cups, which is a couple of thousand pounds. We should see the benefits in the years ahead, but right now that's a lot to spend. We're into the tens of thousands of pounds of sustainability spending across the business.' Sustainability costs management thinking time too, he says. 'I'm in the fortunate position that my colleague Lucy Scrase is doing most of the hard crunching and thinking. But there's definitely a management cost. It adds up.'

And the solutions are never as simple as they sound. How do you deliver 3,000 litres of water an hour to runners going through the mountains on a hot day, without using tonnes of plastic? And do you hire a generator that runs on biofuel instead of a normal diesel generator, given that the biofuel one needs a battery pack, which needs an additional trailer and another vehicle, so you've doubled your transport costs and emissions? 'Doing the right thing isn't always simple. It's about really understanding where your inputs come from and that's why doing carbon accounting has been really useful for us.'

Overall, Shane feels both optimism and pessimism for our climate and ecological emergency. 'The vast majority of runners I know are really lovely, great people who have all the right motivations and they want to see a sustainable industry in terms of clothing and events, races that are brilliant and they can be passionate about. But as a global population, are we going to make the sacrifices and changes required to get us on a sustainable footing in terms of being on this planet? I feel a bit more doubtful about that. The trajectory is not good. I'm very pessimistic. But I don't think that's a reason not to take action.'

---

41 It's estimated that music-festival attendee travel constitutes 80% of total festival emissions, totalling over 78,000 tonnes of CO_2e, the equivalent to driving to the moon 760 times or driving at 60 miles per hour non-stop for 354 years.

The good, the bad and the ugly

In the UK, several trail-running event companies at least have sustainability policies. As with sportswear brands, and in fact all companies now, there's something to be said for simply how quickly you can spot the word 'sustainability' on their home page, if at all.

Some races I've loved doing, such as Ultra-Trail du Mont-Blanc, look at best a bit out of touch or at worst knowingly irresponsible now. UTMB has made runners carry their own cups and laudably laid on buses for supporters for years, but thousands of runners come from over 100 nations, and a UTMB World Series has just been launched, encouraging travel to China, Australia and Patagonia. The Salomon Trail Series is a similar idea, and the Spartan Trail World Championship has nine events in five continents, including in Australia, Argentina, the USA, Malaysia and Sweden.

Marathon des Sables has the vast majority of the 1,200 participants fly to Morocco from the UK and France, get bussed to the Sahara Desert, then have their camp taken down and erected a few kilometres away by an army of jeeps over six days[42] – plus two helicopters are primarily there for media purposes.

I'm reluctant to get the pointy finger out, especially as it's easy for me to be an eco snob when I've done several exciting foreign races. While I don't wish to deny the experiences I've had to others, pan-continent race series sit very uncomfortably with our times. I'm not sure what the answers are exactly, but it probably starts with events openly acknowledging they're part of the problem, measuring their impact and working on solutions to lessen it and spread awareness. Gone are the days when it was morally okay to fly to four or five races around the world in a year.

And as for the World Marathon Challenge, where (very rich) competitors (not that there's much competition, because hardly anyone can afford it) run seven marathons on seven continents in seven days, spending at least 52.5 hours in the air … Most runners will also need to fly to the start and away from the finish too. I can't even bring myself to calculate the unnecessary harm done to the planet from that one. It needs to stop.

The idea of jet-setting to the World Marathon Majors, clocking up some 34,360 miles to reach Tokyo, Boston, London, Berlin, Chicago and New York – oh and soon Chengdu in China too – now seems woefully out of step with the zeitgeist.

The trend for parkrun tourism – travelling about the country, or even the world, to collect different parkruns – needs some reflection as well. The Facebook group has 7.9K members. The point of having so many parkrun locations is surely to make it more accessible for local areas and *stop* people travelling long distances for it.

42 Technically, I'm not sure it's the jeeps that put the tents up.

And parkrun itself? Tens of thousands of people driving, hopefully only a few miles, but just to run 5K, every week? As much is it's a wonderful initiative in many ways, those 773 parkruns have a pretty big carbon footprint.[43] A fairly well-hidden blog on the parkrun website does encourage runners to reduce their footprint by cycling, walking or running there, and parkrun's view is that 'it's more beneficial overall to get people out running, even if that results in more car journeys'.

Apart from the grotesque World Marathon Challenge, I'm not suggesting these events need to end. But at the very least they need to be educating participants about the impact of their travel. And ideally do more than that, incentivising low-carbon travel.

'A strong sustainability message from an event can be completely undermined by a sponsor,' an experienced industry insider told me. Ben Ainslie Racing were doing loads on sustainability when they were sponsored by Land Rover, but with their newer sponsors, global chemical company Ineos, not so much, unsurprisingly. 'When they came in, pretty much overnight their sustainability programme was dismantled.' Ineos also sponsor British Cycling, and elsewhere the London Marathon distributes plastic bottles partly due to a sponsorship obligation. 'It's such a shame when really big high-profile teams and some sports events get sponsorship from companies that don't help. The Olympics has Dow Chemicals, Coca-Cola and McDonald's sponsoring them. **Sportswashing** is on the rise.

Virtual races may be loathed by some, but they have a dramatically smaller carbon footprint. 'No need to travel halfway across the world, and your streets won't be covered in a sheet of rubbish and plastic bottles,' writes Sean Ross, on his Sustainable Running blog. He's writing a Master's thesis on the impact of virtual races towards sustainable development goals. 'Taking part can feel as good as running in a crowd,' he insists. 'I believe more needs to be done to reduce the carbon footprint of running events, and virtual races are a step in the right direction. If people can start substituting just one race for a virtual run, they would be moving the sport of running towards a more sustainable future.'

Earth Runs (*earthrunsmedals.org*) hosts virtual races that, rather than rewarding people 'with crappy, cheap medals', plants trees for them instead. Runners open an online account and accumulate real-life trees, with regular impact reports, 'so they know the difference their miles are making'. And if they still want a medal, they can get one of the world's first biodegradable seeded medals.

43 A high-profile parkrun ambassador admitted as much to me, without me having raised the subject – though they suggested parkrun is more for new runners making lifestyle changes, rather than us more seasoned types, which seems fair. Running can be life-changing and should welcome as many people as possible.

For peat's sake

I've run the notoriously boggy 268-mile Pennine Way four times, twice during the Spine Race, which does provide an environmental impact briefing advising runners on how to run creating minimal erosion, sticking to paths being the obvious one. Peatlands are a wetland habitat found in almost every country, from the permafrosts of Siberia to the tropical peatlands of the Congo Basin. In the UK, peatlands are most familiar as blanket bog: a classic British upland habitat such as the Pennines. This treeless, often squelchy landscape hosts rare and unique plants and animals, is a drinking water source (a whopping 43% of the UK population relies on peat-fed water supplies), and a huge carbon sink. In fact, it's the world's largest natural, terrestrial carbon store.

Peatbogs hold an estimated one third to one half of global soil carbon, equivalent to about 60% of atmospheric carbon, yet cover a tiny proportion – just 2.84% – of land surface. Like trees, a wet, pristine peatbog soaks up CO_2. But unlike trees, it does so limitlessly, whereas trees only capture CO_2 until they are mature. However, a dry, degraded bog – like many in England – *releases* CO_2. Carbon oxidises and peatbog emissions are responsible for almost 5% of global CO_2.

There are over 3 billion tonnes of carbon stored in UK peatlands, as much as all the carbon stored in the forests of the UK, Germany and France put together. It's a non-renewable energy resource, like fossil fuels, and grows incredibly slowly, about a millimetre a year. However, in spite of its importance, it gets ripped up willy-nilly for gardening and gets burnt by landowners to 'manage' the landscape for grouse shooting. And, regrettably, we runners can go charging thoughtlessly through it, churning it up and releasing precious CO_2.

'It's definitely made me notice issues linked to my own personal footprint,' says Jess Williams-Mounsey, a runner and postgraduate researcher in the School of Geography at the University of Leeds, who recently authored the first global review on how roads and tracks affect peatlands. She cites the area between Skiddaw and Blencathra in the Lake District, known as leg one of the Bob Graham Round, as an obvious example of runner impact. The Fell Runners Association is trying to think of ways to reduce impacts.

I was horrified to learn a single footprint on peat can last up to five years. 'I think we should be encouraging RDs and runners to consider contributing to peatland restoration schemes to offset damage,' Jess says.

She also suggests minimising time spent doing training or recces in sensitive areas and doing them with fewer people, sticking to marked pathways – not only does exploring damage bog, but it disturbs breeding birds. Runners are also encouraged to report any illegal activity, such as dirt-biking and any suspicious burning activities. 'We can be both damaging but also useful, in observing problems,' she says.

Coastlines are another particularly British terrain seriously under threat, and again I'm as much to blame as anyone. In 2016 I ran the South West Coast Path (SWCP), which rises and falls almost constantly for 630 miles from Poole in Dorset to Minehead in Somerset. In this instance, crashing waves and more frequent extreme weather are bigger factors than runners' footsteps, but nevertheless the coast is visibly eroding. Houses are literally tumbling into the sea. Millions are being spent on sea defences. Diversion notices are constantly in place for walkers and runners. The places we love to run in are disappearing.

What's encouraging in the running events world is that there's real collaboration between competing parties. 'All mass-participation sports organisations are collaborating on sustainability,' says Kate Chapman. 'There's a recognition that sustainability shouldn't be something that we compete on. There's a lot to be said for acting together rather than individual organisations making a decision to, say, limit the number of overseas participants. It would be more powerful if as a group we all did that.'

Most of the mass-participation event companies genuinely get it, she insists. 'It isn't just lip service. I've worked for organisations where it is lip service and it's like, "Oh, yeah, let's get some good comms messaging out here." They genuinely see the need for this, the benefits for it, and it's a real priority. It isn't just a fad or a token effort. They've got real budget and resource commitment. And rightly so.'

To the non-runner, events like the London Marathon may sound like a huge amount of unnecessary emissions. But while I'm sure they can reduce CO_2e further, let's not forget that even watching the London Marathon on TV can be life-changing for people. It's common for contemporary world-class runners to recall seeing athletics golden moments when young which planted that crucial seed. And it gets thousands more off the sofa, and London especially raises millions of pounds for charity too. With big media coverage – millions watching online and on TV – it's also a platform heavily pregnant for raising awareness of environmental issues.

'There's a balance,' argues Kate Chapman. 'At the really big events, there's incredible amounts of money raised for charity. And what's also so incredible is the ability to inspire, when you've got 40,000–50,000 people out there running through the streets and you see how that brings people together, brings communities together and inspires people watching from their balcony to have a go next year. How many people have got into running because they saw some lunatics in fancy dress? All those positive mental and physical health benefits.' It does, though, seem very slow to confront its elephant in the room.

Similarly, multi-stage races which require most participants to fly to the other side of the world fit awkwardly with our times, but I have some sympathy for these companies. It seems a shame to deny these potentially life-changing experiences to people. At the same time, events like these clearly need to change with the times – as BTU and Ultra X are doing – at the very least educating their customers about what their travel emissions are and the consequences of them, and incentivising low-carbon travel and lifestyles. Races are in a key position of influence.

How different will running races be in the future? 'Mass-participation events are trying to move away from giving out stuff and instead enhancing the quality of the experience,' says Kate Chapman. 'Giving people fewer things, but things like post-race massages, photo opportunities, opportunities to run in places you wouldn't otherwise get access to. Those sorts of things as alternatives to T-shirts, medals and goodie bags. Goodie bags are on the way out.'

Megan Hunt from LME thinks runners will have to get used to being more self-sufficient, carrying their own water, their own nutrition and putting it in a bin when they're finished – 'you know, things you would do in training anyway. Environmentally it'll be a lot different, but socially it will be just as good as it is now.'

With those almost irrelevant-seeming changes to plastic and T-shirt waste, it is more than just the action. It's the message too. It's spreading awareness, making people think, making them question, encouraging them to make personal changes, or better still making them push for change (more on page 111). They may seem like small actions. But oak trees grow from acorns.

But do runners even care?
Some races have made significant changes towards greater sustainability, but people need to be along for the ride, or they won't work. Some runners didn't like running while carrying a refillable bottle and didn't like cupped water, according to research by the Bath Half, although 78% who tried the compostable cups said they were 'excellent' or 'good'.

It feels like the message is getting around about T-shirts and the ironically named goodie bags. Only a third of runners (37%) consider their goodie bag an important part of a race; while 62% say it's not very or not at all useful, according to David Moulding's timely Master's research, involving a survey with 1,200 responses.[ix] One per cent said a goodie bag is 'very useful'.

It can be difficult to manage expectations, says Ashtead 10K organiser Robert McCaffrey. 'People even complain about our wooden medals – they want a big, shiny, metal one.' However, 54% of runners are likely or very likely to forgo a medal if it meant reduced entry fees.

Tellingly, less than two-thirds (63%) of Cardiff Half runners said they reused their race T-shirt. When the Manchester Half Marathon did away with T-shirts altogether in 2019, the response was strong from both sides, says RD Chris Atkinson. 'It's been really interesting understanding how important this issue is to people.' Now, those who want a tee can pre-purchase a finisher top made from recycled material, at a low cost. 'This will allow us to order the correct quantities, reduce wastage and keep the entry price reasonable for others who are less concerned about receiving one.'

One RD pointed out there are several risks when it comes to car-pooling with strangers, even aside from the recent pandemic. 'Unless the race is going to vet drivers in the same way Uber would, I wouldn't feel comfortable offering this service or using one myself.' Hathersage Hurtle signed up to the car-sharing website *racelifts. org*, but just a handful joined up. 'This fact illustrates one of the most important points about "greening" races,' wrote *Runner's World*. 'They only work if we, as runners, play our part too. It may require a change of habit, but that is surely possible.'

'Organisers can place signs telling you where to put your banana skins, but a lot depends on the behaviour of the participants as well,' says Kate Chapman. 'A lot of the sustainability is dictated by what the event organisers say. But some of it's also dependent on participants. These important changes need runner pick-up too.'

Some of the pushback is inevitable and understandable. It doesn't feel like there's a great deal of awareness in the right places. Running events have to change and it may be a little abrupt for some, but awareness of the issues surely helps. **Communication is key**, agrees Kate. '**It's about helping people to understand why you're doing things.**'

The Royal Parks Half is a good example of how it can go wrong. The event announced it wasn't providing bottled water on the course, though there would be refill points. 'They were doing that for sustainability reasons, but it blew up in their faces,' Kate says. 'People said, "Oh, this is a cost-saving exercise – and it's dangerous."' In the end, it was a hot day and they did provide water. 'But that messaging, that understanding of why you're doing it is crucial … **Sustainability doesn't always mean taking things away.** We're battling with the widely held perception that being sustainable means having less fun. It's costing the same, you get less for your money. So we need to work on still having brilliant experiences. **Races should focus on the quality of the experience, rather than the quantities of goodies given out.**'

Kate's local running club does a Christmas pudding 10K. 'You don't get a medal; you get a Christmas pudding sitting there at the end, made by a local company. And it's great! It's sold out every year and people love it. It just goes to show that you can get behind something simple, useful and edible, and it gives them a lot of fun and joy. And people probably like that better than another crappy T-shirt.'

Anyway, though the events stuff doesn't feel nearly as depressing as the kit stuff, it's time for a joke …

> *I saw a climate scientist eating pasta out of a pink leather bowl. She was eating carb on dyed ox hide.*

Yeah, but what can race directors do about it all (in approximate order of impact)?

1 Have a qualified external body do a carbon audit of your company, create a sustainability policy and an impact report. Know your emissions and have measurable targets to reduce them, in a transparent way.

2 Help make good choices easier for runners, by incentivising travel by bike, public transport or car-pooling (try the GoCarShare app) and disincentivising those who drive solo or fly.

3 Help spread awareness that participant travel is the biggest source of CO2e emissions, for both running events and runners.

4 Consider cancelling your T-shirt and medal orders, or at least offer them as paid extras for quality items. Consider signing up with Trees Not Tees or similar schemes.

5 Does your event cater for plant-based diets? That will further reduce emissions and send the right, planet-based message.

6 Can you reduce or ideally eliminate your event's plastic and other waste, from bottles, food wrappers, signage, tape and so on?

7 Do you really need a goodie bag? Most runners don't want one and it ends up as waste. If so, could it be more sustainable?

8 Share news of your sustainability improvements, to help runners make better choices, such as signing up for your event rather than a less conscientious one.

9 Find more ideas and guidance for RDs in Resources (page 202).

6

GREAT TRAINING?

The biggest footprint-cutting action runners can take
is less and low-carbon travel

*'We can't rely on the big people making the right decisions.
So we've got to do it as the little people.'*
Chris Zair

It's very painful to admit now, but in 2019 I took *seven* running-related return flights. Five were short-haul (i.e. in Europe) for races and a recce, one was to speak at ISPO on behalf of inov-8, and another was for a trail-running festival I was invited to in the Czech Republic, which doubled as a family holiday. That was an unusual year. For the handful of years before that, I averaged three flights for running and often a fourth for a family holiday.

Flights were – and still are – incredibly cheap, foreign mountains are incredibly enticing, it felt like my peers were all doing the same (not any kind of excuse, really) and I was only vaguely aware that flying wasn't great for the environment (ditto). I also saw competing in international trail-ultramarathons as my job. I guess my hands were over my ears. How can something be so cheap and easy if it's so bad? Surely it would be more prohibitive? It was only towards the end of 2019 when Extinction Rebellion woke (pun intended) me up a bit that I started looking into things more.

We know a running event's CO_2e emissions are over 90% from participant travel (if we include scope 3, which after all are very much real emissions and have to be accounted for somewhere). If we flip the coin, in most cases, **a runner's highest portion of CO_2e emissions each year will be from their travel**.

A pro runner doing the Skyrunning series might fly to six international races and a few training camps per year, estimates Rosie Watson, in a thought-provoking piece about a more sustainable outdoor community on AdventureUncovered.com.[i] If they 'only' took four return flights from the UK (perhaps to Italy, New York, Greece and Australia), she estimates that would emit about 5 tonnes of ghg through flights alone.

'These emissions are the same as the global average emissions per person for an entire year – for everything.' Five tonnes is also what Mike Berners-Lee suggests we should be aiming for in the UK (down from 13).

Unlike T-shirts and plastic bottles, travel is a hard thing to avoid. The good news is that once we know and understand the consequences and our choices, we can do quite a bit about it, and get more out of travel too. As low-carbon travel will often be the largest portion of a runner's footprint, it seems worth delving in further. First, that mandatory reality check …

Sky-high statistics

Travel is responsible for one fifth of global emissions. In richer countries, the transport sector emits more ghg than any other – it's 28% of the UK's footprint. Travel is also at least one quarter of an individual's footprint and often the largest segment overall.

Most runners will be aware that flying is bad for the planet. How bad? Well, here's the curious thing. From one angle, actually not that bad. 'Aviation's contribution to climate change … is often less than people think,' says Oxford University's invaluable Our World in Data.[ii] From a global perspective, flying is commonly calculated to be only 2.5% of total CO_2e emissions. There are some significant caveats, though.

Flights tend to be more damaging than other ghg emissions because they're released above the protective ozone layer, potentially doubling their impact. So Our World in Data estimates that due to 'effective radiative forcing', flying is actually responsible for 3.5% of the world's CO_2e. Another study puts the industry's contribution to our climate and ecological emergency at 4%.[iii] That still doesn't sound like a huge number against all the hullabaloo. However, if you take a consumption-based approach to the carbon footprint of the UK population, Mike Berners-Lee estimates that the figure is 8%. And 4–5% of global emissions.[iv]

And here's the thing: 80% of the world don't currently fly. In fact, **just 1% of the world causes over half of aviation's emissions**, the frequent-flying super emitters.

Up until the Covid pandemic anyway, flights were increasing inexorably. In 2019, almost 40 million flights departed from airports worldwide, amounting to more than 100,000 trips per day, and CO_2 emitted by airlines has doubled since the 1980s. The 32% increase in flights from 2013 to 2018 is equivalent to building fifty coal-fired power stations, and they're expected to triple by 2050. To achieve net-zero emissions in the UK by 2050, as pledged, government advisory body the Climate Change Committee says there's room for no more than 25% growth in aviation passenger numbers on 2018 levels. Yet planned airport expansions for Heathrow, Gatwick, Luton, Bristol, Stansted and others will result in nearly three times that number. Globally, it's by far the fastest growing cause of ghg.

At the same time as harmful CO_2e emissions from flights are taking off like a drunken pilot, we're slowly waking up to the fact that, unlike fashion and automotive, aviation is the hardest industry to decarbonise. You can buy an electric car, but the batteries needed to power planes are currently too heavy to be viable for anything other than short domestic flights, while various alternative fuels are a little way off, although Denmark thinks it will have fossil-fuel-free flights by 2030, with easyJet making similar noises.[44] But when you hear airlines are flying 100,00 near-empty 'ghost flights' – generating up to 2.1 million tonnes of ghg, as much as 1.4 million cars emit in a year – simply to retain EU airport slots, in what a *Guardian* podcast labelled 'an environmental disaster', it's hard to feel any sympathy for their plight.

When it comes to picking up boarding passes, the UK flies higher than most. Though the average Briton flies short-haul once a year and long-haul once every three years, in 2018 **more flights were made by Brits than any other nationality**.

The UK is behind only the US (24%) and China (13%) in aviation emissions. How can that be? Well, nationally we mirror the same global pattern of elitism, with 1% responsible for nearly a fifth of all flights abroad and 15% of people snaffling up 70% of the chances of some duty-free shopping.

Like with race T-shirts, flights are so cheap we barely value them. Half of leisure flights were not considered important by the traveller, found a 2019 study.[v] 'A lot of travel is going on just because it's cheap,' summarised the *Guardian*.[vi]

'Some people … are really gallivanting all over the place,' Mike Berners-Lee told *Business Travel News*.[vii] 'If those people were to be more selective, that would make a huge dent in [emissions].'

Though globally the industry is overshadowed by other polluters, **from an individual perspective, flying is the most carbon-intensive activity we can do**. The return flight from London to San Francisco I did in 2019 emitted around 2.58 tonnes of CO_2e, about the same emissions as a family car in a year and more than the average person in numerous countries produces annually. Meanwhile, a return flight from London to Berlin emits around 0.6 tonnes of CO_2e, three times the emissions saved from a year of recycling. Even a short-haul return flight from London to Edinburgh contributes more CO_2 than the average annual emissions of someone in Uganda or Somalia. With that in mind, the damage caused by flying doesn't sound quite so tolerable.

---

44 As far as alternatives are concerned, hydrogen, sustainable aviation fuels, waste and synthetic e-fuels show *some* promise, as does, er, kelp. While biofuel gets mooted, it suffers from seriously inefficient land use; it's the same amount to fuel a car for 1.1 miles, for example, as would feed a person for a day.

Runners' highs

Most runners I know do a handful of races each year, with perhaps one or two abroad, but I was still surprised to discover what a large industry sports tourism has become. Having boomed for the last two decades, travel for sport, as a participant or spectator, now accounts for over 10% of all international tourism expenditure, is worth £610 billion, and may be the largest growing sector in tourism. **With UK runners' attendance at international marathons at an all-time high, regrettably the activity is a huge contributor to our climate and ecological emergency.**

What contribution does a runner's travel make to their overall footprint? Well, I'm glad you asked. 'Marathon running is an activity that corresponds to a significant carbon footprint,' concluded a 2021 study, 'The Carbon Footprint of Marathon Runners: Training and Racing'.[viii] The research aimed to estimate the CO_2 footprint of the common scenario of a person training and competing in an international marathon. Researchers calculated impact from the hypothetical runner's shoes, clothing, books, magazines, insurance, travel, hygiene (eh?), laundry, electronics and food, and estimated **a France-based runner taking part in the New York City Marathon would emit 4.3 tonnes of CO_2e from their hobby.** However, 3.5 tonnes of that comes simply from the return flight to America – 83% of his running footprint.

The annual carbon footprint of an average citizen in France is around 11 tonnes of CO_2e (it's 13 tonnes in the UK), and they estimate that **being a runner adds 40% to it.** 'The global impact of this activity is not climate friendly,' the study concludes.

A runner travelling to the five international Abbott World Marathon Majors from London would create 9.2 tonnes of CO_2e from flights, the same as driving two cars for a year (assuming a generous 22,800 miles each) and would take 11 acres of forest to sequester.

However, there's some good news. In the study of the French runner, simply by replacing the New York trip with a domestic marathon that could be reached by train in a 1,000-kilometre round trip, *CO_2e emissions are lowered to six times less* and 0.7 tonnes. The domestic marathon option brings his running footprint down to just 7% above the average citizen.

Also, if that runner does daily run commutes instead of using public transport to get to work, *their impact becomes almost carbon neutral.* Andrew Murray makes the same point in his Running On Carbon blog. In 2019 he did fifty-four 8-mile run commutes, potentially saving 93 kilograms of emissions from car travel or 42 kilograms of emissions from train travel.

The travel element of running is potentially by far the biggest negative environmental impact. It can be huge. But it can also be small. When Andrew calculated his running footprint, travel for the activity amounted to 46% of his overall running footprint (albeit a comparatively modest 291 kilograms of CO_2e – he's more conscientious and carbon wise than most and cycles a lot). Andrew raced six times, with just one international flight, but used public transport for all domestic races and to return from France. 'If you flew a few times specifically to run … this alone could add at least 1–2 tonnes to your running carbon,' he says. 'You might fly to Berlin or Seville to knock two minutes off your marathon PB, but is it really worth that much carbon?'

Similarly, when Our Carbon calculated my family's footprint for 2019, I was aghast to see my flights that year amounted to *6 tonnes of CO_2e*, over half of my footprint and over a third of my family's.

The Swedish have a word, *flygskam*, meaning 'flight shame', an ethical movement which started in 2017 when singer Staffan Lindberg announced he was giving up flying. Other celebrity advocates include Olympic-medal-winning biathlete Björn Ferry. They all trail in the wake of *The A-Team*'s B.A. Baracus (played by Mr T), though, who was saying, 'I ain't getting in no plane, fool!' back in the 1980s.

I too started to feel that creeping sense of guilt. I initially told myself I was doing my job as an international ultrarunner. I had to fly for work, right? But it dawned on me that I couldn't carry on like this. Once you see it, you can't unsee it. Cutting down on flights significantly shrank my carbon footprint (in fact, I haven't flown since, though the pandemic helped). And I feel a tiny bit less guilty about my contribution to the Big Kerfufflefuck.

Ethical flying?

Should we stop flying altogether? It's between you and your conscience, says Mike Berners-Lee in *There Is No Planet B*. 'Nobody is saying "no flying", but the hard reality is we don't know how to put a big passenger airline up in the air on a long-haul flight without burning through something in the order of 100 tons of aviation fuel which turns itself into over three times its weight in carbon dioxide.'

We're going to have a few decades where we have to think more carefully about when we do and when we don't fly, he says. He would like to see a culture where people are 'using their own consciences a bit. That doesn't mean we can't all get to see the world and have fantastic cultural experiences and keep our businesses thriving. It just means we need to think a bit differently about it.'

Go to Berlin for the Marathon and hit your PB. 'But then get a train to Budapest and have a nice European break, spend more money locally,' suggests Andrew Murray. 'It's about combining events, an adventure or experience with something else – a work trip, a family holiday, a wedding, a marathon – so there's proportionally less carbon. We should be seeing flights as unique trips, one-offs, annual opportunities. Use that carbon budget for something big. Flights should be a rare treat, like a bottle of champagne, or beef.

In fact, Berners-Lee says he wouldn't want a flight-less world. 'I wouldn't want to see people running countries who haven't explored the world to understand other cultures and I wouldn't want to see my kids not understanding people from other cultures … Go for a long time, have new experiences and meet people who see, think and live differently to you.'[ix]

Ultimately, we're never going stop people wanting to travel internationally, says Andrew. 'And travel is a fantastic thing. Some of the best things you can do for climate change are economic development of really low-income countries: spend money there, which might help build schools. Women's education is number three on the list of top things to do. Travel is a really great fact of life. The problem is, some people do way too much of it. Flying is a necessary evil in some situations, so it should be weighted and costed accordingly, and it isn't.'

What about that argument that the plane was going to fly anyway, so us not being on it makes no difference? One individual choice won't impact the plane flying, agrees Andrew. 'However, as planes only make economic sense to fly as full to capacity as possible, it doesn't take many people not flying to make it less profitable to fly that route or frequency, which would lead to fewer flights overall. It's a classic example of a single individual action not making significant difference because it's so small, but **all the actions add up and can shift the system through collective action**.'

People who might take one or two short-haul flights a year aren't the real problem. After all, **the world's richest 10% are responsible for 49% of global emissions** and in the UK 70% of flights are taken by 15% of people, not forgetting the 1% of binge fliers. That's surely where the brakes need to be applied. Individuals who care have a tendency to shoulder the blame and make sacrifices, while the people who don't continue to cause far more harm. And that doesn't seem fair.

Another problem with flights is the absence of a tax on aeroplane fuel, kerosene. 'It's the only fuel in the world with zero tax, which is incentivising cheap but a very harmful form of travel,' says Andrew, who's a big fan of the idea of a frequent-flier tax, progressively punishing those who fly five or six or more times a year, rather than once for a family holiday.

Currently no country's plans include flying in their national decarbonisation plans, because of air travel's international nature, so there's less pressure to reduce all those harmful gases being pumped directly into the sky. 'It's an example where governments, rather than individuals, could make huge impactful changes quickly', Andrew says. And some are. The French government (like the Scandies, they always seem so much more on the ball) have moved to reduce the amount of domestic flights, while the Swedish government have introduced an 'eco-tax' on aviation and is investing in sleeper trains. If the UK government really cared about our climate and ecological emergency, you sense they would introduce a frequent-flyer tax or disincentivise aeroplane travel. But they're heavily subsidising airlines and building new runways. They're killing the planet.

In the meantime, how much air time is ethically okay? Kilian Jornet's Outdoor Friendly Pledge allows runners to emit 3 tonnes of CO_2e for travel a year, which amounts to four or five short-haul flights and seems pretty generous. German public interest group Atmosfair recommends limiting air travel to about 3,100 miles per year, a return trip from Los Angeles to Mexico City. Perhaps one flight a year is reasonable, suggests Trees Not Tees' Chris Zair. Take no more than one short-haul flight every three years and one long-haul flight every eight years, says a 2022 study, as part of six lifestyle changes that could keep global heating down to 1.5 °C.[x] Maybe 'how often' isn't the right question? Perhaps it should be: 'How vital is it really?'

If you do fly, there are some ways to reduce CO_2e. See page 130 for more details.

Planes, trains and SUVs

In a way, navigating the aviation maze is the easier end of low-carbon travel. Planes aren't the biggest slice of the planet-poisoning pie. Remember, transport overall is responsible for almost a quarter (21%) of global CO_2e, but flying is just 4% of that.[xi] **Road travel – cars, buses, motorbikes, lorries – accounts for three-quarters of the world's transport emissions and 15% of the world's total CO_2 emissions**.

In developed countries, car ownership feels like a civil right. Globally, we sure do love our fossil-fuel-powered, four-wheeled boxes. I had assumed cars aren't nearly as bad as planes. But the thing is, driving isn't much better, especially if we are the sole occupant. **While an average long-haul flight emits 195 grams of CO_2e per kilometre, the average diesel car with one passenger in emits 171 grams per kilometre.** In fact, **sometimes a car journey is environmentally worse than a flight**. If the journey is longer than 1,000 kilometres, flying actually has a slightly lower carbon footprint per kilometre than driving alone.

When it comes to runners, **80% of us usually use a car or motorbike to travel to races**, according to David Moulding's research, and only 11% use public transport.[xii] It's fairly easy to improve here. Adding a passenger to a car halves the emissions per kilometre and **a car with four passengers (43 grams per kilometre) is almost as efficient as a train (41 grams per kilometre)**, in most cases the best option otherwise (more anon). So car-pooling really is a climate-friendly option.

SUVs aren't, though. A Chelsea tractor can emit a whopping 85% more CO_2e per kilometre than a small car and is responsible for the second-largest cause of the global rise of CO_2e over the past decade, eclipsing shipping, aviation, heavy industry and trucks combined, and easily cancelling out any decarbonisation gains. **If SUV drivers were a nation, they would rank seventh in the world for emissions.** That's another one to repeat out loud.

But they're safer, right? Erm, nope. A person is 11% more likely to die in a crash inside an SUV, and their height makes them twice as likely to roll in crashes. They're also twice as likely to kill pedestrians and they're proven to lull drivers into a false sense of security, encouraging them to take greater risks. I do find it pretty funny when the brave folk from The Tyre Extinguishers go on a splurge of deflating SUV tyres.

Battery Electric Vehicles (BEVs) and partially electrical vehicles/hybrids are thankfully also being bought in record, albeit far fewer, numbers. They produce zero CO_2 if charged via a renewable energy supplier (as 39% of the UK is), which also means zero exhaust pollution and that electricity is much cheaper than petrol or diesel (which are at record high prices at the time of writing).[45] **In the UK, the lifetime emissions per kilometre of driving a BEV are three times lower than the average conventional car.**

Incidentally, 40,000 people die prematurely from air pollution in this country each year, with 8,900 deaths attributed to vehicles, and diesel cars produce fifteen times as many harmful particles as petrol cars.[xiii]

However, some experts, including Mike Berners-Lee, say we need to rethink our relationship with automobiles and predict a move away from ownership. Car sharing, fractional ownership, rental initiatives and subscription models are the future. Schemes which allow you to rent a car without owning one, such as Zipcar, are increasingly an option for those in cities and towns and could significantly reduce the number of cars on the roads. Most cars sit there unused 90% of the time. Indeed, as a one-car household, I rent a car a few times a year for running-related reasons. I'd love to be supporting one of these schemes but they're urban-centric at the moment. I'd also love to hire an EV, but my local rental company tell me they only have one and it's pot luck whether I get it. But there's progress.

When it comes to other types of public transport, **taxis** are 47% worse than an equivalent private car ride, due to the extra passenger-free driving, known as 'deadheading'. Travelling by coach scores surprisingly well, emitting 27 grams of CO_2e per person per kilometre, compared with 41 grams on a UK **train** (but only 6 grams on Eurostar). **Ferries** are even better, at 18 grams for foot passengers (but

---

45 In conversation with Mike Berners-Lee he pointed out that not all renewable energy is as good as it sounds. See *How Bad Are Bananas?* for more.

won't get you from London to the Lake District very quickly). Travelling on light rail or the **London Underground** emits a sixth of the equivalent car journey; while a **local bus** emits a little over half the ghg of a single-occupancy car journey – and helps to reduce congestion, which should improve as electric and hydrogen buses proliferate. That local bus currently emits more than a coach because these buses travel at lower speeds and pull over more often.[46]

Great training

Trains are brill! **Using a train instead of a domestic flight would usually reduce a journey's emissions by around 84%.** Another example is that a return flight from London to Moscow would use a fifth of your 'carbon budget' for a year (the amount each person can emit in 2030 while keeping ghg down to safe levels), while going by train would use one-fiftieth of it. **In a nutshell, trains are often the most low-carbon way to travel, domestically and internationally.**

We don't always feel we have the time for a train journey, but maybe we should make it. The burgeoning slow-travel movement is largely centred on trains and revelling in slow, deliberate journeys, making the locomotive aspect part of the holiday. The Swedes, again, have the word *tagskryt*, which translates as 'train bragging', a point of pride.

Sleeper trains are coming back into fashion, with investment and lines opening up Europe, including a planned link between Edinburgh and Portugal. 'Rail's brilliant,' says Mike Berners-Lee. 'The last time I went out to Berlin I took the train and it was great. Such a relaxing experience. I did a lot of work and it was really chilled out. And we've been on holidays with the kids where we've taken the sleeper out to Italy – it's a really nice thing to do … For trips around Europe about half the time it works for me to take the train.'[xiv]

Yet, frustratingly, train fares on popular UK routes are 50% more expensive than plane fares, according to *Which?*, which (arf) says passengers face a 'near impossible' choice between low prices and climate-friendly travel.[xv] We are currently incentivised to make the worst decisions for the planet. You can't blame people for taking the half-price option. As with so much of this mess, government intervention could make a huge difference. We need to be incentivised to make good decisions. Studies in the US have shown that cheaper fares on public transport lead to greater use. New Zealand halved the cost of all their public transport in April 2022, while the Spanish government have made all short-to-medium train journeys free (partly funded by a windfall tax on energy and finance sectors).

---

46 As with all these calculations, it depends on journey duration, whether the transport is electric, the number of travellers and other variables.

Damian (right) meets Charlotte Jalley and Dan Lawson at ReRun Clothing.
All photography © Stuart March.

The massive scale of ReRun's trainer mountain, with a handy reminder that the most sustainable running kit is the kit you're already wearing.

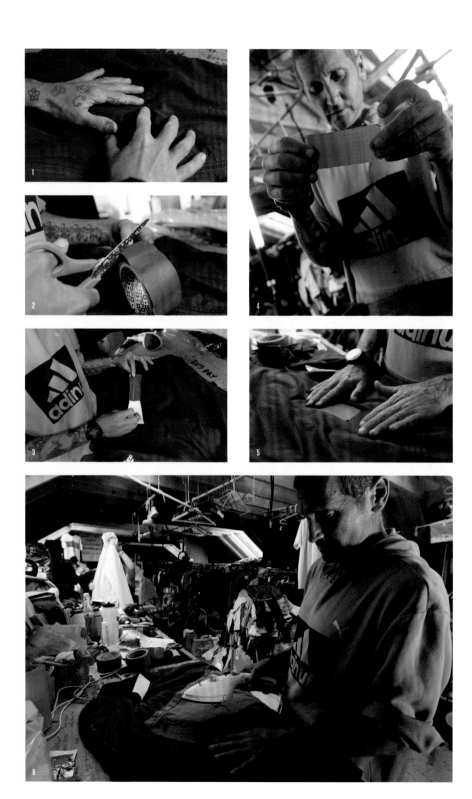

To repair a tear, you'll need clothing repair tape, scissors and an iron. Assess the size of the hole (1). Cut the tape, ensuring an overlap of at least 1 centimetre around the hole (2 & 3). Place the patch, making sure there are no wrinkles on the tape or the garment (4 & 5). Put a tea towel over the repair and fix the tape with a hot iron (6).

To repair a hole in knit trainers, you'll need a darning or sewing needle and polyester thread. The thicker the thread, the easier the repair! Assess the damage (1 & 2). Use a running stitch to sew lines across the hole in one direction (3). Do not pull too tight. Weave the thread in the opposite direction over and under to form a net; then weave back in the opposite direction (4). Secure the thread by weaving through the patch a few times in different directions (5).

Do you really need another race T-shirt? ReRun have thousands of them and Charlotte says they're 'the most unwanted and unloved items in the running industry'.

Yesterday's trainers become today's plant pots.

Walking and running are, unsurprisingly, the lowest-carbon ways to travel. The footprint of cycling is only a tiny bit worse, with 1 kilometre usually costing 16–50 grams of CO_2e, depending on how efficiently you cycle and what you eat – **if fuelled by cheeseburgers, the journey emits about the same CO_2e as a car**. In the US, elite ultrarunner Dakota Jones has got into the habit of cycling hundreds of miles to races, and still winning them. We can all be low-carbon travellers. In reality, that's often as simple as swapping a plane or a car for a train.

There are further nuances to low-carbon travel. The type of car matters, as does a country's electricity grid (for electric cars and electric public transport) and whether you fly business or economy (better environmentally), plus some domestic flights emit more CO_2e per kilometre than long-haul ones (as taking off uses more fuel than cruising and they tend to have more empty seats). There are more low-carbon travel tips on page 129 and if this stuff interests you, check out the amazing *OurWorldinData.org/travel-carbon-footprint*.

Becoming a low-carbon athlete

Perhaps before thinking 'Can we travel better?', we should be thinking 'Do we even need to travel?' **Is our race calendar fair on the planet? 'To really attack the 98% of CO_2e from participant travel, it has to initially come from changing the way the runners choose their races**,' says Chris Zair from Trees Not Tees.

'You have professional runners, where racing is their job', says Chris. 'And day-to-day runners, who maybe only fly to a race once a year. But you get a small percentage who fly to several races, and that's where we see a bigger impact. We don't need to do that as runners. We don't need to go to these races, not all the time. If you want to run a cool race, there's hundreds of them right here in the UK.'

Chris is frustrated by influencers. 'How often do we see them on social media racing in what feels like a different country every weekend? The Golden Trail Series and similar create this glamorous view of trail running across the globe, and I've only seen Kilian Jornet and [this author, ahem] actively talk about reducing their footprint, by either not racing, or making a serious effort to decarbonise travel. How do we make people conscious of that travel impact? **We all need to be more vocal** on the impact of booking that cool race that's a four-hour flight away three times a year, and pushing people to #runlocal.'

After considering whether you really need to do that faraway race, think about how you're going to get there, says Chris. 'Calculate what that carbon footprint is, think about the impact you're going to have and how long you're going there for. Is there a chance to build in four days before and five days after, rather than flying out Friday, coming back Sunday? Are there other runners you can get in touch with to share a vehicle with? If there's a Facebook group, ask in there. If not, message the race director. If not, is it really worth the carbon footprint?'

However, we don't want to ostracise people, he says. 'If someone currently flies to eight races a year, then next year flies to three, then two, that's success. That's the decarbonisation we need. We don't exclude people who love their running, who've got dreams of doing big international races and want to go away for summer, and may have to fly there. Making positive changes is the goal. It's about being better every year.'

I'm not perfect by any means, but I've made progress. When plotting my race calendar, now I ask myself, 'Can I really justify doing this race or challenge? Is it really worth the CO2e?' For years I've very much wanted to run Diagonale des Fous on Réunion Island, for example, but now that just feels too far for me. (However, if I could turn it into a family holiday, it might just about become more ethically viable.)

I've largely swapped international races for domestic ones and I'm having a blast. There are plenty of epic challenges to be had on this lumpy island. Domestic races – while sometimes, but not always, a little less prestigious and exciting terrain-wise – are easier to train for and recce, offer a more familiar climate, are cheaper, and I won't be away from my kids as much. (Plus, as they're usually a little less competitive, I have a better chance of making the podium!)

I'll fully admit that it's easier for me to cut back like this, having already done several of the biggest ultra-trail races around Europe and spent years travelling the world. I'm not telling anyone else what to do and I won't judge you if you fly (well, not much).

Secondly, after really questioning whether I 'need' to do it, I'll look at whether I can practically get there without flying, which is often much easier than I thought (more anon). Though I know some runners who've given up flying, including record-breaking fell runner Finlay Wild – and huge plaudits to them – I haven't yet sworn off flights for good. As well as not wanting to limit my children's experiences too much, there are some once-in-a-lifetime races and challenges in places it'd be very difficult to get to without a flight, such as the US. But even typing that makes me feel uneasy.

I'm very reluctant to fly again, but like Shane Ohly says, we're not yet at the point in the emergency where we have to forego all pleasure. When I do fly for running, it'll be because it's a bucket-list race or challenge that has huge meaning to me and because alternative travel methods really aren't practical. I'll make sacrifices elsewhere in the year to keep my footprint low, I'll make the most of the trip and I'll feel really bad doing it.

There's been a behavioural change, with my flights dramatically reduced and train journeys replacing car or plane journeys whenever feasible. For 2021's Ultra-Trail du Mont-Blanc, in Chamonix, France, instead of the usual flight from Bristol to Geneva, I caught the train. Well, okay, several trains. It only took two hours longer door-to-door, and was more comfortable, relaxing and enjoyable (flying isn't actually much fun when you think about it: cramped seats, crap food and getting your penknife confiscated by Customs). I was perfectly happy doing some work, listening to football on the radio, doing a spot of sightseeing in Paris, and I arrived with less guilt, feeling happier about my contribution to the world. However, at around £400, the trip was over twice the cost of flying, proving that conscience is a middle-class luxury.

I'll admit I struggle with car travel for running journeys. It'd feel good to give up our car, and if it was just me, I could. Living in the Wiltshire Alps, the idea of no car – the second most effective thing we can do, after not having children (oops, too late), saving 2.4 tonnes of CO_2e a year – just feels, while not impossible, prohibitively awkward and limiting. The school run, numerous local clubs and weekend trips would be hugely inconvenient, time-consuming and unfair on my kids by forcing them to hang around at bus stops a lot. I still feel bad about it, even though there's no practical alternative.

For running-related trips, car use feels unavoidable sometimes too. I am compelled towards running and racing on fells and big hills. Finding that stuff has been life-changing for me and is far more than a hobby. It's integral to my livelihood and happiness. But those enticing lumps tend to be in the north or Wales. I can't think of a year where I haven't done a race, running challenge or some type of event in at least one of the Lake District, North Wales or Scotland. Using a car means I can travel at unsocial hours, setting out after the kids' bedtime so I minimise missing out on them. (In fact, I've set off at 2 a.m. before for a 10 a.m. race in the Lakes and been back for their bedtimes.) Driving is also usually cheaper and much more time-efficient, and often public transport simply doesn't get to the places I want to go to.

The almost 600-mile round trip from Corsham to Keswick in my diesel car costs 90 kilograms of CO_2e. A running shoe, remember, costs about 14 kilograms. I could be super parsimonious with my kit, but if I make journeys like that frequently, it counts for little. However, in context, neither my wife nor I commute, and I do drive significantly less nowadays. It's not perfect, but it is progress. Yet somehow our 2021 family footprint from car travel is still 4 tonnes of CO_2e.

When feasible, I now take train journeys instead, which are usually around a quarter of the CO_2e emitted from driving. If I book a few weeks in advance it's affordable and I can work or read as I travel. It may take a little longer, but it's far safer too, especially if returning after a tiring race.

I try to combine trips as well. Recently, I travelled to the Yorkshire Dales to recce a race, then to Snowdonia to help a friend on a Paddy Buckley, or I combine a meeting with inov-8 with a race in the Lakes, trying to get more value from those regrettable emissions. I also try to do most local journeys on two wheels or feet.

Thirdly, and reluctantly, I offset (more anon) all my family's emissions. But that's the last action on the list, only after reducing CO_2e everywhere we feasibly can.

We shouldn't feel guilty for existing. It's not our fault we live in a system so reliant on fossil fuels. 'When I put diesel in my van, I'm not making a profit from it,' says Huw James, a science communicator, activist and athlete who co-founded the Athlete Climate Academy with Kilian Jornet. 'I think there's a distinct difference there. Fossil-fuel industries who are making profits from burning fossil fuels are different to those who consume it to go about their daily lives within the structure society has built around us.'

Context matters too. 'If a runner from London drives up to Snowdonia a couple of times a year, goes into the mountains to run, does a mountaineering course or whatever, but every single day they commute via public transport, that's the larger context. Around 80,000 people commute every day into Cardiff by car. So is it right to have a go at a bunch of runners who drive up to Snowdonia to go running? Or is the problem that 80,000 people drive a single journey in and out of the same place every day?'

There has to be a balance, a small ghg allowance, for the carbon-conscious runner who still wants to actually do some running. And let's not forget, the very lowest-carbon form of travel is on our own two feet. And we runners do that quite a bit.

After considering our race calendar and travel options, perhaps we could start selecting races on their green credentials, as Shane Ohly suggests. Which at the moment is tricky, because so few know or publish their carbon accounts or even have sustainability policies.

There's an element of imposter syndrome around too, perhaps. I know one RD who's doing amazing environmental work behind the scenes, but hasn't yet made any of it public.

There's also the conscience-assuaging but controversial practice of carbon offsetting …

Some offsetting news

When I book a train ticket via trainline.com I've recently started being given an estimated CO_2 cost for my journey. When I hire a rental car online I'm now offered the chance to 'offset it' for £2.50 (without any further info). The UK's largest airport group gives everyone who flies through Manchester, London Stansted and East Midlands the option of offsetting the emissions from their flights.[47] I carbon-offset all my travel with Our Carbon, as part of my family's total emissions. I'd reduced them as much as I felt I realistically could. But I still want to take my kids on holiday. And I guess we should probably take them to school too. In truth, if I don't train in the Brecon Beacons sometimes, I won't be the athlete I hope to be. Sounds a little selfish as I type it out, but in part it's how I support my family.

When I first heard of carbon offsetting it sounded like a brill idea. Paying someone to take my guilt away. Now, though, it's seen as buying our way out of trouble rather than addressing the actual problem. A fig leaf to cover business as usual, our continuing reliance on fossil fuels – when that's the thing that needs to change.

'Seems everyone is going "green" through offsetting,' says Andrew Murray. 'BA offsetting domestic flights, Shell offsetting their UK loyalty-card customers' fuel, celebrities flying around to "do good" then claiming "it's OK, I offset it".'

Greta Thunberg dismissed offsetting as greenwashing, 'a dangerous climate lie', giving polluters 'a free pass to keep polluting', albeit referring to businesses rather than individuals.

'I'm really wary of any kind of offset,' says Mike Berners-Lee. 'It's methodologically flawed. At its worst ... it's just salving consciences in an unrealistic way and is used to encourage people to fly more while taking an action which is not meaningful.'[xvi] Offsets are not a substitute for cutting emissions in the first place. 'Even tree planting doesn't count because we need to plant all the trees we can in the world *even with* a big reduction in flying.'[xvii]

'In the hierarchy of actions, offsetting is the lowest and should only be used when other avoidance, efficiency and renewable sources have been fully realised,' agrees Andrew. 'Remember, the climate is already fucked, the oceans are dying and ecosystems failing. Let's take this seriously, not a frivolous thing that can be solved for the price of a pint of beer.'

But planting trees is good for the planet, right? They soak up some of that dangerously excessive CO_2. Plus trees are cool. One of the big problems with offsetting is the timing. When you fly, those emissions are created instantly and remain in the atmosphere for decades. When you plant a tree, it needs time to grow, some twenty to thirty years to reach maturity; meanwhile, your emissions have been warming the planet all along. Plus aeroplanes also produce nitrogen oxides, which are damaging to public health, and trees don't help with that.

---

47 Supporting projects such as woodland creation and the distribution of efficient charcoal cooking stoves.

The credibility of carbon-offset schemes has also come under scrutiny.[48] 'Are they really happening?' asks Berners-Lee. 'Can you verify them? Are you just planting monocultures of trees where there should be biodiverse savannah? You could be doing something that's good for carbon but bad for the world.'

Also, regrettably, trees die, burn and get chopped down, meaning all that lovely stored carbon is released (carbon stored in soil remains). 'If the tree does survive to old age, this is only 50–200 years, what then?' asks Andrew. 'That tree and all its lovely locked-away carbon needs to be fixed for good, maybe via being made into furniture, CO_2 collected and stored geologically underground (bioenergy carbon capture and storage) and how do you guarantee that?'

Berners-Lee says there are 'high-quality nature-based solutions' in the UK, like planting mixed woodland and peat restoration. 'Those are really good things to do. We absolutely should be doing those.' But another problem is that all those solutions are finite. 'And we need to be doing them anyway.'

'Better to take the carbon on the chin and face that you can't offset it,' he told me. 'That doesn't mean it isn't a good thing to give money to good causes – very carefully selected land management projects, some of which also remove carbon. But maybe consider higher-leverage stuff, like protest groups or legal action such as Client Earth.'

Once all practical avoidance and reduction steps are taken, offsetting is the only remaining option, agrees Andrew. 'So it does have a useful place in the toolbox of solutions, if done well' (see page 131).

In fact, all future 1.5 °C emission-reduction pathways from the UN and others require offsetting to be in with a chance to avoid much greater warming. This is especially true for hard-to-decarbonise sectors such as flying, shipping and concrete manufacturing.

'The same is true for our personal footprints: when there is no other option left, and only then, high-quality carbon offsets can be part of reducing your individual impact and is better than doing nothing,' says Andrew.

Offsetting doesn't have to be tree-planting. As well as cookers for developing nations and other energy efficiency schemes, renewable energy, waste management and land-use projects are available. But even with a credible carbon-offsetting project, such as The Future Forest Company, there's no such thing as harm- or guilt-free flying or high-carbon lifestyles.

---

48 Some programmes are Compliance, which is firmly regulated; some are Voluntary, which are not subject to strict regulation, though they're the options available to individuals, rather than corporations. (The Task Force on Scaling Voluntary Carbon Markets is currently establishing an independent governance body.)

Difficult decisions

It starts with education. The number-one thing runners can do to reduce their personal carbon footprint is to travel more responsibly. Yet, when asked what races should do to reduce their environmental footprint, **only 8% of runners mentioned public transport ahead of reducing plastic, goodie bags, T-shirts and medals**.

The participant travel problem isn't necessarily up to RDs to solve, agrees Chris Zair. 'It comes from the decisions by runners to run a specific race. Races with a high footprint are victims of their own success. Western States or London Marathon never set out to have a huge footprint, but now everyone around the globe wants to tick them off.'

But RDs can play a vital role in helping us to reduce our emissions. 'Unless it's a serious disincentive if you fly, people will still make the trip,' says Chris. 'It sounds extreme, but limiting or even banning people who fly, and incentivising low-carbon travel, may be the way forward.' Chris lives in Barcelona, where some races give discounts to locals. 'Maybe we also need to disincentivise runners from further away? Maybe popular races could have a cap on overseas competitors?'

A first step would be races doing more to spread awareness. Even if a race website does include public transport information, which is rare, it won't be at the point of purchase. 'It needs to be really clear,' says Chris. '"Where are you coming from?" Okay, "this is your footprint". Currently they get you to sign up first. I'm not seeing anything like, "Do you need to do this race?"'

'Runners need to be aware of their impact,' urges sports-event sustainability expert Kate Chapman, 'and that it's a choice they're making. You're choosing to travel long-haul, to fly to an event. Are there events closer to home that you could do, or could you get to the event by a train instead? I wouldn't ever want to be pointing the finger and saying you shouldn't go on holiday. But maybe it's setting yourself a limit on how many events you might go to that are a long way away?'

Clearly, individuals have a role to play, and most of us can reduce our footprints fairly easily. We could all reconsider our race calendars, reconsider our travel options, do eco-friendly races, and potentially offset CO_2e if we really can't see any other way. But there are times when low-carbon travel is either impractical or impossible and that's where events themselves could do more to help us runners make good decisions.

How can runners effect change? Simple, really. Talk politely to RDs. Email them to ask how you can get to their race using public transport. Ask if they cater for plant-based diets. As ReRun Clothing urge, say a polite 'no thanks' to a T-shirt and medal – at the finish line if you can't register your choices at sign-up. Ask them what they're doing to make their event more sustainable. Celebrate races making a difference.

'We're seeing a lot of races come to us because someone's mentioned in Instagram comments that they should be using TNT,' says Chris Zair. 'So pressure is good. As soon as some races start doing it, you reach a point of runner pressure. We can look to do the same with other initiatives, such as car-pooling.'

Talking of which, encouragingly 75% of runners have car-shared en route to a race, and 80% are likely or very likely to car-share again; while 65% would use public transport if it were subsidised, according to David Moulding's research.[xviii] **Also, 60% of runners are likely or very likely to choose a running event purely for its low environmental impact.** Another study found that a runner's concern for the environment and the impact of a running event influenced the event and locations they were willing to travel to.[xix]

'Feedback is effective,' says Shane Ohly. 'We collate all comments – from email, social media and so on. I personally read all the feedback carefully after each event and anything that really stands out I'll investigate.' Some feedback is painful to read, he admits, such as 'Your food is bad; I wouldn't feed it to my dog'. When you get very harsh comments like that, it's important to reflect, but also to have confidence in your principles (a meat- and fish-free menu). But we carefully consider feedback and we've had some brilliant suggestions over the years.'

Former RD and current Open Tracking director James Thurlow remembers his inaugural Lakes in a Day race, where a colleague thought medals were a waste and didn't order any. 'I didn't know until it was too late and spent twelve hours at a finish line *not* presenting medals. I got A LOT of grief,' he chuckles. 'At the time, though, you could have been mistaken from reading online groups that medals were a waste and not wanted.'

But, yes, he always listens to feedback, 'Even if it's not what we want to hear ... As a back-of-the-pack runner, 50% of ultras I took part in ran out of food at checkpoints and irritatingly the RDs would be proud they had no waste. It's a sore point and an easy win for me when I started putting on ultras, with any excess simply going to local food banks.'

Shane thinks a sea change in runner attitudes is needed. 'When a runner enters a race, they need to start thinking, "Okay, this event cost me £100, but I'm travelling 200 miles to get there; how am I going to do that sustainably?" When they're thinking about races to do, that should be the second question, maybe even the first one. That's something all runners can take personal responsibility for from today.'

But do individual actions even matter if there's a coal power station down the road? 'We can each control what we do ourselves,' says Chris. 'We control our footprint, and then by doing that and sharing it, we have an impact. Little ripples can create bigger waves, and that also creates a conscience. You don't know who that next person is and what their job is. They could be a decision-maker, or they could put pressure on a decision-maker to make a change, and something that small company does influences the rest of the society. If we all control the little things, we can have a much, much bigger impact. We can't rely on the big people making the right decisions. So we've got to do it as the little people, and shout about it, to bring about change in the brands we wear and the races we run.'

Thankfully, when it comes to running travel, there's a lot we can do to make fairly easy and significant improvements. It doesn't seem fair for me – and, more importantly, my children – to have to give up everything we enjoy and benefit from in life, just because some very rich selfish white middle-class men insist on flying a lot and getting richer from extracting fossil fuels from our planet when they know it's causing immense harm. At the same time, now that I know what I know, I'd like to live – and run – a little more responsibly. And you know what, you feel better when you do. And one last thought:

Is climate change leading to more wildfires? Without a drought.

Yeah, but what can we do about it?

1   Do we really need to do the race? Do we need to race so often or so far away? We don't have to cancel our dream races, but less travel, especially flying, massively reduces both our footprint and a race's. And sends a message to others.

2   Race less and race locally. There are tons of ace local and domestic races. You're away from home for less time, spending less money and the aid-station food won't be so weird. There are lots of domestic challenges that have no entry fee: see *gofar.org.uk*. If you can cycle or run to a race, even better!

3   Try to support events that are making the effort. Do they have a sustainability policy? Have they had the emissions audited? Do they help runners arriving by public transport? Less importantly, do they use single-use plastic? What's the policy on T-shirts and medals? Let's celebrate races making the extra effort – it'll often cost them more.

4   Be a race activist – speak up by simply emailing RDs to politely ask what they're doing about waste and how you can get to their event using public transport. Add to this templated letter (about T-shirt waste) from ReRun Clothing: *rerunclothing.org/pages/take-action*

5   Low-carbon travel
    - *routezero.world* offers different options for bespoke journeys and associated CO_2e costs.
    - Companies such as Byway (*byway.travel*) specialise in booking your travel to be as sustainable as possible.

- Using a bike instead of a car for short trips reduces your travel emissions by about 75%.
- Ditch the car and explore by bike, foot, kayak or public transport.
- For accommodation, opt for a small, local-owned guesthouse – even better if it's renewables-powered.
- Eat more plant-based and local produce while you're away (and limit food waste).
- Opt for tours that support local conservation or rewilding initiatives.
- For car-sharing, try *liftshare.com*

6 Low-carbon driving
- Save up to 33% on your fuel bill with low-carbon driving.
- The smaller the car, the smaller the footprint. Electric is even better.
- Avoid sudden accelerating and braking to save fuel, brakes, tyres and the planet.
- Driving at 70 miles per hour uses 25% less fuel than eighty miles per hour. Driving at 50 miles per hour uses 15% less than 70 miles per hour.
- Ensure tyre pressure is high.
- Keep windows up when driving fast.
- Take off roof boxes and racks and empty the boot of those golf clubs or anything heavy.
- Go easy on the air con.
- Avoid rush hour.

7 Low-carbon flying
- For long-haul flights, emissions per passenger per kilometre are about three times higher for business class and four times higher for first class.
- Reduce your flight's emissions by 20–45% by:
  » booking economy and flying with an airline that uses the newest aircraft possible, which is often a budget airline (see *atmosfair.de/de/fliegen_ und_klima/atmosfair_airline_index/*).
  » reducing the amount of stuff you take. The heavier your bags, the more fuel burnt.
  » avoiding flying on either very small or very large planes – both are less efficient.
  » choosing direct flights without stopovers, as take-off is fuel-intensive.

8 The EcoPassenger calculator, launched by the International Railways Union in cooperation with the European Environment Agency, is a reliable resource for calculating travel emissions.

- *ecopassenger.org* is a great starting point for European trains, which can be booked via *trainline.com* too.
- *coolclimate.berkeley.edu/calculator* is another trusted carbon calculator.

9 Offsetting

- Offsetting should be the last resort, but if you want to, look out for the UN's Gold Standard certification, and the UN Climate Convention keeps a portfolio of dozens of projects around the world you can contribute to: *offset. climateneutralnow.org*. Ensure the following key principles apply:
    - » It's additional – you're paying for something new.
    - » It's permanent – it will last centuries, not just a few years.
    - » It's certified/registered.
- The Oxford Offsetting Principles are a good place to get more specifics on what makes a good offset. You'll find them at *smithschool.ox.ac.uk/research/ oxford-offsetting-principles*
- 'The only truly good ones in my opinion are direct air capture and geological storage/usage,' says Andrew Murray. 'But they are the most expensive and least widely available.'
- The American Carbon Registry and Verra are reputable standards bodies, writing rules that carbon offset projects must follow in order to be certified. Trees Not Tees, ClientEarth, Treedom, myclimate and Earthchain are also reputable.
- Mongabay has a transparency tool and has put together a database of more than 350 tree-planting projects in eighty countries, showing whether tree-planting and reforestation projects publicly disclose key criteria: *news.mongabay.com/2021/05/how-to-pick-a-tree-planting-project-mongabay-launches-transparency-tool-to-help-potential-supporters-decide/*
- Or just run.

7

THE PLANET-BASED DIET

Tucking in to running's Protein Problem

'It's not possible to be an environmentalist and eat meat.'
Cowspiracy

Chocolate milk. That used to be my favourite post-workout refuelling strategy. Not after every run. But after the faster ones. And the long ones. And, er, a few of the other ones too. I told myself it was a great recovery option (and it is). But really I just loved chocolate milk – because it's all milky and chocolatey and deliciousy. I'd spend the last thirty wobbly minutes of the run fantasising about it cascading joyously down my neck, the sweet silkiness cascading down my throat, luxuriating my taste buds. And that exemplifies **running's Protein Problem**.

Runners need more protein than sedentary types and animal-based options are the most popular. But meat and dairy have a surprisingly catastrophic impact on the planet, so runners could be adding to the problem more than most. In some ways, a McDonald's is worse than a flight to Melbourne.

The arguments for swapping bacon for facon, or at least significantly cutting back on burnt animal flesh and stolen bodily fluids (I'd better admit now that I've become less than impartial on this one) are overwhelming. Consuming animal products has a terrible impact on animals – like, duh! – yet I'd had my hands over my eyes and ears about this all my life. Secondly, food derived from our four-legged friends has a potentially terrible impact on our health too – which I was also wilfully ignorant about. Because chocolate milk.

And then there's all that planet-cooking CO_2e the industry creates, which is beyond epic. 'We must change our diet,' says Sir David Attenborough in his 2020 documentary *A Life on Our Planet*. 'The planet can't support billions of meat-eaters.'

'There is great concern that active, westernised populations consume protein, and specifically meat, in quantities beyond the need for optimal health, muscular development, and performance, while negatively impacting the environment,' said the only study to date on the environmental impact of athletes' diets. 'Athletes may exceed this number on a daily basis.'[1]

The study called for a rise in 'urgency and awareness in athletes, teams and organisations that food for athletes impacts the environment, especially at higher training loads and if rich in meat and dairy products', and recommended a reduction in animal protein and an increase in plant-based options. 'Recommendations for athletes and active individuals cannot be exempt from the urgency to address the sustainability of diets.'

- **If all the cattle in the world were a country, it would be the world's second-biggest polluter.** The world's top five meat and dairy producers – JBS (Brazil), Fonterra (New Zealand), Dairy Farmers of America, Tyson Foods and Cargill (all US) – cumulatively emit more greenhouse gases than ExxonMobil, Shell or BP.
- **Meat and dairy use 83% of farmland yet provide just 18% of global calories – and only 37% of protein.**
- 50% of the world's habitable (ice- and desert-free) land is used for agriculture.
- 40% of croplands are used to grow feed crops for farm animals.
- 70% of global freshwater withdrawals are for agriculture.
- 78% of global ocean and freshwater eutrophication (pollution of waterways) is caused by agriculture.
- **94% of mammal biomass (excluding humans) is livestock, outweighing wild mammals by fifteen to one.** There are thirty farmed animals for every human on the planet.
- Livestock production constitutes the largest use of land by humans.
- Loss of wild areas to agriculture is the leading cause of the current Sixth Mass Extinction. If meat and dairy companies continue to grow based on current projections, by 2050 they will be responsible for 81% of global emissions targets.
- There just isn't enough land on planet Earth for everyone to consume the average Western meat-based diet.

Protein shake-up

Right then. Food production is responsible for somewhere between 21% and 37% of global CO2e. **Meat and dairy alone account for 58% of that and a whopping 18% of global ghg – more than all transport put together.**[ii] It's worth repeating that last bit. We know Big Fossil Fuels is incredibly destructive, but the fact that Big Agriculture is chasing them hard at the top of the Planet-Destroying League has been overlooked.

Well over half of Big Ag is animal flesh and juices, which are largely protein, and runners need more of this macronutrient than non-sporty types. 'A regular intake of high-quality protein is essential for repair, recovery and adaptation after exercise through muscle protein synthesis,' says renowned sports dietician and runner Renee McGregor in her excellent book *More Fuel You*.[iii] The recommended protein intake for runners is 1.2–1.4 grams per kilogram of body weight per day, around 150% higher than for the average person. For a 70-kilogram athlete, that's a little over 90 grams of protein per day, just under two small chicken breasts.

'Avoiding meat and dairy is the "single biggest way" to reduce your impact on Earth' was a *Guardian* headline that caught my attention just as I was becoming aware of my own footprint.[iv] Oxford University's Joseph Poore originally began studying sustainable animal agriculture practices, but after collecting four years of data from 38,000 farms in 119 countries and 40 food products, he couldn't ignore a different picture emerging in front of him.

Poore switched tack and produced an epic, jaw-dropping assessment of the full impact of nutrition from farm to fork, published in the journal *Science*.[v] He discovered that **the environmental impact from animal-based food is twice that of plant-based foods**. 'Avoiding consumption of animal products delivers far better environmental benefits than trying to purchase sustainable meat and dairy,' he concluded.

It's not just ghg doing the damage. It's also acidification, eutrophication (water pollution – in the run-off from manure, fertiliser, nitrogen and phosphorous), land use and water use. **Cutting out meat and dairy is more significant than cutting down on flights or buying an electric car**, as those actions only cut CO_2e emissions. We Brits individually create on average 3 tonnes of carbon per year, or 8.2 kilograms per day, from food and drink. **Switching from a conventional diet to a vegan diet could reduce a person's footprint from food by 73%**, Poore's research found. A vegan diet uses half as much CO_2e as a meat diet, one-eleventh the amount of fossil fuels, one-thirteenth the amount of water, and one-eighteenth the amount of land. **Compared to a heavy meat-eater, a vegan saves 1.6 tonnes of CO_2e a year, or half the impact on the planet.**

CO_2e emissions per person by diet:
- Meat-heavy diet (defined as upwards of 100 grams of meat per day): 7.19 kilograms of CO_2e a day (or 2.6 tonnes a year)
- Medium meat diet (50–99 grams a day): 5.63 kilograms a day (2 tonnes a year)
- Low-meat diet (less than 50 grams): 4.67 kilograms a day (1.7 tonnes a year)
- Fish-eater: 3.91 kilograms (1.43 tonnes a year)
- Vegetarian: 3.81 kilograms (1.39 tonnes a year)
- Vegan: 2.89 kilograms (1 tonne a year)

A vegetarian has half the footprint of a heavy meat eater.

What's the beef with beef?

Beef is by far the biggest offender. The production of it is just terrible for the planet, over twice as bad as any other food. One kilogram of cow meat costs the same CO2e as a car driving 780 kilometres. Or eating a steak is the same CO2e as fifty bananas, calculates Mike Berners-Lee – 150 bananas if the steak came from Brazil, which may sound unlikely but Greenpeace alleges that Tesco, Sainsbury's, Asda, McDonald's, Burger King and KFC buy their meat from companies owned by Brazil's JBS – the largest meat-processing company in the world.[vi] 'JBS produces around half the carbon emissions of fossil fuel giants such as Shell or BP, and is driving deforestation in the Amazon.'[vii] Sounds like we should try to avoid JBS like we would IBS.

The CO2e cost of beef is 60 kilograms per kilogram of meat. Next worst is lamb (24 kilograms) – indeed, beef and lamb are responsible for half of all farming emissions – then cheese (21 kilograms), with dairy-herd beef fourth most impactful (also 21 kilograms) and chocolate (19 kilograms), coffee (17 grams – no sign of tea on the list!), then prawns (12 kilograms), palm oil (8 kilograms), pig meat (7 kilograms) and poultry meat (6 kilograms), which have significantly lower emissions than beef and lamb because those animals don't burp and fart methane – which is also why dairy milk (3 kilograms) is three times worse than plant-based milks.

Cow flesh is a triple whammy. First, our bovine brothers and sisters release **methane** – ditto sheep – which though it lasts about twelve to twenty years in the atmosphere, is *seventy-six to eighty times worse than CO2* (over a twenty-year period). **One cow emits 100 kilograms of methane every year, almost the same CO2e as two return flights between London and New York, or driving 7,800 miles.**

As with running apparel, most of the harm is done at the production stage, and the second prong of the beef devil's fork is **nitrous oxide** (N2O) emissions from nitrogen fertiliser and other 'farming processes'. *N2O is about 300 times more potent than CO2.* Nitrous fertilisers add significantly (43% of it) to the footprint of eggs too.

The third whammy, and Big Ag's biggest source of CO2e, is land-use change or **deforestation**. The world's forests form an enormous carbon store, holding 861 gigatonnes of the stuff. But when trees are cut down, they release their carbon into the atmosphere. In the Amazon we're losing a football pitch of land every minute, with thousands of hectares of trees cleared primarily for beef pasture – 72% of it, and growing at the rate of half the size of the Netherlands a year (just for beef) – and soy, with large quantities imported to Europe.

The Amazon is fast approaching a tipping point, 2022 data shows, after which the rainforest would be lost, with profound implications.[viii] Tipping points will be disastrous, irreversible and once it's detected that we've reached them it's too late to stop them. The Amazon is a key one, along with Greenland's and West Antarctica's ice sheets (the former is also on the brink), Arctic sea ice, Siberian permafrost and others. Indeed, the Amazon now emits more carbon than it stores.

Beef and soy are the biggest drivers of deforestation (globally and in the Amazon), which rose to a fifteen-year high in 2021. Woodland is often cleared through fire, which releases even more CO_2, and activity in the Amazon has been **linked to slavery, human rights abuses, land-grabbing and illegal deaths of Indigenous peoples.** Deforestation is obviously **very bad news for biodiversity** too and is linked to pandemics. Three quarters of **new diseases** affecting humans come from animals, with yellow fever, Ebola, malaria, Lyme disease and HIV all linked to forest clearances.

Over 96% of soy is fed to cows, pigs and chickens, according the UN Food and Agriculture Organization.[ix] The biggest soya users are chicken producers; the bean makes up a quarter of the birds' diet and is key to producing fast-growing, cheap chickens.[49] Just 1 kilogram of chicken meat takes 3.2 kilograms of crops to produce.

Palm oil, cocoa, rubber and coffee are also leading causes of tropical forest loss. Palm oil, as hopefully everyone's aware, is horrendous for deforestation and is in about half of all products on supermarket shelves, both food and toiletries (sustainable options are certified by Roundtable on Sustainable Palm Oil).[50]

Beef production uses amazing amounts of precious fresh water too, twice as much as any food other than farmed fish. But here's the most baffling thing. **Meat and dairy are crazily inefficient. They account for 60% of agriculture emissions, yet they provide just 18% of our calories.** Animals eat a lot, need lots of calories to stay warm and wander about burping and farting methane, but hardly any of that is converted into calories for humans. All those resources, all that harm, to feed livestock, when **the average animal converts just 10% of the calories it uses into meat and dairy products.**[51] For beef *just* 3% of the calories that go into a cow are turned into food for us. Ain't that bonkers? What an epic waste of resources. A process which is rapidly heating the planet and making it unliveable.

It's also a terribly inefficient use of land. Land the size of the US, China, Australia

---

49 There's no internationally agreed definition of sustainably sourced soya, but private certification schemes exist such as the Round Table on Responsible Soy.

50 For balance, it's also incredibly land efficient, 'producing more oil per land area than any other equivalent vegetable oil crop. Palm oil supplies 40% of the world's vegetable oil demand on just under 6% of the land used to produce all vegetable oils,' says WWF. So suddenly switching to another oil could have a negative effect on land use, though we clearly need to use less.

51 Animals contribute an average of 590 kilocalories to the human food chain, *but* eat 3,810 kilocalories of grass and pasture per animal per day, plus 1,740 kilocalories of human-edible food.

and the EU *combined* is devoted to rearing animals for food. **If we stopped consuming meat and dairy, farmland could be reduced by 75% while still feeding the planet's population** – effectively enabling us to rewild the world, which would remove 8 billion tonnes of CO_2e a year, 15% of the world's ghg. Replacing 20% of the world's beef consumption with microbial protein, such as Quorn, could halve the destruction of the planet's forests over the next three decades.

Put simply, eating plants is a far more efficient use of the planet's stretched resources than feeding the plants to animals and then eating the animals. **In fact, a third of all crops grown in the world are destined for animals.** 'It's a disaster for human nutrition,' says Mike Berners-Lee in *There Is No Planet B*. And ironically, 'Gram for gram, a soya bean has more of almost every human essential nutrient than beef or lamb.' Why don't we just leave those poor animals out of it and eat the plants ourselves?

Did someone mention soil? Whole films have been made just about the soil erosion crisis. 'Nearly 25% of all Earth's soil is severely damaged by unsustainable farming practices, such as overgrazing, deforestation, burning, monocropping, and intensive chemical farming [elsewhere referred to as a "pesticide treadmill"],' says *Swole Planet* author Ryan Andrews. Up to 40% of the planet's land is now classed as degraded, said a 2022 UN report, while half of the world's people are suffering the impacts.[x] Most of the damage has come from food production, though from clothing too. 'The root cause of overconsumption happens in the rich world, for instance in the increasing consumption of meat, which takes far more resources than growing vegetables, and fast fashion, which is worn briefly then thrown away,' says Ryan.

There's an additional pollution and health problem. Big Ag uses pesticides, antibiotics and hormones prolifically, which get into drinking water and endanger human health. **In addition, two-thirds of the world's antibiotics are given to animals, coming back to us through meat and milk** – adding to the global antibiotic resistance crisis.

Also, there are three farm animals to every human on the planet and that's a crapload of manure[52] – 300 million tonnes, in fact. Harmful algae bloom are a problem in all fifty US states and pollution washes down to the sea, killing coral reefs and creating 'dead zones' devoid of life. The Gulf of Mexico has a 21,000-square-kilometre one where much of the waste from US beef production is carried down the Mississippi (according to a 400-page UN report, 'Livestock's Long Shadow'), quadrupling the number of dead zones in the last seventy years.[xi]

The combination of fossil fuels and chemical fertilisers is starving oceans of

---

52 Joke borrowed from Ryan Andrews. Sorry, Ryan.

oxygen, reports the World Economic Forum. Oceans are warming by 0.13 °C per decade and as they warm, they store less oxygen. There are 700 additional ocean areas identified as being low on oxygen, up from forty-five in the 1960s, expanding in size by an area the size of the EU, with all sorts of biodiversity disasters.

Oh. And the world's 1.5 billion cattle also produce more than 100 other gases associated with air pollution, including more than two-thirds of the world's ammonia emissions, one of the main causes of acid rain. How are you feeling about that dairy milk in your tea?

Sheepishly milking it

Talking of milk, it takes 990 litres of water to produce 1 litre of it. (Another one to repeat out loud.) Cheese, too, requires lots of water, hence its high emissions. In the UK, at least a quarter of dairy farms are running at a loss. Yet globally between $540 and $700 billion are spent every year on agricultural subsidies. Tens of millions are spent on lobbying by the industry in the US, twice what other sectors spend, as well as on campaigns against climate action, and they're plenty powerful in the EU too. Almost 90% of global subsidies given to farmers every year are 'harmful', found a UN report, with the biggest sources of ghg, beef and milk, receiving the biggest subsidies.[xii] I'm no economist, but as with almost every aspect of this, it just makes no sense whatsoever.

Neither does the size of the sheep-farming industry in the UK. Here's another illogical truth: 51% of the country's surface is devoted to grazing livestock and growing grass, while trees cover just 10% of it. Some 85% of the UK's land footprint from food is associated with meat and dairy production, yet that gives us only 48% of our total protein and 32% of our calories. We have 23 million sheep in this country, which produce just 1% of our calories. *One per cent.*

As well as the disastrous ghg, I hadn't given any thought to how sheep have shaped some of my favourite places to run. In the Lake District, the much-mythologised fells are barren and quiet. George Monbiot in the *Guardian* calls the area a 'treeless waste.'[xiii]

Sheep have done more damage to the ecology of this country than all the buildings, pollution and climate change, says the environmentalist and author. 'They cleanse the land of almost all wildlife.' He writes of the damage caused: 'wet deserts grazed down to turf and rock ... woods in which no new trees have grown for eighty years, tracts of bare mountainside on which every spring is a silent one. Anyone with ecological knowledge should recoil from this scene.'[xiv] Sheep farming in the Lake District operates at a major loss, but is heavily subsidised. Two kilograms of lamb has the same carbon footprint as three months of porridge.

Talking of British biodiversity, we've lost almost half of ours since the Industrial Revolution and are one of the worst-rated nations in the world, certainly in Western Europe and among G7 nations, for the extent to which our ecosystems have retained their natural animals and plants.

What about fish? I lazily assumed they're relatively low carbon to produce (well, kill). But fishing boats that trawl the ocean floor release as much carbon dioxide as the entire aviation industry, around 1 gigatonne a year. As they brutally rake it, carbon is released from the seabed sediment – the largest pool of carbon storage in the world – into the water, increasing ocean acidification and playing obvious havoc with biodiversity. Oh, and the North Sea has lost 80% of its cod population since the 1970s, while 90% of the world's stocks are officially either fully or over-exploited.[53]

Here's another perverse one. Carnivorous fish eat a lot of other fish, and 27% of seafood that's caught is to feed livestock and other farmed fish. And 90% of it is suitable for humans. Some 35% of all fish, crustaceans and molluscs harvested from oceans, lakes and fish farms are wasted or lost before they ever reach a plate, says the UN Food and Agriculture Organization.[xv] If you have to eat fish, treat it as a treat, says Mike Berners-Lee.

The whole system is just maddening, an epic waste of the world's precious resources. 'If you were an alien looking at our food system from outside of the planet, you would have to conclude that we are completely bonkers,' said Mark Stevenson, author and 'reluctant futurist' on the *Jon Richardson and the Futurenauts* podcast. 'Like William Burroughs said, "After one look at this planet you'd ask to see the manager". If planet Earth were a restaurant you'd say it's the most badly run restaurant you'd ever seen in your life.'

There are a few food myths. A popular one is that organic, grass-reared beef is sustainable. But because the cows live for an average of eight months longer, eating more calories, using more water, more land, belching and farting more methane, growing more slowly and producing fewer calories, they're actually worse environmentally, found a German study.[xvi] Organic chicken also fares slightly worse than its non-organic counterparts from a CO_2e perspective, though organic pork is slightly better for the planet.

'If you want a lower-carbon diet, eating *less* meat is nearly always better than eating the *most sustainable* meat,' says Our World in Data.[xvii] 'Whether they are grown locally or shipped from the other side of the world matters very little for total emissions. Focus on what you eat, not whether your food is local.'[xviii]

---

53 80 million tonnes are caught a year, or 12 kilograms per person per year.

Ninety-three per cent of international food is shipped, which is pretty efficient, but air-freighted foods should still be avoided and the ones to watch out for in the UK are grapes and berries from California, fresh tuna from the Indian Ocean, baby vegetables from Africa and asparagus from Peru. Avoid those and you can relax about food miles, says Berners-Lee.[xix]

Another plant to consider avoiding is avocados, as they require up to 320 litres of water for just one of the pear-shaped fruit (according to the Sustainable Food Trust). However, in context, avocados generate a third of the emissions of chicken, a quarter of those of pork, a twentieth of beef [xx] – even a litre of milk uses three times the water.[54]

However, cutting our meat intake down or out doesn't give us an ethical get-out-of-jail card, allowing us to fly around the world to lots of races, says Rosie Watson. 'This needs to happen *as well as* reducing flights,' she writes. 'It can't be used to "cancel out" big impacts elsewhere.'[xxi] We all need to cut emissions from our diets *anyway*, says Berners-Lee.

Health and kindness

Aside from the disastrous environmental impact, the overconsumption of meat has caused an epidemic of disease, with $285 billion spent every year treating illness caused by eating red meat alone. WHO has declared processed red meat such as bacon, ham and sausages to be a carcinogen and unprocessed red meat to be a probable carcinogen. It's linked to heart disease, strokes and diabetes and 'implicated in many cancers', according to studies.[xxii] Yet people in rich nations continue to eat too much of it. Then there are all the antibiotics, hormones and preservatives.

Vegetarians have a 14% lower chance of developing cancer than carnivores, according to a large 2022 study.[xxiii] If everyone switched to a vegan diet, 8 million deaths would be avoided around the world by 2050, found another.[xxiv] Clearly, cutting out red meat and to a lesser extent dairy is reducing our chances of some horrible, painful, life-ending diseases.[55] Oh, and meat is usually a hit to the wallet too.

Plus, I like animals. They're amazing. They're like us, but a bit more furry and a lot less annoying on social media. That said, being a runner, cows haven't always been

---

54 Another popular myth is that much of Britain's terrain isn't suitable for anything other than grazing. But that pasture could instead be used to grow trees and lock up carbon, provide land for rewilding and even grow bio-energy crops to displace fossil fuels, argues the excellently named *Guardian* environment editor Damian Carrington in an article entitled 'Why you should go animal-free' (19 June 2020). And then crops no longer being fed to animals could instead become food for people.

55 If you want to dig further into the health aspects of meat and dairy, Michael Greger's *How Not To Die* is well worth a read.

my favourite animals, as they sometimes chase me across fields. But why should they be forcibly impregnated to maintain milk production, produce ten times more milk than they naturally would, repeatedly have their newborns stolen from them within an hour of birth (the male calves slaughtered), and live a quarter as long as they naturally would have done? Oh and there's 'tail docking, repeated milking leading to infections, unnatural diets, confinement, unnatural living conditions, and the use of antibiotics to treat mastitis from repeated mechanical milking', records Ryan Andrews in the excellent *Swole Planet*.

All just so I can have a splash of their juice, infused with antibiotics and other additives (flavourings, thickeners, carrageenan, vegetable oils and gums), in my tea? 'Non-dairy products, on the other hand, largely (if not completely) eliminate the ethical conundrum of animal welfare,' says Ryan.

The living conditions for the vast majority of farm animals in developed countries are 'deplorable', 'inhumane, unsustainable and frankly cruel', he says. Yet somehow mere animal welfare/cruelty wasn't enough to swing it for me before. The truth is, I lacked moral conviction. But having watched *Apocalypse Cow*, *Cowspiracy*, *Carnage*, *Milked* and BBC *Panorama*'s *A Cow's Life* (spot a theme?), it's a case of once you've seen how creatures are treated, you can't unsee it.

I had been in denial about all of this. It seems decidedly unnecessary to hurt, murder and eat animals when there's ample food around already which (did I mention?) is much better for the planet, and us, anyway. I don't need to dig too much further into this stuff here. Clearly, farming isn't kind to animals. It feels liberating to no longer be a part of a cruel system.

The plan(e)t-based future

'Why hasn't anyone told me [how bad for the environment meat is] before?' asks Isabel Losada in *The Joyful Environmentalist*. 'Why isn't this the very first thing you learn when trying to figure out how you can help the environment?' She finds numerous environmental-leaning websites that don't mention the disastrous role of the meat and dairy industries in accelerating our climate and ecological emergency. Livestock isn't mentioned as an issue in Al Gore's landmark film *An Inconvenient Truth*. 'It's not hard to guess [why]: if you were a meat eater it would piss you off.' Sorry, meat lovers, but it seems a bit late in the day to be tiptoeing around.

It's seriously bad for the planet, it's bad for us, it's bad for the animals. Who's it good for? A handful of rich white men (spot a theme?). Once you know the science, the question becomes, for me at least, why would you choose to consume dead animals and their bodily liquids in the first place? Like Joseph Poore, George Monbiot and Damian Carrington (and me), Isabel turned vegan while writing her book.

Once I learnt about the epic damage Big Ag does to the planet, it was impossible to justify my previous food habits, which I'd never really given much conscious thought to. I just ate the stuff on my plate/at the race aid station.

When I saw just how bad beef and lamb are, it was pretty easy to just give them up. I was uncomfortable with the idea of eating lamb anyway, just lacked the moral gumption, which I think created that existential angst I felt whenever I met a vegetarian or vegan. I couldn't quite express it, but something about the fact they had stronger values than me made me uncomfortable.

After a bit, only giving up cows and sheep felt like a half-hearted gesture.

In truth, I wasn't a big red-meat lover, but I did love chicken, cheese, eggs, and dairy milk in my tea and chocolate milk (non-dairy versions are just as nice). It was tea I was most worried about. Making a cup of the bittersweet brown nectar is the first purposeful act of my day, the first thing I'll put in my mouth each morning and my much-fantasised-after post-run prize. I *really* like tea. The seismic thought of my six-cups-a-day tea habit being disastrously soured by some weird alternative to cow juice felt terrifying.

Yes, the cheese can be rubbery and bland (it's getting better quickly, though). I've found some perfectly good pizzas, some tolerable cheeses, and scrambled tofu is almost as good as egg. Much more crucially, while soya milk is a bit meh, various oat milks taste identical to dairy, if not better.[56] In fact – and I'm shocked I'm typing this – dairy tastes disgusting to me now. It takes about two weeks, in my study of one, to flush dairy out of the system, and now it smells offputtingly strongly of cow.

Veganism is well trendy now and, like a glory-hunter, I got in at just the right time. Plant burgers and nut milks used to be the preserve of musty health-food shops tucked down dark alleys in Totnes, but now you can get all you need from Tesco and Sainsbury's, and from McDonald's to Greggs, everyone's launching vegan options.

Meating in the middle

One kilogram of peas, incidentally, emits one kilogram of CO_2e. Indeed, emissions from most plant-based options are 10–15 kilograms lower than most animal products. Nuts, pleasingly, have an overall positive impact, because they require the planting rather than knocking down of trees, which store carbon. Does the whole world need to turn Full Annoying Vegan (FAV)?[57] Well, if we all went FAV,

---

56 From a CO_2e perspective, a glass of dairy milk is three times the emissions of non-dairy options, which all use less water and land too. Oat milk has the smallest footprint of the popular options. Soya milk, incidentally, has approximately the same amount of protein as cow's milk.

57 Vegans are annoying. That's not just my view (and I am one). Research has shown that only drug addicts face the same degree of stigma. 'How do you recognise a vegan at a dinner party?' goes the quip. 'Don't worry, they'll tell you.'

the world's food-related emissions would drop a stunning 70%. While **eating a vegetarian diet for a year reduces emissions by the same amount as taking a small car off the road for six months**, says the UN.[xxv]

Clearly not everyone is going to go FAV or even vegetarian. Some people really like bloody steaks and cow juice in their tea. No one realistically envisions a meat-free future.

So how much meat-eating is okay for the planet? There have been lots of studies on this, all broadly reaching the same ballpark area. On a macro level, western nations need to cut consumption of beef by 90% and milk by 60%, urges an IPCC report.[xxvi] On an individual level, a **flexitarian diet** – defined as mostly plant-based foods, with one serving of red meat a week – could be key to keeping the planet habitable. A diet that includes meat two days a week but is otherwise vegetarian would reduce ghg emissions, plus water and land use, by about 45%.

The priority is to cut down ruminant animals (cows and sheep), says Berners-Lee, who sees a clear hierarchy of food, with pulses, grains and soya beans 'as the clear carbon winners', then dairy and poultry, and thirdly red meat in 'worst place'. 'There's no need for extremism here, just moderation and a broadening of choice,' he says. 'We just need to start chipping away so that the proportions in our diets change radically over the next ten or so years. Most of us can use this as an opportunity to eat more healthily'[xxvii] – and **going vegan, vegetarian, or flexitarian could reduce your food bill by up to one third.**

Indeed, we need to cut back on meat and dairy from a health perspective too. In the UK we eat 44–55% more protein than we need to each day. Americans, Australians, Argentines and New Zealanders eat the equivalent of fifty chickens or half a cow each year (about 100 kilograms per person – the European average is about 80 kilograms).

Unlike with clothing consumption and travel, the trajectory is at least going in the right direction. At least 3% of the population (at least 2 million people) are vegan now, a pattern growing quickly – with 7% vegetarian and 5% pescatarian, and Britons eat 17% less meat than a decade ago.

I know loads of people who eat a *mostly* plant-based diet. They may, for example, only have meat when they eat out or as a treat. One of the best ultrarunners in the world is vegan, with the exception of occasional eggs. Even meaty Arnold Schwarzenegger is said to be '99% vegan'.

Being flexitarian or Mostly (Annoying) Vegan is surely the way forward. A planet-based diet.

Helpfully, a traffic-light system of 'eco-scores' is to be piloted on British food labels by NGO Foundation Earth, a bit like the nutritional info we already have, to help us assess a food's impact on the supermarket shelf. Non-dairy brand Oatly and Quorn are the only companies I've seen carbon-labelling their items to date.[58]

Plan(e)t-based runners

'As consumers, the biggest difference we can make is to eat more plant-based sources of protein such as tofu, nuts, peas, and beans,' urges Our World in Data.[xxviii] Happily, plants can produce fifteen times more protein than animals.

I'll admit a flask of tofu and beans doesn't have quite the same post-run appeal as chocolate milk. But protein powder mixed with oat or coconut milk, banana and nut butter sure hits the spot for me. I'll admit too that words like 'legumes' and 'pulses' just sound plain boring. But hummus is brill and comes in several flavours, nuts are ace (I plunge my fist into a litre Tupperware box of cashews, roasted, salted almonds and raisins multiple times a day) and frozen peas are very easy to add to a meal at the last minute. Okay, lentils are a bit of a nuisance, but more tasty, healthy and versatile than I'd given them credit for.

In terms of the health benefits of plant-eating, simply cutting out those foods strongly linked to horrible diseases has to make us healthier. There are other pluses too. 'The case for eating more plant-based food with regard to improving our long-term health is well established,' says Renee McGregor. And a plant-based diet is 'likely to make it easier for an athlete to hit their carbohydrate requirements and recommendations for fruit and vegetables' and 'may contribute to some improved health metrics, such as a more balanced gut biome, lower susceptibility to heart and metabolic diseases, and healthier body composition,' she says. 'There is absolutely no reason why a vegan diet could not support an athletic lifestyle if it is carefully constructed.'[xxix]

'The combination of more plants and fewer animal products will, for most people in developed countries, lead to improved health outcomes,' agrees Ryan Andrews. However, Renee warns that the high fibre content of plant-based diets can lead to premature satiety – feeling falsely full –and may lead to runners failing to meet energy requirements. I find the solution simple, though: just have more snacks.

Planet-based runners need to be conscious of getting enough protein in, as well as mindful of potential deficiencies in vitamins B12 and D, iron, iodine and calcium.

58 Regrettably, not only was Oatly, along with Alpro and Innocent Drinks, rapped on the knuckles by the Advertising Standards Authority (ASA), for exaggerating their environmental impacts, but it's 10% owned by Blackstone, which is in turn owned by a Trump financier accused of facilitating Amazon deforestation. It's really quite the quandary for the planet-based runner. However, Blackstone is a passive investor – meaning it has no management control over the brand – and I still think it's worth supporting the principle that plant-based nutrition is great for the planet and we want more of it.

I've found that's fairly easily addressed with supplements, however, and lentils (which have twice the protein of beans) and peas can help provide the branch-chain amino acid leucine, which could be low otherwise. Soybeans, split peas and white beans are some of the highest in protein per serving.

I've had two blood counts since turning FAV and while the first showed a vitamin D deficiency (along with 'a significant proportion of people in the UK', says the government's Chief Medical Officer[xxx]), I merely upped my dose and the second count was my best ever, with every measurement in the Normal range. Ironically, I'd suffered from low iron/ferritin when I was a meat eater.

So with a little care, a plant-based diet is perfectly healthy. Some documentaries – and in fact some elite runner pals – even claim performance benefits from plant-based diets. Tennis aces Serena and Venus Williams, football star Alex Morgan, Formula 1 champion Lewis Hamilton, multi-world champion boxer David Haye and record-breaking ultrarunner Scott Jurek are just a few vegan athletes. There are not yet any conclusive studies showing performance benefits from a plant-based diet. But there are none showing performance detriments either. I was interested to see if I'd feel any performance benefits. To be entirely frank, I haven't detected anything obvious. But nothing negative either. I feel about the same physiologically (but happier overall because I'm less a part of the problem).

When it comes to a runner's CO_2e footprint from food, it's not just about protein. Runners probably consume more calories than less active folk. The study of the French runner training for the New York Marathon (see page 115) calculated an extra 600 grams of food per day, while Andrew Murray estimated his total calorie intake from running for a year was just short of 200,000 kilocalories – an additional 114 kilocalories a day. His assessment of his running's footprint put food at one-third of his total emissions.

Generally, carbs are a lot less *carb*-on intensive, ironically, than animal protein. And by being healthy, a runner is less likely to be a burden on the NHS (though the same can't be said for pestering physiotherapists). From my point of view, a planet-based diet is also one of the easier holes to plug in an individual's footprint. Our energy, travel and diet are the Three Pillars of most people's emissions, making up a quarter each. Energy is usually a quick fix (see page 6). As we've seen, travel is more complicated and compromising. To me, that lack of absolutism felt unsatisfactory, so when it came to food, I was willing to make amends and go all in. I love being a planet-based athlete. It reminds me of my values every time I'm hungry. It's easy and fun and people don't seem to find me any more annoying than previously (I was already pretty annoying). If you can't be part of the solution, at least don't be part of the problem.

Wasting away

So that's that one pretty much sorted, then. However, there's another lifestyle action we can do to reduce the terrible impact food production has on the planet – and it'll save us money. What's worse than producing high-carbon foods? Not eating them. **Food waste accounts for 8–10% of all global emissions**, estimates the IPCC.[xxxi] **If global food waste was a country, it would come third for ghg emissions, after China and the USA.** But what stunned me was, 70% of it happens not at the farms, factories or supermarkets (although some certainly happens there), but in our homes.

After cutting meat and dairy, cutting waste is the next most important thing we can do diet-wise, says Mike Berners-Lee. One study proclaims **food-waste reduction as the single most impactful climate action we can undertake**, potentially eliminating 70 gigatonnes of carbon emissions in the next thirty years.

- **About a third of food produced globally never reaches the table,** about 3.3 billion tonnes of CO2e and $750 billion worth.
- Each year we throw away 4.5 million tonnes of nosh from our own homes, enough to fill eight Wembley Stadiums.
- Between a fifth and a quarter of food bought by consumers in the UK is wasted.
- If everyone in the UK stopped wasting food at home for just one day, it would have the same impact on ghg as planting half a million trees.
- Food waste happens at the harvesting, storage, transport and supermarket stages but **70% of UK food waste happens in our homes.**
- Rotting food emits ghg, including the dreaded methane.
- Bread, milk, cheese, potatoes, bananas and apples are the nosh most commonly thrown away.

Food on planet Earth is causing some epic problems. But really, on an individual level, they're pretty simply solved. We don't need to labour the point. Wasting food is also wasting money and there are a few tips at the end of the chapter. Occasional scraps in our household go into the Daddy Dustbin, whether they're plant-based or not (most animal products are unappealing to me now). Meat production is terrible for the planet, but even worse if it's wasted. When training hard, I seem to be almost constantly hungry and I've always hated the idea of wasted food, to the point of shamelessly finishing people's leftovers in restaurants.

On that note, my other veganism 'cheat' point is chocolate. I've got used to dark chocolate, which is healthier anyway and has a more distinct, satisfying flavour. But I have a sweet tooth, I train hard and sometimes at nine o'clock on a Friday night (my usual long run day), I just *need* a bit of chocolate. If there are no vegan options in the house, I have sometimes been known to accidentally find where my wife has hidden her dairy chocolate and some of it has fallen into my mouth before I've had time to properly scan the ingredients. It's not the dairy I want, it's the chocolate. It's not perfect. But it's progress. Is it true veganism? I don't really care. It's a planet-based diet.

I don't feel as gloomy as I did at the end of those kit chapters (even though there's a lot more bull). But that's no reason, I'm sure you'll agree, not to finish with an udderly brilliant climate change joke I made up on the hoof but you hopefully haven't herd before (I've probably milked that enough now; let's moove on) …

Why did the weatherman blush? He saw the climate change.

Yeah, but what can we do about it?

1 Read *Eating Animals* and/or *Regenesis* by George Monbiot and/or Ryan Andrews' well-brill *Swole Planet: Building a Better Body and a Better Earth*. Try Anita Bean's *The Vegan Athlete's Cookbook* or one of the *Bosh!* ones.

2 If you find the idea of cutting back on animal flesh hard, start with #meatfreemonday. Make spag bol with lentils (with good flavourings my kids barely notice the difference[59]), add chickpeas to curries, tofu to stir-fries.

3 Races and other running events could consider offering plant-based options (only?), to reduce their impact (by over 70% from food) and perhaps broaden some minds along the way (it worked for me at the Dragon's Back Race).

4 Seasonal produce is one to look out for, as items grown out of season will need more artificial heat and light (energy) and more ghg. Root vegetables grown in the UK are mostly in season for many months and store well. Choose Fairtrade (meaning producers are paid fairly) and Organic (which is kinder on the planet, biodiversity and you) and support local independent shops where possible.

5 For planet-based runners
   - Tofu is a good source of protein.
   - Lentils offer huge amounts of dietary fibre, plus thiamine, folate, iron, phosphorus and magnesium.
   - Peanut butter has the highest protein serving of nut butters, plus healthy fats and the antioxidant vitamin E. Soy nuts contain good levels of protein, amino acids and a wide range of micronutrients.
   - Pea proteins have the highest essential amino acid content as a percentage of total protein.

---

59 Admittedly, my son just read that over my shoulder and is adamant that he hates lentils (but I'm claiming he's misremembering).

6 Low-carbon cooking
- Electricity's carbon footprint is falling all the time, due to renewable options, whereas gas is still gas.
- Saucepans are less efficient than kettles.
- Avoid boiling more water than needed.
- When boiling veg, boil gently, cut into small pieces and put a lid on that pot.
- Use boiled water from rice, pasta or steamed vegetables for washing up.
- Weigh out exact portions of pasta and rice.

7 Food-waste dodging
- Plan it, blend it, broth it, freeze it, compost it.
- Revive stale bread by running it under the tap then putting it in the oven at 200 °C for a few minutes.
- Store carrots, celery and kale in water to prolong their life.
- Storing some fruit in the fridge prolongs life, while you can freeze milk, cheese, butter and eggs. Use leftovers and plan meals better.
- Tesco has teamed up with Olio, a food-sharing app.
- Ignore best-before dates – give it a sniff and trust your instincts!
- Start food-waste composting.
- Experiment with growing your own food.

8

FOSSIL FUELLING

Picking up running's Plastic Problem

'Climate change is caused by the cumulative total of billions of insignificant little actions, and we can help to tackle it in the same way.'
Stuart Walker

So travel, food and kit are the three ways a runner contributes most to our climate and ecological emergency. But there are some notable other bits too ...

In 2019 I did some stints as a support runner on other people's rounds (established fell-running challenges), carrying their food, doing some of the nav, telling them they looked ace while they were chundering on my daps. Like Napoleon's armies, the distance runner marches on their stomach. These runs can often be twenty-plus hours and they need thousands of calories. I couldn't help but notice just how much plastic waste was piling up – as it had when I'd done similar challenges.

Gels. Cola. Chocolate. Flapjacks. Carb powders. Crisps. Electrolytes. Custard. Rice puddings. More custard. It all came wrapped in plastic. Most of it single-use or non-recyclable. Sure, fell and ultra runners eat a shedload – distance running is famously a huge picnic with some light exercise thrown in. But even for the road runner, gels and sports drinks, not forgetting all those plastic bottles, are de rigueur come race day.

How much damage might an individual's plastic waste cause? *Turning the Tide on Plastic* author Lucy Siegle estimates a UK citizen's plastic footprint at 140 kilograms per person per year (three times what it was in 1980), which is over twice my body weight. Recycling 'as much as you can' leads to an annual saving of 200 kilograms of CO_2e a year, according to the Ipsos Perils of Perception study (though that's not just plastic).[60] Add a few helpings of gels and plastic cola bottles and the average runner may feasibly create as many emissions from single-use plastic as a return flight from London to Rome (234 kilograms). Let's not forget that the 2018 London Marathon used an epic 920,000 plastic bottles and another 5,200 kilograms of rubbish.

60 For every kilogram of fossil-based plastic produced, between 1.7 and 3.5 kilograms of CO_2 is released, so a back-of-a-beer-mat calculation of emissions from an individual's plastic consumption could be more like 364 kilograms of CO_2e a year.

This sport, to put it mildly, creates more than its fair share of plastic waste. **Running has a plastics problem.** The 'vast majority' of plastic is made from fossil hydrocarbons, or fossil fuels.[i] We're fossil fuelling.

I felt mildly traumatised by the waste we were creating and became much more conscious of my own rubbish. I was curious to see if things could be done a little better – hence my winter Paddy Buckley Round in early 2020 where I attempted to get there using public transport, fuel on vegan nutrition for the first time and avoid creating any plastic waste. Train travel was easy. Vegan nosh was easy. Fuelling without plastic waste was not easy. All my favourite snacks came wrapped in fossil fuels. My self-imposed petrochemicals ban counted out all my usual gels, chocolate, flapjacks and other bars, chocolate milks, smoothies and crisps.

Instead, I bought trail mix in paper bags (which cost more CO2e to create than plastic ones[61]) from dispensers in a Corsham health food shop, penny sweets from my local post office, chocolate bars with recyclable packaging online (which cost extra emissions from delivery) and home-made brownies. Plastic-waste-free fuelling was a hassle and certainly imperfect, even counterproductive. But it was possible.

I repeated the non-fossil-fuelling tactic on subsequent long-distance challenges, such as the 260-mile Pennine Way, and again found the plastic-waste-dodging trickier than plan(e)t-based fuelling. Most food comes in plastic, certainly most sports nutrition, but so does most of what ultrarunners call 'real food', i.e. bread, pies and pasties, custard and rice puddings, even some fruit. Ever found crisps in recyclable or compostable packets? I found one brand called Two Farmers, but it required a Sunday afternoon driving around Wiltshire to find them, which likely caused more emissions than I'd saved. I ate quite a lot of sandwiches (bread bags can usually be recycled with other plastic bags at supermarkets[62]), but it was a nuisance finding plastic-free avocados and bananas (the former aren't amazing for my footprint, but far better than any meat or dairy). I managed to, just about, run for sixty-one hours on the Pennine Way without generating any plastic waste. But it was expensive and required lots of research, time, planning, extra car journeys and emissions.

'A world without plastics, or synthetic organic polymers, seems unimaginable today, yet their large-scale production and use only dates back to ~1950,' begins the biggest study into plastic waste to date. 'Plastics have outgrown most man-made materials.'[ii]

---

61 Paper bags are often seen as more eco-friendly than plastic bags, but to replace plastic bags with paper ones requires 2.7 times more energy, 1.6 times more CO2e and 17 times more water usage. Plus they're not nearly as durable.

62 Which can be something of a red herring, incidentally, because eschewing a plastic bag but buying a steak undoes all your good work.

Plastic is especially visible to us runners, because as well as our bespoke nutrition wrapped in the stuff, we see its potential harm in the form of litter at races and when out gallivanting in the hills. Who doesn't feel annoyed at the sight of an ugly crisp packet or cola bottle on a hillside? I've never seen CO_2 or methane. But I see plastic waste all the time. It feels upsetting that people don't value these special places as they should. Unlike most aspects of climate change, the petroleum-based material is tangible and emotive.

However, as we've seen with races and our kit, plastic packaging and waste is usually only a small percentage of a product's footprint. A study asked people to rank nine climate actions in order of impact and respondents voted recycling as the most effective, when really it was the seventh, showing people overestimate the role of plastic in our climate and ecological emergency.[iii]

Mike Berners-Lee's *There Is No Planet B* has in-depth sections on food, energy, travel, but not plastic. Mark Maslin's *How to Save the Planet* has fourteen action points with the only vague allusion to plastic being a minor point about avoiding food packaging.

I was confused. I had stopped using a nutrition sponsor as their gels (like all gels, still now) came in single-use plastic. But they pointed out that all of their supply chain was local, so the company likely had a low carbon footprint overall. Which stumped me. I didn't know which was worse, the emissions or the plastic.

So in the grand scheme of things, **how bad is plastic really?** How much does it contribute to the warming of our planet and our ecological crisis? How significant is it in a runner's footprint?

The Plastic Age

When you step back for a minute, plastic is pretty amazing. It's cheap to produce, lightweight, colourful, versatile and almost indestructible. So much of our technology, life-saving medical equipment, crash helmets, bulletproof vests and of course our running shoes, T-shirts and jackets are made from plastic. Not forgetting Lego, which gave me many happy hours as both a child and parent (who still thought he was a child).

Plastic helps protect and prolong the life of foods, saving them from adding to the waste crisis. Plastic is brilliant.

But the same features that make plastic so useful make it such a big problem. It's when it's designed for single-use then discarded that it becomes an issue. A really big issue. Scientists say that after the Stone and Bronze Ages, we're now in the Plastic Age – or the Plast-a-cene, as Dale Vince jokes.

- **8.3 billion tonnes of plastic has been created. 9% of it has been recycled. 12% has been incinerated. 70% is in landfill (all 2015 figures).**
- **8 million tonnes has leaked into the ocean – the equivalent to dumping the contents of one rubbish truck every minute.** Without action, this is forecast to increase to two per minute by 2030, and four per minute by 2050.
- 70–80% of ocean plastics come from land-based sources via rivers; 20–30% come from the fishing industry.
- Rivers carry plastic out to sea, where it does untold harm to ecosystems and biodiversity, killing wildlife and irretrievably polluting the oceans.
- The plastic we throw away each year could circle the Earth four times.
- Plastic waste is now so ubiquitous in the environment that it has been suggested as a geological indicator of the proposed Anthropocene era.
- Plastic takes centuries to degrade.
- More than half of the plastics ever made have been produced since 2000.
- Plastic production could reach 1.34 gigatonnes a year by 2030, equivalent to 295 coal-fired power stations.
- In England more plastic is burnt than recycled (11.6 million tonnes in 2019), which creates highly toxic dioxins, linked to horrible health outcomes.
- Just twenty companies are responsible for producing more than half of all the single-use plastic waste.
- ExxonMobil is the biggest single-use plastic waste polluter in the world, contributing 5.9 million tonnes so far.
- Coca-Cola produces 200,000 plastic bottles a minute and sells more than 100 billion a year, with PepsiCo and Nestlé the next two worst offenders.
- Plastic pollution has been declared a planetary crisis by the UN.

Clearly, plastic production and waste are out of control and transparently (pun unintended, arf) unsustainable. Plastic drives our climate and ecological emergency, because the vast majority is made from fossil fuels.

The plastic plague hurts the planet three times over. Firstly – and to me this is the clincher in why plastic is a huge part of the Big Kerfufflefuck – **plastic production generates 1.8 billion tonnes of CO2e each year, which is 3% of global emissions.** That's clearly massive. Plastic creates huge harm during its life (the second whammy), and in its after-life (ker-pow!) too, whether that's incineration, landfill or in the natural environment.

Secondly, plastic's largest market is food packaging, but in addition to 'protecting' our food and drink it's often leaching toxic chemicals into our calories and bodies.

And thirdly, plastic pollution has reached epic proportions. In the oceans it's predicted to outweigh fish by 2050.

Like most things in the Big Kerfufflefuck, the trajectory isn't great either. If current production and waste management trends continue, roughly 12 billion tonnes of plastic waste will be in landfills or in the natural environment by 2050. **Plastic production is currently 6% of global oil consumption and if that continues at current levels will account for 20% by the middle of the century.** Big Oil is getting around the fact it needs to be phased out by making us reliant on it in other ways, primarily our clothing and food packaging.

We come into contact with micro-sized plastic particles every day, via ingestion, inhalation and skin contact, unknowingly consuming up to 5 grams per week, while plastic particles are detected in our rain, the air, even placentas and just, well, *everywhere.*

One litre of bottled water emits 400 grams of CO2e and is 1,000 times more carbon-intense than water from a tap. Mike Berners-Lee calls bottled water 'An unavoidable disaster that keeps on growing'.

Food packaging is alarming. From phthalates to PBDEs, PPAs and PCBs, most plastic food packaging contains potentially toxic chemicals, concluded a report which looked at yoghurt containers, coffee cup lids, plastic wraps and similar.[iv] BPA is also found in plastic storage containers and the lining of food cans.[63] Don't store food in plastic and don't heat it in plastic, urges the report. The 'disastrous' (that word again) way in which plastic is used in farming across the world threatens food safety and potentially human health, says the UN.[v]

Frustratingly, food packaging is sometimes a necessary evil, as it reduces waste. Using plastic film to wrap a cucumber can extend its shelf life from three days to fourteen and selling grapes in plastic trays has reduced in-store wastage by 20%.

But once discarded, plastic doesn't degrade; instead it breaks down into smaller and smaller particles.[64] Film made from our old friend PET, which most energy gel packets are made of, turns into microplastics, then disintegrates further into nano-sized plastics too small for the human eye. These tiny particles make their way into

---

63 BPA is linked to metabolic disease, obesity, infertility, and disorders like ADHD, while studies in animals link it to prostate and mammary cancer, and brain development problems. 'You're not going to just drop dead [from ingesting plastics], but it could contribute to diseases that may manifest over decades, or it could affect unborn embryos and foetuses,' said Professor Laura Vandenberg of the University of Massachusetts. (Kevin Loria, 2 October 2019, 'Most plastic products contain potentially toxic chemicals, study reveals', consumerreports.org)

64 When it breaks down into microplastics in rivers, harmful microorganisms can attach and colonise on these microplastics, creating biofilms. If these microplastics are ingested by any aquatic (or human) life, it can release the harmful microorganisms inside that body.

our soils and waterways, where they are ingested by organisms and begin their journey back up the food chain towards larger animals and us humans. Soils contain more microplastic pollution than the oceans, which in turn threatens food safety.

The impact of plastic is far more than just the planet-heating CO2e. It's the chemicals and after-life harm, and simply what do you do with it all? I haven't even really looked into the harm it does in our oceans, but it's enough that Parley for the Oceans, Plastic Oceans International, Oceana and Surfers Against Sewage all have a big presence as campaign groups.

So plastic is terrible. But so too is our travel, food and clothing. I asked my go-to sustainability expert Andrew Murray to explain the comparative environmental cost of plastic food packaging, sports nutrition or otherwise. 'It's a hard one to pin to a number or range,' he said. In high-carbon food such as animal products, the CO2e cost of packaging is comparatively very low, and in a food with an otherwise short shelf life it can even be a big positive. After that, it depends on the type of packaging and the end-of-life treatment. 'Hard-to-recycle foil and plastic composites are more energy intensive to make and can't be recycled, while simpler plastics can be.'

'Travel is worth considering too,' says Andrew. 'For example, am I driving out of my way to collect something just to save a few grams of packaging but causing more harm? Wet versus dry foods is another consideration, with wet being heavy and therefore worse.'

At least we have recycling, eh? Phew ...

A recycling joke

The joke is there is no joke (oh, you're missing them now, aren't you?[65]). Recycling is at best disappointing, at worst a sham, say campaigners. The UK generates at least 99 kilograms of plastic waste per person per year, the second highest in the world after the US. Remember, only 9% of the plastic ever made has been recycled and England only has a 45% recycle rate (Wales does better[66]).

In 2020, 486,000 tonnes of plastic were recycled in the UK. But 688,000 tonnes were sent to Turkey, China and Thailand for them to deal with, which may well have been dumped or burnt. Plastic recycling is cumbersome and expensive.[67] Incineration – sorry, Waste to Energy, as it's officially called – facilities are also expensive and need to be justified, so 11% of waste collected by local councils for

---

65 *Aren't you?*

66 Wales has suspended all new waste incinerators, has a country-wide consistent collection scheme and the third-best recycling rate in the world (24% of rubbish incinerated).

67 Wish-cycling, I thought you might like to know, is a term for tossing something into the recycle bin in the hope it can be recycled, even though it can't.

recycling gets incinerated, often because of long-term contracts between councils and incinerators.[68] Plus it's cheaper, as there's a tax for landfill – which releases more CO_2e than burning coal. Twenty per cent of the world's methane, which remember is over eighty times more potent than carbon dioxide, comes from landfill waste. And toxic PFAS are released into the air, later found in local eggs and mosses.

It doesn't help that we only have capacity to recycle 7% of the plastic the country uses, but even then the items that enter facilities have 'very low recycle rates', says Lucy Siegle in *Turning the Tide on Plastic* – only 10–15%, according to WRAP.

What about those three bent arrows on the bottom of plastic packaging? They don't necessarily mean the container can or will be recycled. The Resin Identification Code (RIC) system is designed to tell recycling facilities what type of resins are found in a given object – it's not a recycling guarantee, which was news to me. Only those with numbers 1 and 2 in the middle are recycled at a significant amount.[vi] That's only bottles, milk, juice and detergent jugs, according to Susan Freinkel, in *Plastic: A Toxic Love Story*, with Greenpeace in agreement.[vii]

Almost all recycling is actually downcycling, made into lower-quality items which usually can't be recycled a third time. While downcycling is better than landfilling or incineration, 'it only delays an item's disposal and does nothing to reduce plastic pollution,' reports campaign group Oceana.[viii]

Unlike glass[69] or metal, which can be recycled almost indefinitely, plastic gets weaker each time and often only has two to three lives – and recycled plastic bottles leach more chemicals than virgin ones. Even when successfully recycled, plastic bottles leach even more chemicals (150 types, with 18 exceeding regulations).

Like with recycling our kit and carbon offsetting, it's the final option on the list, the last resort. 'Recycling can never prevent end-of-life disposal; it can merely delay it,' says Oceana. 'The only way to reduce the amount of material we landfill or incinerate is to **reduce the amount we produce in the first place**.'[ix]

As much as I loathe writing this sentence, Boris Johnson was right when ahead of COP26 in 2021 he told schoolchildren that recycling plastic 'doesn't work' and 'is not the answer' to our climate and ecological emergency.[x] He added, 'We've all got to cut down our use of plastic'. But you'll notice he said 'we' and not 'they', pinning the problem on us as individuals.

Blue Planet

So as a society – and as runners – we generate A LOT of plastic waste. But there is *some* hope.

---

68 It's estimated that 60% of what goes into incinerators could be recycled.
69 The problem with glass is that it's heavier and so emits more CO_2e in transport.

Sir David Attenborough's *Blue Planet*, the most watched UK TV show of 2017, was something of a sea change (sorry, that's a bad one), opening our eyes to the plastic crisis in our oceans. The programme showed the horrifyingly epic Great Pacific Garbage Patch, one of at least five gyres in the world's oceans and a symbol of the planet's wasteful overindulgence if ever there was one.

Attenborough predicted polluting the planet would 'soon provoke as much abhorrence as human slavery' and the Blue Planet Effect has led to much greater awareness of plastic consumption in the UK, the banning of various small, actually fairly insignificant items, such as straws and microbeads, and a charge for plastic bags. Meanwhile, France, which always seems to act quicker, has banned fruit and veg packaging.

In March 2022, 200 nations signed up to a legally binding plastics treaty, which is hoped to be a genuine game-changer on a par with the 1989 Montreal Protocol, which phased out ozone-depleting substances. Even though it'll take another two years to actually agree on what's in the treaty.

Bioplastics, biodegradable and compostable options sound promising, but of course it's never that simple. We're increasingly seeing 'compostable' packaging, so that's good, right?

'Compostable is okay if people have home composting, but industrial compostable can't be recycled, it spoils other recycling and can cause methane in landfill,' says Andrew.

'Compostable packaging makes us feel better,' says record-breaking fell runner, Runners Against Rubbish's Chief Binner and marine renewable energy and plastics research fellow Dr Stuart Walker. 'But if you buy a takeaway and it comes in vegware, for the vast majority of people the only option is to put it in the bin. Then there's the guilt, so maybe we put it in the recycling, so we inadvertently feck up that waste stream. We would've been better with an aluminium tray, or even better to take our own Tupperware to the takeaway.'

In addition, a plastic can be made from plants but not be biodegradable, or the other way round, explains Stuart. 'They are very different things, but they're all called bioplastic. Also, you can call it a bioplastic if just *some* of the ingredients come from plants.'[70]

It's a lot of work to make plastics from plants, so this often has a bigger carbon footprint than fossil plastic. And in the environment, bioplastics can be just as harmful to wildlife, with the same level of chemicals. In landfill, they act the same

---

70 Put simply, PET has two parts, one of which is 30% and one 70%. The 30% part can be made from plants and the whole bottle called 'plant-based'.

way as regular plastics, and if they enter a recycling stream, they can ruin a batch.[71] The European Commission has recommended a ban on oxo-biodegradable plastics, because of fears that they break down into microplastics. 'The fact that these materials have an eco-friendly image is testament to the power of greenwashing,' says Oceana.

Again, the issue seems to come down to that distinctly unsexy message of **simply making and consuming less**. As ever, governments could make huge changes for the better. As could companies. 'Reducing our consumption of plastic – and not merely substituting it with another flawed single-use material – is the only way to tackle this crisis head-on,' says Oceana.[xi]

Plastic-free fuelling?

It's a bit cliched, but my wife took the lead on greatly reducing our household plastic after reading *The Sustainable(ish) Living Guide*. She did it in four ways. Firstly, getting milk delivered to the doorstep in glass, just like the good old days (a familiar theme), by Milk & More, who have non-dairy options and orders can be tweaked online the day before.[72] We adopted the middle-class luxury of Riverford deliveries of delicious organic local food without plastic waste (Abel & Cole offer similar). For our children's school packed lunches and similar we bought beeswax wrappers instead of those plastic sandwich bags, which I find useful too and have proved a real hit. We started getting toiletry refills from the Faith In Nature range from a local health food shop. The last one of the four is the only one that takes regular extra effort and we're less good at maintaining (it took a hit during lockdowns). We haven't calculated as such, but there's a very visible reduction of plastic waste in our kitchen, bathroom and recycling bins, with the lack of big dairy-milk containers being the most obvious omission.

Other ways to reduce plastic waste include some magical materials called aluminium and glass. Or even just plastic designed to be reused. Oceana's research shows that refillable bottles, which Coca-Cola has recently restarted, lead to less marine plastic.[xii] The cola brand, very popular at race aid stations (preferably flat), has some making-up to do. It's been named the planet's top plastic polluter for four consecutive years.

71 In some cases, once made, they *are* the same as plastic, chemically, says Stuart Walker. 'Some bioplastics (bio PET and bio HDPE – bottled water bottles and milk bottles) are chemically the same as fossil-based PET and HDPE. Some of the ingredients are made from different raw materials, but once you have made the ingredient, the product it makes is the same.'

72 In fact, milk bottles were being recycled before we even knew the word – and delivered via electric-powered vehicles. As an ex-milk-delivery person myself, I can see now that Benny Hill was more of a pioneer than any of us realised.

What about us runners? 'I feel sickened by the amount of plastic in sports nutrition', says Todd Mackintosh, a runner and a remarkable one-man anti-plastic campaigning machine. 'Especially how many packets are made from non-kerbside-recyclable materials and poor packaging design which leads to littering.' Some packaging needs specialist recycling, yet the user won't know, as it's absent from the packaging, he says. 'Changes to design or materials would address a lot of single-use waste issues.'

He conducts social media polls for runners about sports nutrition and, armed with the data, approaches manufacturers 'to encourage progress'. Though he has some sympathy for brands. 'I've learnt it's hard for them to make changes at scale or speed. It's a complex issue.'

He adds, 'Take responsibility for the waste you produced and treat the package as an education space, not a marketing space – if a product needs specialist recycling, make it very clear on the packet.'

He urges runners to seek refillable, reusable products. 'And ask brands, "Is this recyclable?" If not, ask why not. If we all did just one little thing, like ask a company about their packaging on social media, things will happen … '

For Todd, it's about more than just plastic waste, though. 'If we start to care about little things, we begin to notice more and more things we can, and should, do for a fitter planet.'

My fuelling isn't plastic-free year-round. I'm human. Sometimes I'm lazy. Sometimes I just really want some salt and vinegar crisps. But I use much less than I used to. Once you see the harm caused, it's impossible not to make more conscientious decisions.

I'm a bit biased, but it feels like the fell/trail-running scene is leading the way a bit again here. As with shoes and clothing, it's often the newer, smaller brands doing the ethical pioneering, such as Unwrapped Bars (who, brilliantly, use beeswax wrappers you post back to them) and Nurhu (who make remarkable edible packaging).

Since banging on about stuff on social media, I've been approached by brands who make products in compostable packaging, such as the wonderful Outdoor Provisions (who make addictive nut butters and bars) and Lucho Dillitos (Colombian-style energy jellies wrapped in dried leaves).

Elsewhere, some brands go out of their way to ensure their packaging gets recycled, by sending prepaid envelopes, such as Supernatural Fuel (a sponsor) and Veloforte, both of whom do mostly plant-based options (stick some beef in compostable packaging and you've kind of missed the point). Other brands making the effort, and usually shrinking their profit margins to do so, include 33Fuel (another sponsor), who again offer mostly plant-based fuelling in kerbside recyclable packaging. Like 33Fuel, Rawvelo only use organic ingredients and make recycling of their packaging easy too.

Gels are a staple for most runners, though, and so far there's no truly waste-dodging solution I've found. The liquid nature of the nutrition requires tougher packaging, several brands have assured me. Foil-lined polypropylene needs specialist recycling that's not widely available in the UK yet. However, brands such as HIGH5 allow you to return wrappers for free and ensure they get recycled via TerraCycle. Elsewhere, Hammer Nutrition, GU and Active Root allow bulk-buying options and reusable gel pouches, so at least there's less packaging overall.[73] In the US, schemes like TerraCycle's Performance Nutrition Recycling Program mean runners can download a free shipping label and send sports nutrition packaging off for processing (it currently costs £108 in the UK, which is prohibitive to most individuals, but perhaps not to races), and there are similar schemes here, such as First Mile (*firstmilehome.com*).

It's possible to buy maltodextrin and fructose independently without single-use packaging, or simply make your own gels.[74] I'll admit I've been too lazy to attempt to make my own, but combos of ingredients such as dates, honey, jams, salt, agave, chia seeds, coffee and molasses work for some. Bananas are brill too. Some gel packets are designed so the ripped-off top is still attached and doesn't automatically fall to the floor, which shames the other brands and should be standard.

A lot of my own hill nosh is banana and nut-butter sandwiches, home-made brownies and flapjacks (or failing that, cafe-bought or made by the ace folk at Delushious, which is local to me). As well as those beeswax wrappers, reusable silicone bags can be useful.

Back in the real world, supermarkets now collect various plastics for recycling, Ella's Kitchen has collection points for babyfood pouches (popular with ultra-runners) and Gualapack, one of the largest babyfood-pouch suppliers, has recently developed a fully recyclable polypropylene pouch.

So things are improving, but it feels like a bit of a minefield for now, especially with so many brands producing deliberately misleading packaging that suggests it's recyclable locally, when it isn't.

'My overall approach is avoid the excess packaging around food through bulk buying,' says Andrew Murray. 'And making sure you understand how to dispose of

73 Although ultimately GU products are shipped from America. And, frustratingly, while the pouches work well, Active Root's delivery arrived swaddled in as much bubble wrap as the plastic I'd saved with my purchase.

74 Maltodextrin and fructose are the predominant calories in most gels and what sports science says is the most efficient fuelling for runners (up to marathon distance, anyway).

it properly – i.e. never letting it enter the environment. **But overall the food itself will be a much bigger impact, so it's a minor consideration against the food type choice.**' In other words, if you have beef three times a day (goes well with porridge, right?) and are chucking lamb in the bin, strategically avoiding plastic means eff all.

Andrew concludes, '**Choosing low-impact food, over any packaging, is best.** Then bulk buying. Then making sure we dispose of or recycle packaging.'

Accordingly, it should be standard for support runners on fell-running rounds and other long-distance challenges to tuck into surplus snacks, as Nicky Spinks may or may not have caught Jasmin Paris doing with a rice pudding one time, and it's a good job John Kelly doesn't count his doughnuts. It's not cos we're greedy. We're doing it for the planet.

Not for the first time, I was feeling progressively angry (I'm a very unangry person usually, honest). We're being asked to shop smart, pay more, in some cases not buy the foods we want, and diligently wash up our hummus pots (our dishwasher seems half full of plastic rubbish). But is that fair?

US scientist and *The New Climate War* author Professor Michael Mann details how in the 1970s, Coca-Cola and the beverage industry deflected the issue of plastic waste on to the public, to convince us we don't need regulations on waste disposal. The 'Crying Indian' public service announcement convinced the public that the real problem with packaging pollution was their own individual littering, not this industry's business model. Keep America beautiful – drink Coke but don't litter. 'Because of that we now have a global plastic crisis,' he says. 'The same tactics are evident in the gun lobby's motto, "guns don't kill people, people kill people", which is classic deflection.'[xiii] Big Oil have adopted the same idea, asking us to concentrate on our personal footprints, not theirs.

In response to a story I tweeted about the world being 'addicted to plastic', Mary Gillis replied, 'People don't buy products in plastic packages because they just can't get enough plastic. They buy them because there's no other choice. Corporations are addicted to plastic and governments are addicted to not regulating corporations.'

Like so much of this climate Kerufflefuck, it's Not Our Fault. Why are we the ones tasked with trying to solve it?

Plog on

That said, few things feel better than taking action into our own hands.

As ever, the Swedes have an ace word for it: 'plogging' – picking up litter as you jog. When I found the excellent bunch called Runners Against Rubbish – 'Because binners are winners' – on social media, I joined them for a small fee and got sent some excellent car stickers and badges (which WILL NOT end up as litter).

After record-bothering litter-picking runs, interviewers have invariably wanted to talk trash (in a good way). Plogging was almost an afterthought, in truth, but it gets people's attention and was an invitation for me to talk about our climate and ecological emergency on BBC and ITV. I felt like a fraud, being held up as a climate champion, because the car travel on some of my runs had caused more harm than any of the plogging. Collecting a cola bottle didn't actually stop Antarctic ice shelves from breaking off, did it?

'No, but it's a practical step we can easily do, and it can make more of a difference than you might imagine,' says Stuart Walker. 'We can sometimes feel powerless. But remember, climate change is caused by the cumulative total of billions of insignificant little actions, and we can help to tackle it in the same way.'

There are three reasons why picking up rubbish is worthwhile, he thinks. Firstly, it has a damaging effect on the environment and our animal friends. There are over 7,000 reported incidences of this every year, says the RSPCA, and probably many more unreported. 'Our rubbish kills animals and birds. There's also the impact of rubbish on soil and anything that grows in soil,' adds Stuart.

Secondly, there's the broken windows effect. To human brains it seems less bad to drop rubbish when there's already a pile of it. But thankfully this works the other way round too. 'We recently studied the link between awareness of air quality and climate change and found that when people have the equipment to monitor their air quality, they are more likely to act on climate change,' says Stuart.

Finally, if we see – or, better still, pick up – litter, we become more aware of it. 'Ultimately, we start to change our behaviour, perhaps stop buying certain brands or types of product, which is in itself good, but also drives bigger change. The clever people at companies who want to sell us stuff notice we've stopped buying so many and change the way they do things, to try and make us buy them again. If the correct regulations based on good science are in place (i.e. not just greenwash), this reduces the impact of the product. And if we pick up litter and talk about it, we involve other people and the effect is multiplied.'

Also, adds Stuart, dropping rubbish makes extra work for race organisers and landowners, potentially jeopardising future running events.

On the Pennine Way in 2020 we collected about 8 kilograms of rubbish, which was nothing compared to the inaugural Plogging World Championships, where a whopping 795 kilograms was collected over 1,780 kilometres of trails in the Italian Alps. Now that's far from rubbish.

As well as ditching as much meat and dairy as we can, er, stomach, to me, planet-based fuelling means minimal single-use plastic, routine plogging and any activism (more anon) a runner chooses to do on the topic, like the amazing Todd Mackintosh.

Our behavioural changes definitely influence those around us. Sometimes we may not realise for ages, or even ever. But countless people have told me they've reconsidered their dietary, shopping or travel habits in recent times and that's all been triggered by someone else's actions or words.

It does work. Things are happening.

Were you expecting a joke here? I thought about it, but decided it might be too rubbish.

Yeah, but what can we do about it?

1 Read Jen Gale's *The Sustainable(ish) Living Guide*, which has excellent tips on all of this. And Lucy Siegle's *Turning the Tide on Plastic*, for an overview.

2 Watch *Trashed*, if you dare.

3 Buy less stuff in plastic packaging, such as a veg box of stunning organic nosh from Riverford or Abel & Cole.

4 Consider ordering milk and dairy from a delivery service such as Milk & More, who have non-dairy options and all kinds of produce which can be ordered online, and the milks come in glass.

5 Consider shopping with the pioneering Good Club (*goodclub.co.uk*), who do carbon-neutral doorstep deliveries of zero-waste products at supermarket prices for a small subscription, including food, drink, household and hygiene products – and you're not even asked to clean packaging before returning it.

6 Use beeswax wrappers or silicone bags for sandwiches and other hill nosh.

7 Bulk buying saves money and packaging, for both sports and everyday nutrition (some just call it 'food').

8 Support brands making an effort to reduce plastic waste.

9 Use the Scrapp app to see if packaging is recyclable when buying and check *recyclenow.com* for local kerbside options.

10 See plastic as a resource, not waste – plastic boxes and bags can be incredibly useful and last for years.

11 Properly wash recycling, or there's a chance it'll get rejected and sent for incineration. And squash plastic bottles and cardboard boxes, so they take up less space.

12 Be a little bit activist and avoid products/brands with excess packaging – and email them to complain.

13 Join Runners Against Rubbish and/or go plogging! (Honestly, you'll feel better for it.) Or do a #2minutebeachclean

14 For more on plastic, visit *breakfreefromplastic.org* and/or read *No. More. Plastic* by Martin Dorey (founder of #2minutesolution).

9

WELL STUFFED

Our running stuff, non-running stuff and social media stuff

'Runners are great ambassadors for our planet –
we have an obligation to share those experiences.'
Huw James

While researching this book, I did a Carbon Literacy course online, delivered by the excellent folk at Protect Our Winters UK, which was great for clarifying parts of this Big Kerfufflefuck and galvanising us attendees. During it, we were asked to do a personal footprint calculation, via the respected WWF calculator.

My footprint score of 8.14 tonnes of CO_2e was smaller than the average of 10.8 tonnes for my postcode and a 2.4-tonne improvement on the previous year, even if it was still some way off Mike Berners-Lee's recommendation of a 5-tonne lifestyle.[75] As you would expect, my emissions were spread between food (25%), travel (18%) and home (25%). However, the remaining 33% was 'Stuff'. And my Stuff is equivalent to two medium-haul flights.

According to the questionnaire, my Stuff includes one new appliance in the year, a hypothetical spend of up to £50 per month on clothing (most of the year I don't buy or receive anything new, but I did the Spine Race, which requires a lot of mandatory kit), we have pets (two cats, two rabbits and several fish), I/we spend a bit on online entertainment and subscriptions, and that's about it.[76] Though the majority of that is non-running purchases, it was still disheartening to learn my Stuff could be up to 3 tonnes of CO_2e.

How much of that is running-related? All you need to run, famously, is a pair of daps. But that's a myth, or at least we've come to believe it is. 'I used to think running was a low-cost pastime, until I realised I own more running clothes than day-to-day clothes,' says Andrew Murray. 'Clothes for all weathers and spares for when I'm behind on the washing. Multiple pairs of shoes for different conditions, uses and

---

75 For the record, Our Carbon calculate 13.3 kilograms for my family, which is a more sophisti-cated process and would be more accurate, but doesn't give a figure for me as an individual.
76 Pets can have a surprisingly big footprint (or should that be pawprint?), with a cat estimated at 310 kilograms per year and a dog at 770 kilograms, mostly because of their meat-scoffing.

avoiding repetition. Bags, vests, watches, headphones and torches, all with additional environmental impacts from the electronics and batteries. Ever so many socks, and even more race shirts. This all adds to the total carbon, as well as other significant environmental and social impacts.'

Andrew calculates that products account for a fifth of his running impact, but being a sustainability professional, he's more conscientious than most. For many runners, our footwear and clothing combined with the rest of our running Stuff could well equate to a quarter of our overall running (or even overall) footprint. **Our passive overconsumption is doing great harm.**

A trail/ultra runner will have a lot more, partly because races have mandatory kit to be carried for safety reasons. Waterproof jackets, waterproof trousers, mid-layers, warm base layers for winter, wind shirts, caps, hats, buffs, gloves, sunglasses, water bottles/soft flasks/bladders, trekking poles, navigation devices and bags to carry all that stuff in. The races I prefer usually have extensive kit lists. At the extreme end of things, the Spine Race has thirty-plus items on its notorious list: waterproof mittens, microspikes, goggles, sleeping bag, bivvy bag, sleeping mat, cooker, GPS unit, torches (plural), trowel (no, really) and on and on, many of which I'll admit I have more than one of. The Ice Ultra requires you to run with glow sticks and tampons (long story). That's quite a lot of Stuff, though much of that will also be used in non-running contexts (especially those glow sticks, obvs). But a lot of it just sits there unused for months on end.

That kit is much less of a burden on the planet if it's actually being used, and I'm determined to either pass items on or make them last and last. I make an effort to lend sleeping bags, sleeping mats, packs, trekking poles, head torches and even snowshoes to friends and coaching clients, saving them from buying yet more items they might only use once a year. Black Trail Runners have started a gear exchange of sorts, and it feels like there's room for a place where runners can hire or swap expensive, little-used bits of kit (even if the postage means more CO_2e created).

Trail-ultramarathons are still fairly niche, so does the average road runner cause much CO_2e from their Stuff? Well, the study of the French runner training for the New York Marathon[i] (see page 115) calculated his 'purchases' – shoes (four pairs), T-shirts (five), shorts (three), socks (ten), waterproof 'track suit', hydration pack, head torch, GPS watch, one book and two magazine subscriptions – at 490 kilograms.[77] It's easy to see how quickly kit can pile up.

---

77 As well as additional food, they estimate a runner takes five additional hot showers a week (which seems like an overestimation to me – I have just one most days, post-run) and two additional laundry cycles a month (which seems like a massive underestimation to me), which would all be filed under home/energy.

We've done shoes and clothes to death, but every runner I know also has a watch, usually a very sophisticated GPS or smartwatch worth hundreds of pounds. I can't find a life-cycle analysis, but as it's created from virgin metals with numerous parts, it must be fairly labour- and therefore carbon-intensive to produce.

I've had four watches in my eleven years as a runner. In my defence, the technology has improved markedly over that time, especially in terms of navigation and better battery life, which is genuinely useful when a race or challenge goes beyond twenty-four hours.[78] But as with all of this stuff, whenever there's a new version out, it's easy to start reasoning with myself why I need that very slightly shinier one. I wish I didn't. Knowing the harm caused usually stops me from following through, however. 'If your running watch still functions, do you really need a new one?' asks @sustainablerunning. 'The desire for the latest technology is wasteful and unsustainable.'

Most runners own a head torch or three and, at risk of oversharing, I own two iPod Shuffles, a GPS unit, three small phones (they're built to be smuggled into prisons – best not to ask how exactly) and several pairs of earphones (are they the least durable tech product ever created?), all for running purposes. Oh and four kettlebells, two dumbbells, a pull-up bar, three foam rollers (they're all different!), a muscle gun, a weight vest, several resistance bands ...

Oh heck. In my defence, those items have been collected over several years. But still. It's a lot of Stuff, some of it doesn't get used and I need to pass those items on.

I wish it didn't, but a smartphone plays a huge role in my athletic life, from podcasts and music to Strava, Training Peaks and Garmin Connect apps, taking photos, various running-specific WhatsApp groups and social media, which for me is very running-centric (more anon). **Smartphones are responsible for around 1% of the world's CO_2e**, 690 million tonnes of it, and 69 kilograms of CO_2e per device (for typical use of 195 minutes per day). Storage of all those selfies generates 355,000 tonnes of CO_2e every year (deleting the ones photobombed by your thumb does actually help here). I'd guess a GPS sportswatch has about a quarter of that footprint?

Tech waste or WEEE (I almost kept a straight face as I typed that) is a huge problem. Fifty-seven million tonnes were discarded in 2021, a 'mountain' of tech heavier than the Great Wall of China.

I was jogging round a central Glasgow park at COP26 with record-breaking fell runner and GP Finlay Wild as he told me about the surprisingly huge impact of inhalers. Five million people in the UK, including lots of runners, have inhalers,

---

78 For some of my challenges it's an advantage to wear two watches: one for live stats and recording the activity as means of proof, and one to help avoid topographical embarrassment, something I'm quite good at not avoiding.

and those little puffy devices, while potentially life-saving, have a disproportionately high carbon footprint. Standard aerosol spray inhalers – also known as pressurised metered-dose inhalers – contain a powerful ghg called hydrofluorocarbons, which is between 1,000 and 3,000 times more potent than CO_2. Each dose from the inhaler is equivalent to driving one mile in a family car, so one inhaler is close to driving 200 miles, while around 4% of the NHS's entire carbon footprint comes from asthma drugs.

Thankfully, dry powder inhalers are available, often allow better control and the equivalent emissions are about a twentieth of the standard inhalers. In fact, many European countries with similar health outcomes predominantly use dry powder inhalers, and the UK is an outlier in its continued high use of the high-carbon metered-dose aerosol ones.[79]

Runners may also wish to consider time online: ogling race rivals on Strava, registering for events, watching trail porn on YouTube. **The carbon footprint of our gadgets, the internet and the systems supporting them account for 3.7% of global ghg emissions and 1.7 billion tonnes of CO2e**, estimates Mike Berners-Lee. Not far off aviation's contribution. Partly it's the energy to power our gadgets, partly the production process for our phones and laptops, but also the energy and intense cooling needed for the vast servers and data centres. That's around 414 kilograms per person.

Andrew Murray didn't buy much in the year when he analysed his carbon emissions from running, but even 'a few items' added up to 18% of his total impact, a weekly average of 2.4 kilograms. 'If you buy or receive a lot of stuff (race shirts, sponsor/gifted items), you should really consider refusing or passing on items, as the environmental impact very quickly adds up!' he says. 'Do you really need another low-quality 10K finisher shirt sitting in a drawer?'

Cripes. We seem to have gone full circle and landed back at those cursed race T-shirts again (groan). But several of those things surprised me, certainly how much of my running footprint might come from tech and add to my Stuff.

---

79 However, 'the most effective inhaler is the one which is right for the patient and used appropriately, and for some patients that will still be a metered-dose inhaler,' Finlay warns. 'Changes to inhaler devices should be done carefully. No one is suggesting denying asthmatics treatment; this is just about shifting to more sustainable devices.' Also, suboptimal asthma control and even asthma deaths are linked to an over-reliance on the short-acting reliever inhalers and underuse of longer-acting preventer inhalers. So if you are going through a lot of blue reliever inhalers (e.g. salbutamol) it's likely your control could be much better on different medicines, which is a triple win – better health with less frequent reliance on inhalers, and shifting to using the dry powder low-carbon variety where appropriate.

Sponbassadencers

Talking about the online world, running is built for social media. It's usually a crap spectator sport and has nothing like the media support of, say, football, so a lot of it – both the races and the pretending we're doing twenty-milers in the mountains twice a week – happens online. Social media is a very silly place. But we don't need studies to tell us it has a great deal of influence too.

The lifestyles of sponsored athletes, ambassadors and influencers [all three are a little different and I'm going to use the word *sponbassadencers* for short] inspires us to act like them, says Rosie Watson, whether we're conscious of it or not. 'There's a trickle-down or ripple effect of influence. It shapes what we aspire to and the whole outdoor culture.'

The bottom line of sponsorship is product sales. 'Runners with a social media following are a really cost-effective way for brands to advertise their kit,' says ReRun Clothing's Charlotte Jalley. 'They need you more than you need them.'

'I would hope that anyone working as [a sponbassadencer] is representing a brand that reflects their beliefs and has true faith and respect for the products or events they are promoting,' Charlotte says, adding that sponbassadencers can have an influence both on their following and, back the other way, on a brand. 'They should remember it's a two-way relationship and to feed back honestly with thoughts, opinions and recommendations.

'If more influencers bravely ask brands, "Who made these clothes?" or "What happens to these trainers when they are done?", it will create a shift and make them more accountable. If brands have to answer these questions, they will have to have adequate answers.'

Sponbassadencers make a brand's products seem personable and trustworthy, says Rosie. 'Some brands have repair schemes, lifetime guarantees, use recycled materials, ethical work practices, have sustainability reports. But if the same brand's website is full of product-pushing sales, Christmas lists, "New Season, New Product!" posts, and their ambassadors are regularly promoting new jackets on social media, this is still pushing an unsustainable consumerist model. We need cultural change.'

Science communicator Huw James, who co-founded The Athlete Climate Academy with Kilian Jornet, wants athletes to turn to their sponsors and say, '"I'm currently not comfortable with how much you are doing; we need to do more." And then go back to their audience and say, "I'm pushing these guys to do more. I'm trying to do more. Neither of us are perfect, we all make an impact on the environment. Let's not point fingers at each other; we're all working towards a common goal."'

Sponbassadencers who care about the Big Kerfufflefuck can have a really positive impact, says Charlotte. '**I love to see posts of well-used clothing, dirty trainers, tips on repairs and hacks to make clothing and gear last longer!** I would like to see before and after shots of muddy–clean trainers. Images of where you donate your clothes. More about a brand's sustainability policy and things they are doing for the greater good. Questions to the community for their thoughts about a product or event and how they could do better.'

In terms of climate-emergency hypocrisy, this is the area that personally troubles me most. I hate getting my pointy finger out, but to me it's not okay to bang on about how much you care about the planet, then in the next post rave about a new bit of kit you've just got for free – knowingly creating consumer lust. It often looks like the kit hasn't even been tried out yet and certainly durability can't be vouched for. There seems to be a distasteful eagerness to boast that we got a free thing. And, sure, I've been guilty of that in the past.

I've stopped doing those 'Look everyone, my sponsor sent me some new daps!' posts, which are pretty unhelpful. I've decided to celebrate loved kit just as much as new, which I very rarely promote directly anyway and when I do it comes with a (pious) warning about overconsumption and I have to have confidence in its durability or sustainability credentials. These brands get great marketing from us for peanuts and we should value that and not feel overly grateful. Though I get that it's hard to shake that feeling of gratitude when you're new to it.

It's not perfect. I'm aware I'm still implicitly promoting a brand. But I can certainly do so in a more planet-conscious way. I've pushed back on all my sponsors, following Rosie's practice of asking to see their sustainability policy, which hilariously and happily led to me losing one. Another made some marked improvements. I had to press pause on a relationship with one brand because they weren't acting quickly enough on a particular issue – a decision that cost me a fair bit of money. But it feels like the right thing.

I was initially nervous about challenging people who support me, but it's vital that I'm working with brands who share my values, and most conversations have been surprisingly fruitful, open and productive. A couple were doing far more behind the scenes than they were saying publicly – a common imposter-syndrome theme I see among races and elite runners too. I've also got better at simply saying 'no thanks' to new products if there's nothing wrong with my current version. I'm not promoting a product just because it's new. It has to be a worthwhile improvement. Social media can be pretty unhealthy anyway, so the more authentic we can make it, the better for all concerned.

'Sponsored athletes have a massive reach; they're role models for many, many people,' says Huw James. 'Kilian Jornet is a great example. The amount of times I've seen comments like, "It's nice to see Kilian take a stance on things and talk about it." It just makes a difference. It makes you get up and take a look. Us runners are great ambassadors for our planet and I think we have an obligation to share those experiences with people, to continue the conversation of how we can better protect the environment that we experience first-hand. I think we forget that many people don't experience it.'

Let's not promote something just because we got it for free. Let's promote it because it really is durable or has good repair options. Let's show off repaired and well-loved kit. Let's raise the bar and not contribute directly to the overconsumption crisis fuelling the climate and ecological crisis. There needs to be a middle ground, where we can care deeply about the Big Kerfufflefuck and still have relationships with some brands that are productive for them, us and, more importantly, the planet. If we force people to choose between the two, we'll likely lose people. Let's be better sponbassadencers.

'When I think about my role as an activist, I like to remember that the movement doesn't need more perfect environmentalists,' said ski mountaineer and activist Caroline Gleich on Instagram. 'When we shame one another for not living up to standards, we shrink the climate movement. Fighting climate change means working to create a cleaner system where people don't have to hate themselves for living their lives.'

Other stuff (we can do)

On the subject of lives, our Real ones invariably overlap with our Running ones and many of our actions affect both. So it's probably worth knowing that **the number-one thing we can do to reduce our contribution towards climate change is …** (drum roll please …) not have children. Saving 58.6 tonnes of CO_2e. Oops! Too late for me.

So should we really consider not having children – or having fewer? The former instinctively doesn't seem fair. But overpopulation is often cited as the issue underpinning our planetary crisis. 'It's not just about the number of people, it is about how they live,' says Mike Berners-Lee. It takes 500 Malawians to clock up the carbon footprint of just one person in the UK. So is it bad to have kids? No. But a big family seems irresponsible. 'What matters is what lifestyle your children have.'

This feels like a good moment to hammer home the point that **overconsumption is the issue, not necessarily overpopulation**. Our money is inexorably linked to CO_2e. The more we spend, the more we pollute, and the more waste we create. People in rich countries consume up to ten times more natural resources than those in the poorest countries and we are devouring the planet's resources at a rate 1.7 times faster than it can regenerate.[80] Around two-thirds of global ghg emissions are directly and indirectly linked to household consumption. And **70% of ghg could be linked to the manufacturing and use of products**. 'We're consuming too much – and it's the root cause of climate change, biodiversity loss and plastic pollution,' says Jane Shaw in a powerful blog on ethicalbusinessmarketing.com.[ii] **'Consume less to save the planet. It really is that simple.'**

It's not easy, though. We get an addictive dopamine hit from the anticipation of a purchase. Less so from its actual arrival. On top of that, for the runner, FOMO is real. There's always a new shoe or watch claiming performance benefits.

If we, like smokers trying to quit, simply put money in a jar every time we talk ourselves back from the consumption cliff, I wonder whether the visual evidence of what we spend, or rather save, on unnecessary consumption, would keep the momentum going and help us save up for something really rewarding. Like a private jet or something. #ClimateBantz

After having one less child, the next most impactful non-running changes we can make are: to go car-free (saving 2.4 tonnes), avoid a long-haul flight (1.6 tonnes), switch to a renewable energy supplier (1.5 tonnes), switch from a fossil-fuel-powered car to an EV or hybrid (1.1 tonnes), go plant-based (0.8 tonnes), recycle as much as possible (0.2 tonnes – but note how the amount of CO2e saved is really dropping off), hang-dry clothes instead of tumble-drying them (0.2 tonnes) and replace traditional light bulbs with LED or CFL ones (0.1 tonnes).[iii]

Of course, the last three are worth doing. But not at the expense of time spent on the others. Note the huge differences in impact between those nine actions, from 0.1 to 58.6 tonnes, between mice and elephants. 'People on average underestimate the most impactful climate actions they can take, and overestimate the least impactful ones,' says the World Economic Forum.[iv]

We're at the tipping point for mass adoption of EVs. Switching to a renewable energy supplier was in my experience easy and even saved a bit of money (pre-'energy crisis' anyway) and lifted a big bit off my conscience. I've avoided long-haul flights, or in fact any, since 2019 and I've gone plant-based. Switching to an EV is beyond our means right now, which is frustrating because travel is the biggest area we can improve on, but we will as soon as we can.

There's one more big one: your dosh. Not the spending of it, but the investing of it. Stephen Fry was among a coalition of celebrity and business campaigners calling on the public to harness the untapped power of their pensions to tackle the climate

---

80 A North American consumes 90 kilograms of resources a day, a European 45 kilograms and an African only 10 kilograms per day.

crisis in November 2021. Lots of banks and financial corporations invest in fossil fuels because that used to be a pretty dependable return on the money and **thirty-five of the world's major banks have provided £2 trillion to fossil-fuel companies since the 2015 Paris Agreement**. Which seems disgustingly greedy to me. All that money knowingly funding the direct destruction of life on this planet as we know it.

'It's crazy that our banks and our pensions are investing in fossil fuels, when these are the very things that are jeopardising the future we're saving for,' said David Attenborough in *A Life on Our Planet*. Genuinely, how do those people sleep at night?

Switching your money so it's not being invested in fossil fuels could be twenty-one times more impactful than going vegetarian, giving up flying or switching to an energy supplier, says Make My Money Matter. Apparently, the average individual UK pension saver can bring about a cut in carbon emissions of 19 tonnes a year by switching to a sustainable fund.

Think of your money in three ways: current accounts, Isas/investments and pensions. Nearly £3 trillion is in pensions, much of it in fossil fuels (it could also be abetting gambling, tobacco or the arms trade – makemymoneymatter.co.uk is a great place to start your research).

I'd known about the idea of divesting for a while, but even though I was with Barclays – the worst of the worst – taking my very modest money elsewhere took me ages to get round to. I was nervous about the transfer, because I'm self-employed, paid by numerous accounts each month and envisioned a Kafkaesque nightmare of missed payments, an empty account and a stern letter from my mortgage provider. When I finally plucked up the courage, not one payment went missing, there's been surprisingly little admin and I feel SO MUCH better banking with Triodos, who deliberately target sustainable investments and are transparent about it, the most ethical bank according to our hard-to-please friends at Ethical Consumer.[81] I wish I'd done it sooner. If we can't be part of the solution, at least don't be part of the problem.

There's always more we can do. Around a third of heat in an insulated home is lost through the walls, according to the Energy Saving Trust, so proper insulation, especially in an older building, could save CO_2e and cash. However, even with government grants, that can be costly and sometimes just heating a home more efficiently can save money and energy. Fitting and using heating controls (timer or programmer, a room thermostat and thermostatic radiator valves) properly could save between £75 and £280 a year and reduce annual carbon emissions by anywhere

---

81 I don't have a pension or any investments because I'm too busy being out running to make any real money.

from 320 kilograms to 930 kilograms. Installing heat pumps and/or solar panels might be something to consider too – and with all of these, look into government grants. But, globally, education of young women and improved refrigeration and clean cookstoves will have big impacts. For more insight on a macro level, visit Project Drawdown, a multi-disciplinary coalition of experts on climate-change solutions (*drawdown.org/solutions/table-of-solutions*).

That's about it, really, in terms of a runner's – and a non-runner's – personal carbon footprint. But **there's one more thing we can do and it could have an impact far exceeding everything we've talked about. Find out in the next chapter.** But first, that climate change joke you've been desperately hanging on for ...

> *Fossil-fuel use has increased eightfold from the middle of the last century*
> *– things like coal, oil and gas – which was actually the original name of the*
> *band Earth, Wind and Fire. (With thanks to comedian Matt Winning.)*

Yeah, but what can we do about it?

1 For banks and pensions, use *switchit.money* and *tumelo.com/personal*
2 Pawprint, WWF, Earth Hero and Climate Action Now are all good apps to help you calculate your footprint and show ways to improve it, with Pawprint being especially good.
3 There's loads more that people can do around their homes, but we're into the mice not elephant category. Jen Gale's *The Sustainable(ish) Living Guide* is a great start.
4 Buy less stuff. Buy second-hand. Do you even need to buy at all? Can you borrow it from somewhere?
5 If buying tech, 'consider buying refurbished – you usually can't tell they are used,' says @sustainablerunning. Groups such as @recyclehealth donate used sportswatches to those under-served.
6 Using Ecosia as your search engine instead of that bigger famous one means you're planting trees as you ogle Power of 10 after that parkrun PB.

10

LITTLE BIT ACTIVISM

Should we forget about personal footprints and go superglue ourselves to something instead?

'Imagine if Greta Thunberg had devoted her attention to ditching dairy instead of #FridaysforFuture.'
Emma Pattee

It's my sister's fault. Like many, I saw news coverage of Extinction Rebellion (XR)'s captivating central-London protests in November 2018. They had a striking, easy-to-understand hourglass symbol, big loud drums and giant pink boats. They blockaded bridges and brought traffic to a standstill. The protestors seemed very well organised and happy to be arrested, singing 'we love you' at the police handcuffing them. They were calling on the government to 'tell the truth' about climate change. (Their other two main demands are to 'act now' to aim for net zero by 2025 and to form a citizens' assembly – a structure successful elsewhere.)

XR were back bothering the capital again in April 2019. They glued themselves to roads. Again, they were willingly arrested – which can have serious consequences, not least financial. It was somehow both humorous and calmly alarming how serious and concerned these people were, the lengths they would go to. And they weren't green-haired hooligans or hemp-honking crusties. They were mostly middle-aged professionals, acting with stoic, non-violent, civil disobedience, like the great civil justice movements had before them in India and the American South. Plus they called themselves Rebels, like in *Star Wars*.

My sister was involved. Of course she was. She lived in Bristol, or rather Brizzle. That's just what people in Brizzle do. I learnt XR had formed in Stroud, where I went to school, so XR was in my family and my heritage. It's no coincidence Forest Green Rovers sits between the two, in Nailsworth, where I mostly grew up. The small, hilly town is home to the world's first carbon-neutral and vegan football club, owned by eco-energy entrepreneur and former New Age traveller Dale Vince. I remember his first giant wind turbine going up, controversially, in view of our house in 1996.

When we were growing up, my sister would ask our parents to buy her bits of the

Amazon for her birthday, to guarantee their conservation, which was impressively prescient. But that was her thing, not mine. In my mid-twenties, seeing the rampant destruction of magnificent ancient rainforests in Tasmania was the first time I felt politicised. I was shocked by how little these treasures, these magnificent Ents, were valued. I read about the activism that prevented the damming of a major river and the formation of the world's first green party, in Tassie. As a travel writer I did a tour that deliberately showed us the island's polluted rivers and miles of felled tree stumps. My best friend in Australia was a Canadian named Ryan Sengara, who was passionate about growing organic food, reducing plastic waste and using natural cleaning products. I gently mocked him, to be honest, but was impressed. People doing more than you are kind of annoying, aren't they? Some seeds were sown.

I can see now that several more were too: my friend, fellow ultrarunner and journalist Matthew Maynard adding 'Environmentalist' to his email signature, ReRun's Dan and Charlotte, hearing about Finlay Wild giving up flying, Clare Gallagher's 'Earth-raging', Andrew Murray and Rosie Watson's writing. I followed a trail of breadcrumbs. We can all be dropping breadcrumbs …

Time to Rebel?

Anyway, XR seemed really quite insistent that this 'climate and ecological emergency' as they were calling it, really was, well, an emergency. The phrases 'climate change' and 'global warming' both lack a little urgency, don't they? So I visited their website, followed up on the links, signed up for the mailing list.

I learnt this stuff really is a lot more urgent than the government, corporations and most of the media are saying. Really fucking urgent. The film *Don't Look Up* is not a comedy. That's what it feels like to those of us who can see what's hurtling towards us.[82]

I knew more protests were planned and had this strong urge to be involved. I'd seen Finlay Wild, record-bothering fell runner Es Tresidder and Shane Ohly all refer to XR subtly online or in interviews, which helped make the idea of activism seem accessible. I felt like a hypocrite, though, because I'd flown to a lot of races that year. 'It doesn't matter,' said my sister. 'It's about politics, not people. XR are all about **pushing for system change**, not nitpicking about whether you left your laptop on standby overnight.'

Nevertheless, I thought I should probably use public transport to get to London.

---

82 As I type, in July 2022, meteorologists are warning of 'absolutely unprecedented' 40 °C in Britain – driven by climate change – and consequent deaths. A TV presenter responded with: 'John, I want us to be *happy* about the weather … something's happened to meteorologists to make you all a little bit fatalistic, harbingers of doom.'

I was in several exciting new chat groups, on WhatsApp, Telegram and Signal. Naively, I was willing to get arrested. That would be quite cool, I thought, show my commitment to the cause. I had been radicalised by an extreme organisation.

London was surprisingly quiet at first. I mostly walked around a bit on my own, till I followed a lead on Twitter and arrived at a courthouse to see eight pensioners standing outside, hands glued together, with police passive-aggressively reading them their legal rights. Some of them looked frightened but they all appeared magnificently unflinching. The police were advising them their lives would be much, much easier from this point if they chose to detach themselves from their comrades (if they even could?) and leave. But they wouldn't. One by one, they were unglued, via some mysterious liquid poured on to their hands by police, and led to a waiting paddy van. It was an act of heroic, moving defiance and deep moral conviction. I was awed.

My other sister and her partner arrived in the afternoon and we joined a good old-fashioned march. Songs were sung, loud drums were played, colourful flags were waved. It felt inclusive and that strong sense of shared mission was powerful. The march culminated at Trafalgar Square at dusk, where short, impassioned speeches, mostly by young people, detailed what frightened them about what we are facing. There was more singing too and the mood was optimistic, if calmly angry. Most people didn't have unconventional hairstyles, rainbow trousers or sandals. They just looked normal. I was very happy to be a part of it. Much more than washing up my hummus pots, it felt like I – we – were actually doing something.

I posted about it on social media afterwards and Charlotte got in touch to say Dan had been arrested there – willingly. Though I hadn't spotted an opportunity to be handcuffed, I felt like I hadn't shown the necessary conviction, even if I had at one point been asked to get off a wall by a copper. To my great shame, a little surprised by the request, I'd meekly obliged.

Since then, I've joined some Fridays for Future protests in Bath and gone to some XR meetings, where as well as delicious vegan food and a bit more singing, I was struck by how very well organised everything is, despite it being a decentralised structure, and very welcoming too – even if waving hands in the air rather than verbally agreeing to ideas takes some getting used to. I went to some more XR protests in London, then headed up to Glasgow for COP26 and two huge protests there.

Dan and I co-formed a WhatsApp group called Runners for XR and recruited around fifty like-minded runners with the idea of some sort of protest run in Glasgow. However, I was a reluctant organiser and never really got a coherent idea or the logistics together. But a few of us met and ran together and other runners joined in virtually, to run 414 kilometres for the 414 parts per million of

CO2e in the atmosphere (#WeCantRunAwayFromThis). Which didn't, er, quite get on BBC News (though the main marches made all the front pages). But it felt good to do a political act, however small. It just felt more natural to combine concerns for the world's future with my passion for running.

I haven't yet got involved in any of XR's controversial direct actions, which usually involve strong glue and occasionally wearing nappies. In Glasgow, three activists tried to recruit me for a sleepover/occupation of the Science Museum to protest about fossil-fuel sponsorship. I half wanted to, as it sounded like proper guerrilla tactics and I'd have had a better story to tell in this part of the book, but was secretly relieved when I realised I couldn't do that date. XR aren't to everyone's taste. But, honestly, they're amazing people: thousands of pensioners and professionals willing to get arrested because they feel there's no other option left but to rebel. It looks increasingly like mass civil disobedience may be the only way to force the systemic changes needed for a liveable planet.

Do XR's civil disobedience tactics work? Well, David Attenborough and Greta Thunberg have chipped in too, but **80% of people in the UK now think the climate crisis is a global emergency**. Parliament and numerous local councils have since declared climate emergencies.[83] XR were never going to win everyone over, and indeed aren't designed to, but public endeavour for climate solutions rocketed after XR protests, showed a study – although support is higher amongst younger than older people (41% of eighteen- to twenty-four-year-olds compared to 26% of over-sixty-fives).[i] But then the oldies won't have to endure the Big Kerfufflefuck for long.

'Activism, including litigation, as well as the tactics of protest and strikes, have played a substantial role in pressuring governments to create environmental laws,' said April 2022's IPCC Mitigation Report.[ii]

Concerns about climate change have gone mainstream. *The Mirror* did a green special. The *Daily Express* has a weekly Dale Vince column. Even the *Daily Mail* has started using the previously self-banned phrase 'climate crisis'. Indeed, the number of editorials calling for more action to tackle climate change quadrupled in the space of three years, according to a study by Carbon Brief.[iii]

The biggest shift took place in right-leaning newspapers, which have switched from predominantly opposing climate action to overwhelmingly supporting it. Google reported that 'impact of climate change' was searched for more than ever in 2021.

Somewhere in amongst experimenting with activism, I started thinking about my own footprint and making changes there too.

---

83 Which demonstrates 'the will of the Commons to act', but isn't legally binding.

Do individual footprints even matter?

If you'll forgive a klunky namedrop, I was out gambolling through soggy Wiltshire fields with Boff Whalley,[84] thrice legendary as a musician, fell runner and author, and we were discussing all this lark, when Boff made a point that cuts right to the heart of the Big Kerfufflefuck. 'Have you heard about the scale of military eco-fuckery?' he asked. I hadn't. But I wanted to.

The fell-running author and musician recommended a book called *The Green Zone: The Environmental Cost of Militarism*, by two-time Pulitzer Prize nominee Barry Sanders. 'The impact of the military is just amazing,' Boff said. 'And I'm equally amazed all this stuff is kept hidden.'

'Here's the awful truth,' wrote Sanders in 2009. 'Even if every person, every automobile, and every factory suddenly emitted zero emissions, the Earth would still be headed, head first and at full speed, toward total disaster, for one major reason. The military produces enough ghg, by itself, to place the entire globe … in the most imminent danger of extinction.'

Sanders investigated the US military, from fuel emissions to radioactive waste, and found the Pentagon is the largest single consumer of petroleum in the world, using enough oil in one year to run all of the transit systems in the US for the next fourteen to twenty-two years. It consumes one quarter of the world's jet fuel, and the world's militaries combined are responsible for two-thirds of the ozone-depleting ghg chlorofluorocarbons (CFCs) – which have more impact on global heating than CO_2. **The US military is the largest single polluter of any single agency or organisation in the world.**

'We are all made to feel like climate disaster is our personal fault and responsibility,' said Boff, 'while the military of every country is somehow left blameless. I'm not saying we shouldn't all do whatever we can, all the time, in everything we do. Just that it's also important – perhaps more important – to actively stop the biggest and worst transgressors, the biggest polluters, who seem to have carte blanche to escape blame.' He agreed it's 'absolutely right' to make runners aware of what they can do, 'as long as one of those things, alongside shoe choice and where to race, is learning who are the biggest nature destroyers and talking about how we oppose and resist their almost invisible destruction.'

Boff was spot on. I felt angry again. Even putting the military aside, let's not forget that **10% of the world's population are responsible for half of all ghg, while the bottom half contribute just 12%.** And the 'luxury carbon consumption' of the top

---

84 Much as I wish it was a regular occurrence, it was an open invite to attendees of the excellent *These Hills Are Ours*, a two-man show with Daniel Bye that perfectly blends running with politics. Go see it if you can!

1% of super-emitters will account for 16% of global emissions by 2030. We're talking private jets, megayachts and space travel. That lot. And **71% of global emissions come from the same 100 companies**, while the poorest 50% will release just 1 tonne of CO_2 a year. And it's not just Global North versus South – even within the same country, such as the US, the gap can be more than seven to one (an average of 75 kilograms of CO_2e versus 10 kilograms). 'The richest 10% … should pay to fix the climate,' suggested Professor Lucas Chancel, author of *Unsustainable Inequalities: Social Justice and the Environment,* in a *Guardian* column.[iv]

It seems bitterly unfair that it's solely on conscientious individuals to make all the sacrifices to try and solve the Big Kerfufflefuck. So should we even try to improve our personal footprint and accept the sacrifices that usually entails, when they are below minuscule in the grand scheme of things, dwarfed by those who don't seem to care and are carrying on with business as usual?[85] That way, aren't we just playing Big Oil's game?

Let's not forget who invented the concept of the personal 'carbon footprint calculator'. It was our fine friends at British Petroleum (BP) in 2004, or at least the advertising firm Ogilvy & Mather working for them. When they tied the concept of carbon footprints to small, feel-good activities, they shifted the narrative from corporate accountability to individual responsibility. They want us to count up our grams of CO_2e and keep washing up our hummus pots, so we don't have time to look at *them* and the epic, unethical, profit-driven harm they're doing.

Today is my animal-adoring son's eighth birthday and one of his presents was a wonderful book about nature, galvanising young conservationists with planet-saving tips such as recycling, avoiding palm oil and telling their parents not to use chemical pesticides and fertilisers on the garden. While it seems smart to plant these seeds in fertile minds, at the same time it feels like the onus is being placed on my children to sort out our climate ecological emergency. And that made me angry too. Governments and corporations, and especially the fossil-fuel industry, got us – *knowingly* – into this mess. And they can do so much more than we can to sort it out. Individual action is meaningless without government action, says Professor Michael Mann in *The New Climate War*.

Sweeping up leaves in a hurricane?

There's some low-hanging-footprint dieting we runners can do, primarily travel, food, kit/stuff. But after that, are we really just sweeping up leaves in a hurricane? Pushing for system change feels more important, and is potentially many times more impactful than concentrating on personal footprints. 'Apart from embracing

---

85 Although to be fair, the UK military is consulting experts about net zero.

trains over flights, and reducing your meat and dairy consumption [and buying less kit and making it last, I'd add], forget individual actions,' says Rosie Watson. 'Focus on wider change.' Indeed, most of our lives were radically simplified during Covid lockdowns, but CO2e didn't drop significantly, which showed that the emissions we need to tackle are systemic rather than lifestyle.

By encouraging environmentally minded folk to use their carbon footprints as guides to fight climate change, we risk them spending all their energy on low-impact actions, turning off lights and recycling, argues US journalist Emma Pattee on Mic. com, instead of putting that energy towards more meaningful work, such as lobbying politicians or erasing wasteful practices at work. 'Imagine if Greta Thunberg had decided to devote her attention to using less water or ditching dairy products instead of creating #FridaysforFuture,' she says.[v]

Another helpful way to think about things is the concept of our **climate shadow**. If one person flies weekly for work and another walks to the office every day, who is doing more for the planet? It's clear who has the bigger carbon footprint. But what if the weekly flier is a climate scientist who travels the world spreading awareness about climate change and the walk commuter works for a marketing agency, making ads for fossil-fuel companies? Who is contributing more to the climate emergency?

Think of your climate shadow as a dark shape stretching out behind you, says Pattee. 'Everywhere you go, it goes too, tallying not just your air-conditioning use and the gas mileage of your car, but also how you vote, how many children you choose to have, where you work, how you invest your money, how much you talk about climate change, and whether your words amplify urgency, apathy or denial.' It includes actions that defy easy calculation, 'which, as Greta's #FridaysforFuture strike showed us, almost all high-impact actions do'.

Pattee explains a climate shadow as consumption, choices and attention. I understand it to mean my sphere of influence, especially workplace but also family, friends and social media.

By promoting the carbon footprint as the most important thing for citizens to focus on, Big Oil ensured we wouldn't put our energy toward what really matters: collective action and activism, she says. 'To know the true expanse of your impact on the planet … **overlook your carbon footprint**. Instead, look behind you, at your shadow.'

Indeed, when a climate action website was launched alongside *Don't Look Up*, with input from Katharine Hayhoe and others, the top six actions all related to climate shadows (talk about it, join a climate group, make your money count, keep politicians accountable, spark ideas at work, push for climate headlines), rather than footprints.[vi]

Individual choices do add up, writes Rebecca Solnit in the *Guardian*.[vii] But vegan diets have not made the beef industry go away or reformed its devastating climate impact, she points out.

'As citizens we must go after the climate footprint of the fossil-fuel corporations, the beef industry, the power companies, the transportation system, plastics, and so much more ... It's not good enough for a bystander to say, "I personally am not murdering this person" when someone is being stabbed to death before them,' she says. 'And those of us in the global north have countless ties to systems that are murdering the climate, so we are not exactly bystanders. The goal for those of us with any kind of resources of time, rights and a voice, must be being part of the solution, pushing for system change. To stop the murder.'

Even the guru of personal carbon footprints, Mike Berners-Lee, agrees. 'Each one of us – as individuals – can be a meaningful force for change,' he writes in the bible for personal footprinting, *How Bad Are Bananas?*, 'both by cutting our personal carbon and exerting pressure on our workplaces and schools, our councils and governments, and on companies and corporations.'

Imperfect activism

'We don't have to beat ourselves up for not being perfect,' says Berners-Lee.

'I'm an environmental hypocrite,' wrote Heather Higinbotham in the *Independent*.[viii] 'I dutifully separate and clean my recycling, knowing it will likely end up in landfill. I compost, but still waste too much food. I have way too much stuff, yet on my hundredth trip to donate random junk I didn't need or use, I ponder clever ad campaigns promising me that "get out of jail free" card, and wonder whether buying new recycled yoga pants is better than thrifting a new-to-me pair.'

Under our current social and economic systems it just isn't possible not to be a hypocrite, says Zoë Rom, environmental journalist and editor in chief of America's *Trail Runner* magazine. The idea we must be perfect before we act 'is one of the most pernicious traps of climate inaction ... None of us is perfect and we all desperately *need to do something*.'[ix]

From the moment we wake, almost everything we do burns coal, gas or oil. Of course, some level of footprint-cutting mitigates against the flawed and damaging system we inherited. But nothing we do as runners really matters, she says, if we don't focus on advocating for systemic change. 'Rather than judging others or feeling guilty for driving to races, we should use that energy advocating for energy policy, food and agriculture policy, better waste management [or in the US] protecting and regulating public lands so that those fossil fuels never leave the ground in the first place.

'Overemphasising individual power downplays the necessity of collective action. **Climate action doesn't need a few more saints. What it needs is a lot more runners willing to do what they can, while making mistakes and trying to do better in a system that works for, and not against them.**'

After all, we can be hypocrites or arseholes.

'Imperfect activism' is a key philosophy behind Jen Gale's *The Sustainable(ish) Living Guide*. 'It's about embracing the "ish",' she writes. 'Making changes one baby step at a time, knowing that we won't always get it right, knowing that no one lives the perfect sustainable life, and that's OK.'

Jen became an accidental sustainability hero after attempting a Make Do and Mend Year, i.e. buying nothing new, which turned into a blog, a *Guardian* column and a book or two.

What I love about Jen's books is there's full acknowledgement that we're all busy, tired and inconsistent.

It feels important to show imperfection.

Indeed, *almost everything we do creates emissions*, so we can't not be hypocrites on some level. So let's embrace imperfection and seek progress rather than the eternally elusive perfection. Waiting for perfection means nothing will happen.

'Driving or wearing shoes or eating cheese doesn't make me a hypocrite,' says Zoë Rom. 'It makes me a normal, flawed person living in a broken system that displaces its own culpability by redirecting guilt towards individuals with less power. If those of us who are trying, really and honestly hard are still fully meshed in a fossil fuel system, that makes clear that **what needs to change isn't individuals, but** *the system*.'

Individual action alone, though important, will not be enough to reverse course in the climate crisis: '**We need runners to advocate for effective, evidence-based collective action and public policy.**'

Berners-Lee is adamant that **individual actions do still matter**, and many of the experts and activists I've read and listened to insist the same. 'Every tonne [of CO_2e] that doesn't go into the atmosphere is relieving human suffering somewhere in the future,' said Mark Stevenson.

'Each time we make a different, more conscious, more thoughtful choice, about what we buy, or what we don't buy (choosing to reuse or repair instead) we are changing the world,' agrees Jen Gale.

'**What you do will be insignificant, but it's very important that you do it,**' said Gandhi.

Those small individual actions matter because they **influence** others.

'Even though each of us is still such a small part of the change that is needed, if we take action, and consciously live a lower-carbon lifestyle, we help create new norms,' says Berners-Lee. 'By finding ways to live better and with less impact, we show others what is possible.'[x] Most of us like to be like most other people most of the time, he says. When we do something brave, it makes it more normal for others to follow.

Among other things, personal carbon-cutting brings **integrity**, he says. For me, I realised I had some strong values, perhaps for the first time in my life. And I want to live by those values as best I can. They affect numerous decisions every day, from what I buy and eat to how I travel. But I feel so much … I'm not sure what the word is – better? – for having a purpose, some clear ethics.

Lifestyle changes can also **build momentum** for systemic change, suggests research on social behaviour. 'People don't spring into action just because they see smoke; they spring into action because they see others rushing in with water' – and that comes from a study with exactly that design.[xi] 'One person skipping a flight will not solve global warming alone, but when one person withdraws from a system that causes harm, they **make that harm palpable to others**.' More solar panels are bought in neighbourhoods that already have them.

The commitment shown by people who don't fly influences others to fly less too, shows a Cardiff University study.[xii] When one person makes a sustainability-oriented decision, other people do too, found another.[xiii]

But we must also push for the big system changes we need, urges Berners-Lee. 'It's not one or the other; we need to do both.' Push for the cultural and political change in every situation, he says. 'How we influence our politicians (not just through our votes), and the things we say and do at work, at leisure and at home.'

Grassroots pressure can change politics, he asserts, citing the UK government's tighter carbon targets as a response to XR, the US youth organisation Sunrise Movement pushing for a Green New Deal in the US (forcing every Democratic hopeful to speak out on the climate), the Jubilee 2000 campaign credited with the cancelling of debt in developing countries. And the biggest breakthrough of all: Greggs' vegan sausage rolls.

Being a little bit activist

'Climate activists are sometimes depicted as dangerous radicals. But the truly dangerous radicals are the countries that are increasing the production of fossil fuels,' said UN Secretary-General António Guterres in April 2022.

What frustrates me so much is that governments could be doing so many obvious things to dramatically speed up CO2e reduction, such as removing fossil fuel, farming and aviation subsidies, incentivising low-carbon travel, plant-based diets and BEVs, regulating fashion and insulating our homes.[86] But they're not. Above all else, we need to get off fossil fuels ASAFP. But they don't seem in any rush about that, despite thousands of scientists screaming at them in panic. We may have to force the change ourselves.

Runners are natural environmentalists. 'Runners should care about climate change, because we so directly interact with nature,' says Bruce Rayner, the founder of America's Athletes for a Fit Planet, in *Trail Runner*. 'If you plan on running on this planet, you should also bank on protecting it,' agrees Zoë Rom.

Activism can be a daunting idea and a bit vague too. It's easy to feel you're doing *something* when you wash up those hummus pots, a simple, commonplace action with a clear (intended) result; while advocating for fossil-fuel divestment doesn't necessarily give that satisfying or immediate outcome. But activism can be countless things, large and small.

We can all be 'a little bit activist', says Isabel Losada in the excellent *The Joyful Environmentalist*, where she too joins in with XR, banging a drum on the streets of London. It's a neat phrase as it doesn't sound overwhelming or daunting. 'But it sounds scarily persistent,' she says. 'I think it's important … that we **find ways to combine what gives us joy and what makes us happy with saving our planet**. And I don't think that's as difficult as it seems. There are many opportunities for creativity and duty within environmental work.'

'**You have to tackle sustainability in a way that makes you feel most alive**,' says Rosie Watson, borrowing from cyclist, writer and environmentalist Kate Rawles.

Find what you're passionate about, Isabel urges in an interview with Jim Mann's The Future Forest Company. 'If your love is clothes, then be activist within the fashion area. If your love is trees and protecting nature, then it's important to be active in that area.'[xiv]

Against individual actions, activism targeting systematic change is a bit nebulous. How do you become an activist? What does one actually do? Do we need to dye our hair green and pink? However, it's less committing and more versatile too, certainly than say giving up flying or going vegan. You can dip in and out. Do what suits you.

'Climate change affects everything, so it shouldn't be hard to find an arena that's personally interesting,' says leadership expert Professor Thomas S. Bateman.[xv] 'Consider how your skill sets can help and figure out where you can contribute best.'

Joining in with boots-on-the-ground environmental protests is the obvious way to be an activist, such as with XR or Fridays for Future, which are 'super fun',

---

86 These may not actually be the most impactful or cost-effective things; they're just the actions that seem most obvious to me.

says Rosie Watson. 'They have an incredible festival-y and positive atmosphere, are extremely respectful, inclusive and safe, and are the easiest way to create change while being very non-committal. You can literally turn up, hang around being a body in the crowd for half an hour, and go again. But numbers of people in the crowd is everything, so just doing that is hugely powerful, much more than agonising for hours over which trainers to buy.'

She's heard politicians directly thank protesters for creating enough momentum that it allows them to make much bolder political suggestions to tackle the climate crisis. The protests at COP26 made front-page news around the world.

Plus it's great spending time with like-minded folk, because sometimes all this climate anxiety feels like a lonesome, depressing and anxiety-inducing prison. You don't have to chant or sing, get arrested or even wave a flag. You just walk along for a bit, in a safe inclusive atmosphere, usually having a good chuckle at humorous banners, and go home feeling empowered and like you actually did something. XR are big on protesting, so just sign up for their emails or visit your local group's Facebook page. Fridays for Future are more frequent and a good way to experience protest without the drama of a huge occasion.

If you're feeling brave, consider joining the amazing, friendly and courageous folk at Just Stop Oil, Insulate Britain, or The Tyre Extinguishers. Civil disobedience and non-violent direct action is historically proven to be the most effective tactic we have, as witnessed in India, the American South and the Suffragette movement. Traditional civic methods, although I feel they're worthwhile, don't reflect the urgency of our plight, so this may be the only solution. We're almost out of time.

'**Be more rebel**,' says self-styled carbon coach Dave Hampton. 'Join (your local) Extinction Rebellion. Join IB. Sit in the road. Engage in activism, civil disobedience, and protest (non-violent direct action) … often. Get yourself arrested. Live a little!'

Friends and family

Mike Berners-Lee suggests focusing on 'our own biggest areas', starting with friends and family. 'We have to find clever ways of moving ourselves and each other in the right direction that brings us closer to the people we care about the most.'[xvi]

Work, schools, community

'The most effective thing you can do about climate change as an individual is to stop being an individual,' writes Bill McKibben, co-founder of 350.org, in *Trail Runner*. 'The most important thing you can do is join with your neighbours and organise. The second most important thing you can do is join with your neighbours and organise.'[xvii]

'All of us can make suggestions, help set the culture of a business or organisation and challenge what isn't right,' says Berners-Lee. Or just consider what groups we belong to and aim to exert some influence there, with the obvious one for most runners being a local running club, event or the wider running community, like ReRun and TNT have.

'I think it's very, very important as environmentalists that we look at what we call our locus of control,' says Isabel Losada. 'In other words, where we have influence and where we don't have influence.'

Politics

It sounds old-fashioned, but emailing our MP is one of the most effective things we can do. Constituency correspondence gets recorded by topic. 'They all need to hear from us that we care,' says Berners-Lee – and not just at election time. MPs report 'limited interest [in climate change] from their constituents', found a 2018 report by Green Alliance.[xviii] Find your MP at *theyworkforyou.com*.

I've emailed my local (Tory) MP several times, usually via Greenpeace campaigns. She always replies, albeit with a copy and paste, and has started following me on Twitter. After emailing my local council about their fossil-fuel divestment, via a POW UK campaign, a sympathetic councillor replied in person, told me he supported the idea and followed it up.

Greenpeace is great for emailing campaigns when something relevant is being debated in Parliament and urging you to send a timely email to your MP. It just takes a minute, but feels impactful. More than ever, we must vote for those with the greenest policies, in local elections too. I joined the Green Party and leafleted for them in north Wiltshire, which was less arduous than it sounds. This may be naive, but what if all those people who would vote Green but think it'd be a wasted vote, actually did? The next election seems like a good time to try that experiment. The election after that will be too late, if we're trying to keep 1.5 °C alive.

Consumer activism (or conactivism?)

'[Climate change] is what we wear. It's what we eat. It's how we travel,' says Isabel Losada. 'It's how we dress. It's how we buy our food. It's how we spend our leisure time, it's every single aspect ... We have an opportunity to bring about change every single time we part with money.'

'Runners can hold brands and events to account, nudge them to be more responsible,' says Charlotte Jalley. 'Write to them. It does work. Even if you can't get to the big guys, if you go to an event and you're not happy with how they've done something, write and tell them. We're led to believe us Brits are good at complaining, but often not to the actual people we need to complain to. So if an event doesn't offer an opt-out for the T-shirt, let someone know. I mean, nicely; like, "I'd really love it if we could have an opt-out as I don't need that T-shirt or medal". And if more of us did that, or wrote to adidas … '

'As an individual, you can really shout for change by calling out anything that sounds like greenwash,' says Rosie Watson. 'And promoting second-hand gear and repairs, and asking brands to do the same'.

Similarly, Jen Gale talks about being an everyday radical. 'Against the constant bombardments to buy more, the act of not buying, buying less or buying better is actually pretty radical … I see these acts as a sort of gentle rebellion against the status quo. Every time I choose second-hand, or reuse or resist single-use, it truly is an act of activism.'

She's a big fan of voting with our money and letting retailers know if you love their product but hate their plastic packaging. 'If you've stopped shopping or going somewhere, let them know, tweet them.'

Clicktivism

Do online petitions work? Natalie Fee, founder of City to Sea and author of *How to Save the World for Free*, who started the campaign to end plastic cotton buds, certainly thinks so. She's spearheaded several campaigns, saving hundreds of tonnes of single-use plastic from entering the oceans, and it all began with a humble online petition.

Slacktivism and social media

If you follow me on Twitter, I pity you, because I'm a doom-mongerer. Almost every day I compulsively retweet a *Guardian* story about our climate and ecological emergency and, let's face it, they're almost never positive stories. To be honest, I do it mainly for my own mental health, to howl into the abyss a bit. I've made mistakes (like just lazily assuming everyone would agree man-made climate change is a thing), but my confidence in talking about our climate and ecological Kerfufflefuck is growing. I've felt inspired by the likes of Kilian Jornet and Clare Gallagher, who seem brave and confident. We can reach a huge audience online.

'I really wanted to engage athletes,' says science communicator Huw James. 'They are just predisposed to care about the environment, but there was a lack of confidence in talking about it. They often don't think they're experts, but they can still have a very valid experience and opinion. The number-one thing we can do is just make sure we're talking about it, but not just in our echo chamber, to friends and family, and in the running community. Keep it on the tip of your tongue. Talk about it on social media. Climate apathy and anxiety is the new climate denialism.'

Live your values – as conspicuously as possible

'Probably the easiest way to broach these conversations is to simply live your values,' writes Jen Gale.

Those everyday acts of radicalism, those conspicuously repaired running shoes, the polite request for non-dairy milk or decline of the race T-shirt, those are conversation starters. 'The more normal we make these acts, the more confident we feel talking about changes we're making and why we're making them, the more people will be inspired and empowered to change too,' Jen says.[xix] Plus being engaged with the problem helps with climate anxiety, says Anouchka Grose in *A Guide to Eco-Anxiety*.

Make climate actions as conspicuous as possible, says a piece in Slate.com about social psychology of climate change. 'With each step, you communicate an emergency that needs all hands on deck. Individual action – across supermarkets, skies, roads, homes, workplaces, and ballot boxes – sounds an alarm that might just wake us from our collective slumber and build a foundation for the necessary political change.'[xx]

It feels like we've come full circle, where those tiny, individual decisions are actually acts of systemic-aimed activism. If you have one minute spare a week, I'd say email your MP, a brand or a race. Those moments of micro-activism are crucial too – especially if it's not done in secret. Those small visible actions are planting seeds, helping build a flowery path for others to follow ...

Talking of which, the Grantham Institute works on climate change and the environment and says we should simply talk about the changes we make. 'Conversations are a great way to spread ideas. As you make these positive changes, share your experience with your family, friends, customers and clients. Don't be a bore or confrontational. Instead, talk positively, and be honest about the ups and downs.'[xxi]

Following the ideas of seeking out what makes me feel alive and where my locus of influence is, for me activism has simply been conspicuously attaching my values to some of my run challenges such as the Pennine Way, using my skills (or lack thereof) to write this book, and using my contacts to be a founding member of The Green Runners (more anon). Oh, and banging on about stuff on social media. Like Clare Gallagher says, it's too late in the day to worry about being annoying. In fact, we *need* to be annoying.

With my latent skills of a hospital radio DJ, that links nicely to one of my favourite climate scientists, the excellently surnamed, US-based Canadian Katharine Hayhoe, author of *Saving Us: A Climate Scientist's Case for Hope and Healing in a*

Divided World, who featured in *TIME*'s top 100 most influential people.[87] In the US, she points out, 70% of people are worried about climate change; in Canada and the UK, it's over 75%. And yet only 8% of people are 'activated'.

'The biggest barrier is not lack of understanding of the science,' said Katharine on the *Sustainababble* podcast. 'The biggest barrier is not fear – we've got lots of that. **The biggest barrier is lack of efficacy**, the sense that people don't think they can make a difference.'

The first step in giving people efficacy is witnessing it, she says, seeing what other people have done. '"Wow, they did that? Well, maybe I could do something too." Then you use your voice to say, "Hey, maybe we could make something happen?" To paraphrase [*Don't Even Think About It: Why our brains are wired to ignore climate change* author] George Marshall, how does social change happen? The first step is when people have conversations.'

Isabel Losada has simpler ideas for fixing a perceived lack of efficacy. 'We rarely feel powerless when baking, walking over fire, enduring a triathlon [yuk – I think she just forgot how to spell marathon] or doing whatever we enjoy to raise money,' she writes in *The Joyful Environmentalist*. 'Campaigning with thousands of others to change the political conversation is also a powerful antidote to feeling that one person is not enough.' She adds, '**It's not knowing what to do that leads to people feeling powerless.** But there are many actions we can take, and not take, every single day.'

Indeed apathy is seen as the new denial, the mass (in)action that may hold us back at the most critical time. The truth is, we can be an activist by doing almost anything. I like the 'not take' reminder. When we refuse to buy beef, don't book a flight or cancel those shoes in the online shopping basket, that's an act of everyday radicalism. However, *just* those individual actions aren't enough. They don't have much impact if they're not shared. It's crucial we talk about it too – the importance of which is reiterated by Anouchka Grose, Huw James and others. Even then, 'After decades of talk and negotiation on climate change, years of personal actions and corporate targets, a mass of rhetoric, greenwash,' says Mike Berners-Lee, 'there has been no dent whatsoever in the rising global carbon curve. Nothing at all. Talking about it has not been enough. Asking for it has not worked. Somehow, we have to insist.'[xxii]

'I want you to stay angry,' Barack Obama told activists at COP26. 'I want you to stay frustrated. But channel that anger, harness that frustration, keep pushing harder and harder for more because that's what's required to meet that challenge.'

---

87 Her TED Talk, 'The most important thing you can do to fight climate change: talk about it', is available at *ted.com/talks*

How we talk about It

Alongside our actions, individual or systemic, everyday consumer decisions, and speaking up about them, have to be productive. When you talk about *It*, though, not everyone agrees. It's a heated subject, remember (sorry). But that's okay. Katharine Hayhoe believes that '99.9% of the time [inactivists] don't think there are any solutions to climate change that are consistent and compatible with their values.' The answer, she says, is to talk specifically about solutions consistent and compatible with their values – and this was the lesson from my POW Carbon Literacy course too. Climate change affects everything. Find out what they care about and start there ...

Online there are bots, digital finger-pointers and keyboard commandos, and people definitely enjoy highlighting inconsistencies, otherwise known as 'what-aboutery'. Doesn't that climate activist realise his shoes are made from plastic? **'Cynicism is apathy dressed up as wisdom,'** said author and 'reluctant futurist' Mark Stevenson on the *Jon Richardson and the Futurists* podcast. If you point out someone else's imperfections, it lets you off the hook from doing anything, right? 'It's really, really, really easy to think we're hard-wired to balls things up, because then it absolves us of any responsibility to do our bit. My answer is, you do what you can, with what you've got, where you are. As Gandhi said, "be the change you want to be in the world". That's all you can do. If you think, "I'm not going to do anything till that lot across the road does", then you're part of the problem.'

'How we best communicate things depends on what you want the outcome to be,' says Huw James, who admits he sometimes indulges in 4 a.m. squabbles on Facebook. He likes 'the Inception model', based on the film. The premise is that you cannot make someone make a decision by telling them to make that decision. 'They have to make the decision for themselves. So you have to go in and plant that seed and that seed will grow and they will make a decision by themselves. Otherwise they rebel against it. That's what I always try and do with my science communication. I try my best to plant seeds, so people go away and do their own research, think about it for themselves and make their own mind up.'

We're not going to change everyone's minds, initially anyway (though often when I've simply asked, 'What do you think the solutions are, then?' a useful exchange takes place). Armed with OurWorldinData.org, IPCC reports (*ipcc.ch/reports*), the BBC and *Guardian* websites and *How Bad Are Bananas?*, I feel I can counter most objections with science. I usually reply once with the facts and leave it there (and usually it ends there) – more for the sake of anyone watching who may be curious.

It doesn't take the prime minister to change the world, says Katharine Hayhoe. 'Individual ordinary people can change the world.' That's how women got the vote, how slavery ended, Apartheid in South Africa. 'It wasn't that important influential people woke up one morning and decided it had to happen. It happened when very ordinary people, who were not famous or influential or wealthy, had the courage of their convictions. And they acted and used their voice, to bring people with them and that's how the world changed.'

Anyway, it's that time again ...

> *Remember when glaciers were cool? That's the joke. (Sorry, I'm scraping the bottom of the sea here.)*

Yeah, but what can we do about it anyway?

1 Join The Green Runners, Protect Our Winters UK, XR, Greenpeace, Friends of the Earth, Fridays for Future, Youth Strike 4 Climate, the Green Party ... Donate to those causes, if you can. Join in with their protests.

2 Email your MP. Email them again. Do the same with your local council.

3 Tweet a brand, politely, asking what they're doing to improve their sustainability.

4 Tweet a brand who've made the effort and celebrate them.

5 Join the Fashion Revolution and ask #whomademyclothes

6 Do a Carbon Literacy course, with POW or another facilitator.

7 Wear visibly repaired running kit – with pride.

8 Live your values. But don't stress about being perfect or being judged a hypocrite. No one is and we all are.

9 Talk about it.[88] Have conversations with family, friends and fellow runners, at your running club or local race.

---

88 If that idea is intimidating even after you've read all this nonsense, the IPCC have six principles to use in public engagement (*ipcc.ch/site/assets/uploads/2017/08/Climate-Outreach-IPCC-communications-handbook.pdf*, which would have been great to find at the beginning of this book-writing nightmare – sorry, journey – rather than right at the end). It's only a page long (jump to page 5) and two leap out at me. The first is 'Talk about the real world, not abstract ideas' (i.e. big numbers bypass people, so relate to common ground and day-to-day experiences). The second one, also suggested by the ace folk at POW, is 'Connect with what matters with your audience' (i.e. studies show values and politics often override how people interpret science, so start with local interest or shared values), which in a lot of cases for a runner, will be how climate change affects the sport and how the sport contributes to it.

11

HOW GOOD IS RUNNING!

Our sport is already making a difference

'Sport has the power to change the world.
It has the power to inspire. It has the power to unite.'
Nelson Mandela

Cheesy quote time! So that's about it, really, in terms of the most significant aspects of running's footprint on our climate and ecological emergency. As we've seen, some actions cause great harm. But should we just stop everything and go live on a remote Scottish island under a rock subsisting on seaweed?

Yes. If you want to. But you don't have to. To allow ourselves to be content – within reason – will have a greater positive impact on society and the environment than any number of solar panels, argues Mike Berners-Lee. We should keep getting out there, enjoying being in those green and lumpy places. And, crucially, sharing the fact we are. And that we're doing it better than we were. Let's make carbon-conscious acts and lifestyles the norm. Let's help running and sport lead the way towards a sustainable future.

Personally, I'm content if my family is safe and well and I can drink limitless tea and still do most of the running I used to do, just in a lower-carbon format. Knowing what I know now, my conscience won't allow me to be jet-setting around Europe, promoting new gear on Instagram and glugging back chocolate milk.

I've made mistakes. I've made a prat out of myself (nothing new there) on several occasions. But I've forgiven myself too. Because it all comes from the right place. I care and I want to understand the Big Kerfufflefuck. Things are just too urgent to worry about being perfect. And we shouldn't try to be, because who even can be? But we can all make progress.

I'm a hypocrite. We all are. Once we see that, it's liberating. Waiting to be perfect can look like apathy and delay. I want to have less impact on the planet, make feasible changes, but feel less guilt for existing.

This whole thing has really depressed me at times, though. Runner pals stopped asking me 'How's the book going?' on runs because the well-meaning question invariably descended into weary rants and I found them suggesting that though they *were* planning to be out for twenty miles, maybe just five would do. But once I'd got it all out on to the page, I felt some catharsis.

For runners, the Big Three are our travel, our kit/stuff and our nutrition (sorry, food) – often in that order (depending on your shoe habit). But activism, in whatever form makes you feel most alive, is better still. With personal footprints, just grab the low-hanging fruit, then go make some noise in the general direction of those reluctant decision-makers.

'All roads lead to less' is a distinctly unsexy message. But a lot of harm – both environmental and human – went into the creation of our kit, so let's make that count for something. Let's impregnate it with special running memories, then protect, preserve and treasure it. Let's be proud of old shorts and socks. Let's celebrate them. Not forgetting other Stuff, such as GPS sportswatches and vibrating toys (ooh, Matron). If we shop less, we'll be less a part of the problem, the Overconsumption Crisis. We'll be happier and have more money too. Brands simply need to make and market less stuff, but build it to last and help us to make things last better too. And just cease the poppycock and bunkum. Marketing is becoming one of the unrecognised evils in the history of climate change.[89]

With our daps and tees, it's such a complex and Machiavellian industry that we're better off ignoring the white noise of marketing – including that 500-mile shoe myth – and the incessant churn of new clobber, and instead remembering that the most sustainable kit is the kit we're already wearing. Mushroom, sugar cane and algae isn't necessarily any better, especially if it's at the cost of durability and, even if it was, if it's heavily marketed and runners buy more shoes and create more waste, it's worsened the Big Kerfufflefuck, not improved it.

It does feel like the outdoor-clothing industry, with its more nature-loving customer base, is being genuinely progressive. With running sportswear, and presumably a more urban and less committed customer, it's less hard to see that ethical stance, and some brands and retailers are entangled with the horror show of Fast Fashion. Less so in the trail-/fell-running scene, which again has a more environmentally aware audience. The Big Running brands need to step up. We're nearly out of time.

A lot of this stuff seems to come down to a dichotomy between Fast and Slow. While we all want to run faster, slow travel, slow food and slow fashion are undeniably better for the planet – and us – than the faster versions.

The elephant in the room, though, is participant travel to races. Now we know the costs to the planet, we need to consider how important each event really is to us,

---

89 Ahem. Except the people marketing this book, of course. They're wonderful, brilliant and
   beyond moral rebuke.

and then whether we can get to it as low-carbon travellers. If we can't but it's important to us, how can we turn the race into a proper holiday experience? As well as a polite 'no thanks' to T-shirts, medals and single-use plastic, we can gently lobby RDs about these important, urgent things. Events need to help runners make the best decisions regarding travel, with real incentivisation, perhaps funded by the high-carbon travellers. I'm trying not to point fingers, but while the London Marathon is a wonderful, potentially life-changing event, it's not only being very slow to confront its huge elephant, but could also use its presence of vast influence more productively. This stuff's too urgent not to. While we're on the subject, the mooted idea that the Sydney Marathon might join the Abbott World Marathon Majors seems flagrantly insensitive to our climate emergency. That's just greed.

Providing vegan food at races will bring the event's footprint down significantly – and with our own fuelling, clearly less meat and dairy is better for the planet, ourselves and those lovely four-legged types. Not everyone needs to go Full Annoying Vegan if we all cut down – though I'm very happy to, not least because it provides some satisfaction in being able to close off one of the key areas that causes harm, whereas travel and kit is harder, for me, to act on conclusively. Avoiding food waste is huge too, and cutting out plastic waste is less significant but still important.

As an ex-member of it, I do think the running media could do a bit better, such as including ratings on durability and (real) sustainability credentials as standard in kit reviews. I appreciate that magazines especially fall into the trap of becoming servants to their advertisers, but over-celebrating new kit is keeping the fires of overconsumption constantly alight. As well as damping that down, let's see more long-term kit tests, with more honesty.

I honestly don't enjoy wagging my finger, because I'm not perfect either, but this stuff's too important to be shy about: sponbassadencers have a lot of influence and most of us could behave more responsibly, more honestly, on social media. We don't need to be fuelling the Overconsumption Crisis. The more authentic our communications, the more trust we'll garner. Let's be honest about durability. Let's show off well-loved kit with pride. Let's make it cool. And let's talk about our climate and ecological emergency more. To me, what we do on social media is really important. It's activism.

We can all make changes, improve, reduce our personal footprints. But as I've looked into this, I've grown increasingly frustrated by how much the onus is on us as individuals to solve the Big Kerfufflefuck. You can sink into a mindset where you feel guilty for merely existing. Last time I checked, it wasn't us making billions by extracting gigatonnes of oil from the ground while knowing that it's making the world a less habitable place and causing epic suffering. And yet somehow fingers are pointed at well-meaning folk to make the myriad sacrifices aiming to fix things, while Fast Fashion, Big Agriculture, Big Oil and Big Money (and Big Marketing?) carry on scot-free.

I'm not naturally an angry person and I don't enjoy conflict. But, honestly, if you're employed in those industries and you're not working towards improving things with a *massive* sense of urgency, then you need to take a long hard look in that mirror. Your greed is fucking this planet up. You are complicit in ecocide and genocide, frankly.

Deep breath. It felt good to get that off my chest.

Activism can have a wildly bigger reach than personal footprint stuff. It may be a vague and daunting idea, but it needn't be. Pick the area you know best (quite possibly within running in some way – your local running club or race), align it with your values, your skill set or passion and … on your marks, get set, go! Venerated author and activist Noam Chomsky recently advised Just Stop Oil campaigners to simply ask themselves, 'How can I make a difference where I am, where I live, with capabilities I have?'

Your climate shadow is more important than your carbon footprint. I'm happy to be a climate-emergency hypocrite, because we're all de facto hypocrites in this disastrous system we've inherited. And don't forget the simple but effective idea of just Talking About It. Don't even try to be perfect. No one is.

To my mind, all runners are environmentalists. We love being outdoors, ideally somewhere handsome, and the simple pleasures of moving simply and naturally. Few things are as primitive and as joyous. We need to protect running, the climate we do it in and the places we love to do it in. If you have one minute available each day to devote to the Big Kerfufflefuck, instead of washing up your hummus pots, email your MP to ask why Big Oil and Big Ag are being subsidised rather than public transport and renewable energy. But if you have two minutes available, do both.

How bad is running comparatively?

'There's no major sporting event that doesn't have a significant impact,' says London Marathon's Megan Hunt. I didn't find a study comparing CO_2e emissions sport for sport, but elite competitions such as tennis, golf, rugby, cricket and Formula 1 involve flying teams on a circuit around the world and, while we're not yet at the stage where we have to think about such things being stopped, they clearly need some low-carbon modifications (some of them have at least pledged to cut emissions, but mind you, even our government said that).

However, a bigger factor will be spectator travel and that'll be huge for the planet's most popular sport, football. Indeed, a World Cup is estimated to cause a whopping 2.5 million tonnes of CO_2e and the sport as a whole is conservatively estimated to have a similar carbon footprint to Tunisia. An Olympic Games has similar issues with transport, though running is only a small part of the Games. A climate-friendly aspect of running is that as it's thankfully such a crap spectator experience, fans aren't travelling long distances to watch it.

As well as sportspeople and spectator travel, venue building and energising will be more of an issue for some sports, says Megan. 'Venues have a different challenge to a mass-participation event where you don't have a fixed venue. You're putting it up and down in a short space of time. Stadiums use a huge amount of energy, but they can also govern that a bit.' Again, running scores quite well there.

While one study suggested outdoor sportspeople could have a 40% greater carbon footprint than other sports, in the study of the French runner who switched his flight to an international marathon for a train to a domestic one (see page 115), he had a footprint only 7% larger than the average citizen. And we saw that some run-commuting made him carbon neutral, so many runners' footprints can be small to negligible if they're largely acting conscientiously. A person playing tennis, meanwhile, is estimated to create 6% more emissions, while for a football fan it's 20%.

If a runner flies to five international races a year, buys new shoes every month and eats beef for breakfast, their footprint could be big, comfortably 20-plus tonnes of CO_2e in total. If a runner races domestically and travels by train, eats mostly plants and doesn't buy much new kit/stuff, it could be under 10 tonnes.

On a societal level (finally, that sociology degree is paying off), running is great for physical and mental health, extending quality of life. Exercise is 'the miracle cure we've always had', says the NHS. Healthcare is responsible for 3% of all UK emissions (8% in the US). Through reducing healthcare provision, points out Andrew Murray, 'running saves associated carbon emissions, costs to the state and even boosts work productivity. I'd call that a win!'

There are thousands of stories of people suffering with various difficulties and turning their lives around through running. You only have to pick up a running magazine to read them and I know of plenty myself. Running saves lives. (Although, come to think of it, that's not so great from a global CO_2e perspective.)

We're inspiring folk to get outdoors, get healthy and enjoy nature. Running has a huge positive impact. Yay running!

Also, says Andrew Murray, it's relevant to ask what we would be doing if we weren't running. In 2019 he spent 322 hours running, he calculates. 'What else would I have been doing with that time? Watching Netflix or other carbon-based

WE CAN'T RUN AWAY FROM THIS

entertainment. It's a bit of a stretch to say running has directly avoided these emissions, but it could be considered.'

How can running help?

Running has its bad bits. But it has its effing ace bits too. Really it was running, and specifically Dan Lawson and Charlotte Jalley, who galvanised me and many others, simply by talking about the Big Kerfufflefuck. Yes, it was going on all around me, but that seemed distant and not directly relevant to my life. **It wasn't until I could see issues in front of me, that involved me, in my beloved running that I suddenly felt affected.** I got interested.

We've heard how in the clothing industry, outdoor brands are leading the way in durability and other progressive ideas. We've heard how in the mass-participation world, they look towards trail and fell running for ideas. Indeed, many of these low-carbon actions are already commonplace among my runner pals, especially plan(e)t-based fuelling, low-plastic fuelling, making kit last and sharing it (it's expensive for many, after all), low-carbon travel, plogging ... (For balance, a downside of ultra-trail running is the glamour of the big races abroad, while in fell running it's the wilful erosion of terrain underfoot on unmarked courses.)

In sports nutrition and events worlds too, there's a bunch of people doing exciting climatey things, even though this initially dents profits. Also, though the clothing industry side of things is the darkest part of all of this, the people I spoke to really do care, have been behind some ethical innovations and are pushing for progress. And that's something.

I also felt a bit defensive of running. As we can see from this admittedly brief and unscientific discussion, running's actually pretty good compared to other activities, despite its inherent ills. And you know what else is ace about running? It's full of effing amazing people.

There's Dan and Charlotte of course, and Jim Mann, who are genuinely chang-ing things. 'Running wasn't setting me free,' says Dan of previous sponsorships. 'I was a cog in a machine. Running should be a simple, beautiful thing.' He felt happier not wearing a sponsor's logo and instead now runs entirely in second-hand clothes and shoes, sometimes mash-up versions (a 'new' shoe made from several others). ReRun Clothing are genuinely changing the world. They've planted some acorns.

It was US ultrarunning star Clare Gallagher who I first noticed discussing the climate crisis on social media, or rather she was 'Earth-raging'. I don't know Clare, but I know she has a marine conservation background, lobbies politicians, is outspoken about air pollution and protecting public lands, is an ambassador for

Winter Wildlands Alliance, is aligned with Protect our Winters and gives climate change talks at schools. She's come off social media, which is an almost unprecedented move for a sponsored athlete, but has an excellent series of well-informed blogs at *clare.run*. She's inspired me greatly, especially to speak out more.

Rosie Watson inspired me early on too. She's worked alongside Mike Berners-Lee as a carbon consultant, before starting her epic, albeit pandemic-interrupted run from UK to Mongolia, 'searching for stories of new ways to live, work and meet our needs in a time of climate crisis'. I thought that was just amazing. She's idealistic, passionate and well informed (watch the *New Story Run* film by Guy Loftus).

I love the phrase 'Tackle sustainability in a way that makes you feel most alive'. Someone who presumably felt very alive but also quite dead at times, is Agis Emmanouil, a fifty-two-year-old Greek man who ran 2,073 kilometres over fifty-one days from Athens to Glasgow for COP26, inspired by Sir David Attenborough's *A Life on Our Planet*. 'I was touched profoundly,' he told *Runner's World*. 'I started feeling humanity was hopeless and that I needed to do something to draw attention to climate change.' His epic run-commute saved 540 kilograms of CO_2e that a flight would have caused. Emma Hazeldine embarked on a similarly environmentally themed run, along the 630-mile South West Coast Path, in part to raise awareness for sea-level rise and coastal erosion in Devon and Cornwall, which became a short film, *Living on the Edge*.

I noticed when Es Tresidder broke the Charlie Ramsay Round record in 2019 that he was raising money for XR and discovered he's a certified Passivhaus designer, helping people build and retrofit houses that use 90% less energy. On his friend Finlay Wild's Instagram account I noticed the GP had been at climate protests, another seed linking running with climate change. 'Fast-paced international lifestyles have been sold as aspirational, and the inalienable right of the successful, but at what cost?' said Finlay, who has committed to only do races he can get to without flying, saying, 'I still have several lifetimes' worth to go at.'

Thirteen years ago, fellow doctor and fell runner Jon Morgan stopped flying and catches trains to races in Europe, while working with his club, Dark Peak Fell Runners, to organise minibuses to European events. 'It doesn't go unnoticed that the climate emergency is also a health emergency,' he says.

Kilian Jornet, the star of the mountain-ultra scene, has done impressive things away from the lumpy stuff too. He declared he's reducing travel to international races and launched The Outdoor Friendly Pledge, encouraging brands, events and athletes to sign up and pledge more sustainable behaviour. Then he launched the Kilian Jornet Foundation, which supports environmental projects such as the World Glacier Monitoring Service. And thirdly, with science communicator Huw

James, he co-launched the excellent Athlete Climate Academy, a series of expert interviews to help inform runners about climate change. His new sportswear range, NNormal, while adding to the huge amount of kit already in the world, looks to have impressive eco credentials which may raise the bar and force others to follow.

As well as doing proper science work on plastics, Stuart Walker started Runners Against Rubbish after feeling frustrated by the litter he found when training in the Peak District. The charity now has over 300 members and last year cleared the 630-mile South West Coast Path of litter in three days. Binners are winners!

Lindsay Buck is an even bigger winner. Known as the Wasdale Womble, she runs up Scafell Pike, the highest peak in England, most days, collecting rubbish. In 2018, she collected over 1,350 plastic bottles, 955 cans and lots of other litter from the Lake District.

Dan Lawson's GB twenty-four-hour running teammate, the record-breaking James Stewart, organises the Antonine Trail Race which offers cupless water stations and wooden medals, while also promoting litter picks. James has also done #OneYearNoGear (as has my mum!).

America's Kasie Enman was World Mountain Running Champion in 2011 and is also a maple-syrup farmer in Vermont who is passionate about land stewardship and sustainability ('an American Jim Mann', I was told) and writes about it for the World Mountain Running Association.

Jasmin Paris, who garnered global fame when she won the 260-mile Spine Race outright in 2019 while expressing milk for her baby daughter, has eschewed sponsor-ship, eats a mostly plant-based diet, uses low-carbon travel whenever possible and is a co-founder of The Green Runners.

Tina Muir is a US-based British former pro-athlete and mum who repeatedly features climate change on her popular podcast, *Running For Real*, and is co-writing a book a bit like this one but probably much better with the awesome Zoë Rom. Rich Roll is another runner with a huge platform, centred on his veganism.

Matt Hill and Steph Tait ran across Canada and around the perimeter of America, totalling 11,000 miles, doing over 420 marathons on the Run for One Planet, an ongoing run endeavour focused on 'Inspiring environmental action, one step at a time'.

Running Up For Air is a running-based climate activism challenge to highlight air pollution, initiated by Tara Warren and three-time Barkley Marathons finisher Jared Campbell over a decade ago and supported by Patagonia. It started as 'just a few friends trudging through the snow' and is now a race series across several US states, and the climbing community have co-opted in too with Climbing Up For Air.

My Santiago-based friend, ultrarunner, environmentalist and investigative journalist Matthew Maynard not only took the Running Up For Air idea to Chile, but had a huge win in stopping multinational mining due to the damage it was causing to glaciers.

Dakota Jones, who has joined Clare Gallagher in lobbying politicians in-person, famously cycles long distances to races where feasible. 'I want to understand my impact on the world and how I can mitigate and improve it,' he says on his website. 'The environmental issues we face today are formidable, but there's no point in going forward without hope … This will be painful, but it has the potential to be incredibly inspiring too, and I'm excited to see what we can accomplish together.' His Footprints Running Camp sees every camper work on a climate-friendly project which they will take home and implement in their own community.

Christopher Gaskin takes on epic running challenges, such as the Wainwrights (214 Lake District fells) and the Pennine Way (quite a lot of bog), but does so solo and unsupported. The former Special Forces man knows this approach saves many kilograms of CO_2e by not having the big support crew these attempts usually have.

Ultra-trail running stars Sweden's Emelie Forsberg (partner to Kilian) and Brazil's Fernanda Maciel have been outspoken about their advocacy. 'The challenge of climate change is too big to be solved by individuals alone', noted Emelie on a blog of sustainability tips on her previous watch sponsor's website. 'System change is required.'

In other sports, gold-medal canoeist Etienne Stott MBE co-founded Champions For Earth, encouraging athletes to speak out about climate change. Equally impressively, he has been arrested ten times and convicted twice for public order offences (i.e. sitting in a road).

Similarly, America's EcoAthletes is a team of athletes and academics, climate scientists, journalists and others 'devoted to identifying & equipping the Jackie Robinsons and the Megan Rapinoes of the climate crisis to lead climate action'. Protect Our Winters sprang up from the US snowsports scene but is doing great things over here too and I feel grateful for their help in educating and empowering me.

Not forgetting Paralympic gold-medallist James Brown, who was jailed for a year for climate protests involving a plane and some strong glue. Kate Rawles and Lee Craigie have done great things too.

I could go on and on. I'm sure I've missed out some amazing people doing amazing things. But the point is that, actually, running is doing a fuckton of good. Instead of asking how bad is running, I find I want to shout, 'How good is running?!'

Also, I know lots of runners, including the very best in the world, who really make their kit last, who are really considerate about their travel and hate the very occasional times they feel there's no option but to fly, who turn away inviting sponsorship offers and/or who are 95% vegan, but aren't necessarily comfortable being public about this stuff. And numerous unfamous runners doing the same and more.

Indeed, several runners and sustainability experts mentioned in this book joined Dan and Charlotte, some other ace folk and me to set up The Green Runners, which launched in April 2022. Let's just say the discussion about whether we should produce T-shirts was a short one.

The community of runners 'making changes for a fitter planet' operates on Four Pillars: how you move (i.e. travel), how you kit up, how you eat and how you speak out – to me the most important one. We launched on Earth Day 2022 and were bowled over by interest, from hundreds of sign-ups, media and brands. All we ask is that members make at least one pledge for the year, according to one of the pillars. That's it, really – though we hope they'll get involved in some collective efforts we have planned too. I'm confident it will turn into something special. It already is. Please come join us. Together we WILL make a difference. We won't stop the ice sheets melting on our own, but we're already planting more acorns.

Other founding members include the irrepressible Darren Evans, Ellie Wardell, Ajay Hanspal (the man with the big idea!), Jasmin Paris, Todd Mackintosh, Nina Davies, Chris Zair, Russell Bentley, Emma Hazeldine, James Williams, Taz Babiker, David Starley and Andrew Murray.

Anyway, I'm in a much better mood now. I feel real optimism. But enough of all that. I'm off out for a run. Thanks for listening. You really should put this book down now. But you didn't think I'd let you go without one last climate change joke, did you?

Why is climate change good for shy people at parties? It's a good ice breaker.
#sorrynotsorry

ACKNOWLEDGEMENTS

Thanks firstly to Dan Lawson and Charlotte Jalley for sounding the alarm in the running world.

Thanks to Greta Thunberg, David Attenborough, Extinction Rebellion and all the scientists and authors for sounding the alarm to the wider world.

Heartfelt thanks to all the utterly ace folk at Vertebrate Publishing, especially Kirsty Reade for being well skill at this stuff in every way and unreasonably patient and well brill to work with, the astonishingly thorough and forgiving Emma Lockley (editing), Jane Beagley and Rosie Edwards (design), Moira Hunter (proofreading), Shona Henderson (ebook and audiobook versions), John Coefield (production and marketing), Lorna Brogan and Becky Wales (marketing), Sophie Fletcher (office manager), Col Perkins (the critical role of actually sending books to customers) and of course their idiosyncratic leader Jon Barton.

Thank you to the wonderful experts and industry insiders who put up with numerous stupid questions and often went above and beyond with time and critical feedback, plus runners and friends who shared ideas, inspired me or read through bits of this nonsense and sagely suggested how it could be less bobbins. They are: Bodil Oudshoorn, Helen Stuart, Andrew Murray, Anne Prahl, Laurent Vandepaer, Charles Ross, Ellie Wardell, Rosie Watson, Stuart Walker, Renee McGregor, Kate Chapman, Megan Hunt, Shane Ohly, Lucy Scrase, Chris Zair, Jim Mann, Kilian Jornet, Huw James, Dave Erasmus, Laura Hendy, Ellen West and all at Our Carbon, Alex Hutchinson, Boff Whalley, Zoë Rom, Danny McLoughlin, David O'Brien, James Thurlow, Kris King, David Moulding, POW UK's Paul Atkinson and Dom Winter, Terry Chiplin, Tim Laney, Finlay Wild, Nathan Roulson, Tim Bevan, Sean Ross, Sophie Power, Jimmy Hyland, David Starley, Tom Hill, Alex Copping, Des Tinney, David Roche, Jasmin Paris, Ella Revitt, Dale Vince, Mark Townsend, Ben Hart and Rob Lewis, the industry folk who spoke to me anonymously and probably some really helpful people who I've forgotten in this very tired moment long after my third deadline, sorry and thank you so much.

Not forgetting all The Green Runners, the Bath Bats, Corsham Running Club, my ace-in-the-hole coached athletes, plus Ryan, Matt, Barbara, Kelvin, Rose, Susannah and, of course, Amy, Indy and Leif.

RESOURCES

How I learnt about the Big Kerfufflefuck

Books

How Bad Are Bananas?, Mike Berners-Lee – the bible for personal footprints and a brilliant introduction to the whole thing. More entertaining than it sounds (and – spoiler alert – bananas aren't that bad).

There Is No Planet B, Mike Berners-Lee – a more societal perspective. What are the most pressing concerns?

The Sustainable(ish) Living Guide, Jen Gale – back to the individual, household, day-to-day stuff, but always with that idea that none of us are perfect.

How To Save Our Planet, Mark Maslin – Just. The. Facts. Makes the problems and solutions all seem simple.

The New Climate War, Michael E. Mann – how Big Oil knew all along and has actively delayed solutions. Warning: this book will make you angry.

Saving Us, Katharine Hayhoe – this one, from North America's joint-pre-eminent climate scientist, is more hopeful.

The Joyful Environmentalist, Isabel Losada – this is brill too. The doom is absent as Isabel tries to work it all out.

Consumed, Aja Barber – good for fashion, overconsumption, inequality, racism and thoughts on why we consume the way we do.

The Future We Choose, Christiana Figueres and Tom Rivett-Carnac – as the title suggests, this is galvanising and optimistic, passionate and well informed.

There were many more, sometimes mentioned in relevant chapters. But those were the most useful.

Websites

Oxford University's Our World in Data (*OurWorldinData.org*) has been a priceless resource, especially for food and travel.

The BBC, *Guardian* and *Independent* websites are all very useful for finding quick info.

co2everything.com is a fun way to determine the CO2e of many things.

runrepeat.com has some ace research on it.

trailrunnermag.com is where Zoë Rom and David Roche write well-brill things.

irunfar.com is also essential reading for distance runners.

Podcasts

Dale Vince's Zerocarbonista

Jon Richardson and the Futurenauts

Sustainababble

Films

A Life on our Planet (2020) – Sir David Attenborough's depressing but galvanising witness statement.

Cowspiracy (2014) – explores the impacts of animal agriculture on the environment.

Don't Look Up (2021) – Leonardo DiCaprio and Meryl Streep star in an alarming, too-close-to-the-bone satire.

Kiss The Ground (2020) – surprisingly undull, Woody-Harrelson-narrated look at earth with a small 'e'.

Milked (2021) – an exposé of New Zealand's dairy industry and its epic footprint.

Rebellion (2022) – a revealing, behind-the-scenes look at XR's early days.

Seaspiracy (2021) – an exposé of the fishing industry.

Trashed (2012) – Jeremy Irons uncovers the horrors of plastic pollution.

Organisations

Athlete Climate Academy, *anturus.co.uk*

Carbon Literacy Training, *carbonliteracy.com*

Champions 4 Earth, *championsforearth.com*

Council For Responsible Sport, *councilforresponsiblesport.org*

Don't Look Up Climate Platform, *dontlookup.count-us-in.com*

Eco Athletes, *ecoathletes.org*

Ellen MacArthur Foundation, *ellenmacarthurfoundation.org*

Ethical Consumer, *ethicalconsumer.org*

Extinction Rebellion, *extinctionrebellion.uk*

Friends of the Earth, *friendsoftheearth.uk*

Good on You, *goodonyou.eco*

Grantham Institute, *imperial.ac.uk/grantham*

Greenpeace UK, *greenpeace.org.uk*

GreenSportsBlog, *greensportsblog.com*

Insulate Britain, *insulatebritain.com*

IPCC (Intergovernmental Panel on Climate Change), *ipcc.ch*

Just Stop Oil, *juststopoil.org*

Kilian Jornet's Outdoor Friendly Pledge, *outdoorfriendly.org*

Our Carbon, *ourcarbon.com*

Project Drawdown, *drawdown.org/solutions*

Protect Our Winters UK, *protectourwinters.uk*, *protectourwinters.org*

ReRunClothing, *rerunclothing.org*

Running On Carbon, *runningoncarbon.wordpress.com*

Surfers Against Sewage, *sas.org.uk*

The Green Runners, *thegreenrunners.com*

Trees Not Tees, *treesnottees.com*

For kit repair

3rd Rock, *3rdrockclothing.com/blogs/news/3rd-rock-repair-club*

Alpkit, *alpkit.com/pages/repair-station* – including re-waterproofing jackets and revitalising down jackets

Berghaus Repairhaus, *berghaus.com/repairs.list*

Buffalo Systems, *buffalosystems.co.uk/advice/faq/categories/special-services/*

Cheshire Shoe Repairs, *cheshireshoe.co.uk*

Cotswold Outdoor, *cotswoldoutdoor.com/repair-and-care.html* – including jackets and sleeping bags

Dannah, *dannah.uk.com*

Down Cleaning, *downcleaning.co.uk*

George Fisher (Keswick, the Lake District), *georgefisher.co.uk* – they offer an in-house, one-day re-waterproofing service, plus testing and even poles

Feet First (Chesterfield, Derbyshire), *resoles.co.uk*

Johnson, *johnsoncleaners.com* – the high-street drycleaners, offer kit repair services

Montane, *montane.com* – including patch and panel repair, stitching repairs, seam re-taping and zip slider repair

Lancashire Sports Repairs, *lancashiresportsrepairs.co.uk*

Llanberis Resoles, *llanberisresoles.com*

Mulch Repairs (based in Sheffield), *mulchandthebrokenthing.co* – kit (including zip) repairs, plus rucksacks, tents, sleeping bags, upcycling options

Oxwash, *oxwash.com*

Patagonia, *eu.patagonia.com/gb/en/home*

Rab, *rab.equipment*

Sheffield Clothing Repair, *sheffieldclothingrepair.com*

Tiso, *tiso.com*

Timpson, *timpson.co.uk* – clothing and boot repairs, including zips, inner membranes and leather uppers

Vango, *www.vango.co.uk/gb* – tents, sleeping bags, etc.

Also see the following list from The British Mountaineering Council: *thebmc.co.uk/where-can-I-reuse-repair-recycle-my-outdoor-climbing-hiking-gear*

For kit reuse

A Mile in Her Shoes, *amileinhershoes.org.uk*

Alpkit, *alpkit.com* – will take unwanted kit from any brand and find it a new home as part of their Continuum Project

Bags of Support, *bagsofsupport.co.uk*

Blue Bird Exchange, *bluebirdexchange.co.uk* – reclaiming, repairing and redistributing outdoor gear, Edinburgh area

Cotswold Outdoor, *cotswoldoutdoor.com*

Crackpacs, *crackpacs.com*

Crisis, *crisis.org.uk*

Decathlon: Second Life, *secondlife.decathlon.co.uk* – marked or quickly tested products

Dirtbags Climbing, *dirtbagsclimbing.co.uk*

eBay and Gumtree can be useful places to pass on unwanted kit

Ellis Brigham, *ellis-brigham.com* – working with homeless charities to give outdoor gear a second life

Gift Your Gear (providing donated outdoor clothing and equipment to communities)

Green Peak Gear, *greenpeakgear.org*

I Collect Clothes, *icollectclothes.co.uk*

Kit Collective, *kitcollective.co.uk* – they encourage diversity in the outdoors and may want your donations

Mountain Warehouse, *regain-app.com* – donate unwanted clothing to a charity and receive discount vouchers

Osprey, *ospreyeurope.com/gb_en/secondlife-account* – ex-sample and pre-loved, repaired rucksacks

Outdoor Gear Exchange and Outdoor Kit Exchange – useful Facebook groups for buying and selling unwanted gear

Outdoor Gear For Good, *outdoorgearforgood.com/who-benefits* – they take excess outdoor clothing, supply approved outdoor-related charities, recycle in the best way that they know, with profits going to charity

Outdoor groups such as Girl Guides, Scouts and Duke of Edinburgh accept functional kit.

Preloved Sports, *prelovedsports.org.uk* – resell your pre-loved kit, with money going to charity

Rab, *rab.equipment* – piloting a down collection scheme for worn-out down products like duvets, pillows, jackets and sleeping bags

Refugee Council, *refugeecouncil.org.uk*

Rohan, *rohan.co.uk/giftyourgear* – they have a Gift Your Gear scheme which supports various charities, as long as gear is useable

Run Again, *runagain.uk* – similar to ReRun

Runners Need, *runnersneed.com/about-us/recyclemyrun.html* and *runnersneed.com/recycle-my-gear.html*

Shelter, *shelter.org.uk*

Shoe Aid, *shoeaid.co.uk*

Snow+Rock, *snowandrock.com*

Switchback Clothing Co, *switchbackclothing.co*

The North Face Clothes the Loop programme, *thenorthface.com/en-us/about-us/responsibility/product/clothes-the-loop* – works with the Stuffstr app to redistribute kit (regardless of condition or brand)

Also consider donating to local homeless (via *homeless.org.uk*) or refugee charities, or council clothing recycling banks.

Perhaps arrange a swap shop at your running club? Maybe fellow runners would happily adopt your unwanted tops? Also see Swap Box (*instagram.com/theswapboxcornwall*)

For kit recycling

The final option. Kerbside recycling is appropriate for most clothing, the next option being clothing banks at council recycling centres. See also:

Jog On Again, *jogonagain.com*

Recycle Now, *recyclenow.com*

SOEX, *soex.de* (La Sportiva also take unwanted kit at limited stores and recycle via SOEX)

TerraCycle, *terracycle.com* – a recycling and waste management company; they will accept almost anything through their recycling programmes. They recycle backpacks and sunglasses to crisp packets (though it can cost).

United Shoe Recycling Company, *unitedshoe.co.uk/cash-for-shoes*

For races

A Greener Festival, *agreenerfestival.com*

Athletes for a Fit Planet, *afitplanet.com*

Council for Responsible Sport, 'Where We Stand: How Responsible Is Your Event?', *councilforresponsiblesport*

Department for Environment, Food and Rural Affairs, 'Sustainable Events Guide', *gov.uk/government/organisations/department-for-environment-food-rural-affairs*

Ecolibrium, *ecolibrium.earth* – has toolkits, a carbon calculator and more resources

EcoScore, from the Council for Responsible Sport, tracks environmental and social responsibility progress of events, via a free app: *councilforresponsiblesport.org/rescore*

GreenSportsBlog, *greensportsblog.com*

International Olympic Committee, 'Sustainability Essentials': various downloads, *olympics.com/ioc/sustainability/essentials*

Kilian Jornet's Outdoor Friendly Pledge, *outdoorfriendly.org*

Positive Impact Events toolkit, *positiveimpactevents.com*

Runners For Public Lands' toolkit, *runnersforpubliclands.org*

SME Climate Hub, a UK government-backed initiative to help small and medium-sized business cut emissions, *smeclimatehub.org*

Sport For Good, 'Environmental Action Toolkit', *laureusuk.blob.core.windows.net/laureus/ laureus/media/laureus/news/2021/environmental-action-toolkit.pdf*

Sports Environmental Alliance, *sportsenvironmentalliance.org*

United Nations Sport for Climate Action Framework, *unfccc.int/climate-action/sectoral-engagement/sports-for-climate-action*

Vision 2025, *vision2025.org.uk*

Zero Waste Scotland, 'How to Plan and Deliver Environmentally Sustainable Events', *energy. zerowastescotland.org.uk*

REFERENCES

Chapter 1 How bad is running?

i   Rosie Watson (26 June 2020), 'Building a sustainable outdoor community after COVID-19', AdventureUncovered.com

ii   Ipsos (April 2021), 'Perils of Perception: environmental perils'.

iii   Richard A. Lovett (30 August 2021), 'The Autumn Olympics? How the Games may have to adapt to globally warming summers', *Outside*. The cited study is K.R. Smith, A. Woodward et al. (2016), 'The last Summer Olympics? Climate change, health, and work outdoors', *The Lancet* 388:10045, pp.642–644.

iv   Paul Ronto (6 August 2021), 'How much is climate change slowing down runners?', RunRepeat.com

v   Niels de Hoog (25 January 2022), 'Rising temperatures threaten future of Winter Olympics, say experts', *Guardian*.

vi   Oliver Milman (9 February 2021), '"Invisible killer": fossil fuels caused 8.7m deaths globally in 2018, research finds', *Guardian*.

vii   P. Wicker (2018), 'The carbon footprint of active sport participants', *Sport Management Review*, 22:10.1016.

Chapter 2 Shoespiracy

i   Original EMF research: Ellen MacArthur Foundation, 'A New Textiles Economy: redesigning fashion's future' (1 December 2017).

ii   Environmental Audit Committee of the House of Commons (19 February 2019), 'Fixing fashion: clothing consumption and sustainability'.

iii   Molly Hanson (23 April 2021), *Outside*. Figures from Danny McLoughlin (6 August 2021), 'All eco sneakers do is kill the planet a little bit slower [study]', RunRepeat.

iv   Global Action Plan #Idontbuyit, 'Social media advertising blamed for teenagers 58 million trainer mountain'.

v   Jennifer Chu (22 May 2013), 'Footwear's (carbon) footprint', MIT News. The cited study is L. Cheah, N. Duque Ciceri et al. (2013), 'Manufacturing-focused emissions reductions in footwear production', *Journal of Cleaner Production*, 44, pp.18–29.

vi   Molly Hanson (13 November 2020), 'Running shoes are part of an environmental crisis. Is change coming?', PodiumRunner.com. A detailed breakdown can be found in: Danny McLoughlin (6 August 2021), 'All eco sneakers do is kill the planet a little bit slower [study]', RunRepeat.com

vii   Tansy Hoskins (30 March 2020), 'What your shoes are doing to the world', traid.org.uk.

viii   Billy Saundry (8 July 2020), 'Ethical Trainers', EthicalConsumer.org

ix   Fraunhofer Umsicht, 'Kunststoffe in der Umwelt: Mikro- und Makroplastik'.

x   Elizabeth L. Cline (13 February 2020), 'Ask a sustainability expert: how do I recycle my worn-out shoes?', Fashionista.com

xi   Centre for Sustainable Manufacturing and Reuse/Recycling Technologies (SMART), Loughborough University (December 2007), 'Recycling of Footwear Products' position paper.

xii   David Moulding (2020), 'A critical investigation into the attitudes and behaviours of runners in the UK towards climate change and the environmental impact of their sport'.

xiii   familiesafield.org, 'Sports injury study: total injuries ranked by sport'.

xiv   *Runner's World* (3 December 2020), 'Do running shoes cause or prevent injury?'

xv   B.T. Saragiotto, T.P. Yamato & A.D. Lopes (2014), 'What do recreational runners think about risk factors for running injuries? A descriptive study of their beliefs and opinions', *The Journal of Orthopaedic and Sports Physical Therapy*, 44(10), pp.733–738.

xvi   W. van Mechelen (1992), 'Running injuries. A review of the epidemiological literature', *Sports Medicine* (Auckland, N.Z.), 14(5), pp.320–335.

xvii   E.B. Lohman 3rd, K.S. Balan Sackiriyas & R.W. Swen (2011), 'A comparison of the spatiotemporal parameters, kinematics, and biomechanics between shod, unshod, and minimally supported running as compared to walking', *Physical Therapy in Sport*, 12(4), pp.151–163.

xviii   L. Malisoux, L., R.O. Nielsen, A. Urhausen & D. Theisen (2015), 'A step towards understanding the mechanisms of running-related injuries', *Journal of Science and Medicine in Sport*, 18(5), pp.523–528.
        B.T. Saragiotto, T.P. Yamato et al. (2014), 'What are the main risk factors for running-related injuries?', *Sports Medicine* (Auckland, N.Z.), 44(8), pp.1153–1163.

xix   C.E. Richards, P.J. Magin & R. Callister (2009), 'Is your prescription of distance running shoes evidence-based?', *British Journal of Sports Medicine*, 43(3), pp.159–162.

xx   L. Malisoux & D. Theisen (2020), 'Can the "Appropriate" Footwear Prevent Injury in Leisure-Time Running? Evidence Versus Beliefs', *Journal of Athletic Training*, 55(12), pp.1215–1223.

xxi   L.A. Kelly, G.A. Lichtwark, D.J. Farris & A. Cresswell (2016), 'Shoes alter the spring-like function of the human foot during running', *Journal of the Royal Society Interface*, 13.
        J.P. Kulmala, J. Kosonen, J. Nurminen et al. (2018), 'Running in highly cushioned shoes increases leg stiffness and amplifies impact loading', *Scientific Reports*, 8, 17496.

xxii   J. Hamill & B.T. Bates (1988), 'A kinetic evaluation of the effects of in vivo loading on running shoes', *Journal of Orthopaedic & Sports Physical Therapy*, 10(2), pp.47–53.

xxiii   B. Nigg, J. Baltich, S. Hoerzer et al. (2015), 'Running shoes and running injuries: myth-busting and a proposal for two new paradigms: "preferred movement path" and "comfort filter"', *British Journal of Sports Medicine*, 49, pp.1290–1294.

xxiv   Hailey Middlebrook (30 April 2019), 'Do mega-cushioned shoes increase or reduce injuries? It's complicated', *Runner's World*.
        C.D. Pollard, J.A. Ter Har, J.J. Hannigan & M.F. Norcross (2018), 'Influence of Maximal Running Shoes on Biomechanics Before and After a 5K Run', *Orthopaedic Journal of Sports Medicine*, 6(6):2325967118775720.
        Alex Hutchinson (7 May 2022), 'Untangling running's shoe cushioning paradox', *Outside*.

xxv   E.M. Hennig (2011), 'Eighteen years of running shoe testing in Germany – a series of biomechanical studies', *Footwear Science*, 3(2), pp.71–81.

Chapter 3 Getting T-shirty

i   According to research by David Moulding for his MSc Sports Business Management thesis, 'A critical investigation into the attitudes and behaviours of runners in the UK towards climate change and the environmental impact of their sport', and to a ReRun Clothing survey of 750 runners.

ii   Hillary S. Kativa (3 October 2016), 'Synthetic Threads', Science History Institute.

iii   Tansy E. Hoskins (2020), *Foot Work: What Your Shoes Are Doing to the World*, p.25.

iv   Pauline Op de Beeck (29 March 2018), 'Three sustainability trends shaping the future of the fashion industry', carbontrust.com

v   Chenxing Wang, Lihua Wang et al. (2015), 'Carbon footprint of textile throughout its life cycle: a case study of Chinese cotton shirts', *Journal of Cleaner Production*, 108(A), pp.464–475.

vi   Helle Abelik-Lawson (29 November 2019), '9 reasons to quit fast fashion', greenpeace. org.uk

vii   Andrew Brooks (2015), *Clothing Poverty: The Hidden World of Fast Fashion and Second-Hand Clothes*, Zed Books Ltd.

viii   Peter Kalmus (4 November 2021), 'Climate depression is real. And it is spreading fast among our youth', *Guardian.*

ix   Ethical Trading Initiative (2016), 'Corporate Leadership on Modern Slavery' report.

x   World Vision, 'Forced and child labour in the cotton industry'.

xi   'Child labour in the fashion supply chain', *labs.theguardian.com/unicef-child-labour/*

xii   Environmental Audit Committee of the House of Commons (19 February 2019), 'Fixing fashion: clothing consumption and sustainability'.

xiii   Tamsin Blanchard (24 April 2018), 'Fashion Revolution Week: seven ways to get involved', *Guardian.*

xiv   Changing Markets Foundation (2021), 'Fossil Fashion: the hidden reliance of fast fashion on fossil fuels'.

xv   Fredric Bauer and Tobias Dan Nielsen (2 November 2021), 'Oil companies are ploughing money into fossil-fuelled plastics production at a record rate – new research', *The Conversation.*

xvi   Tom Perkins (31 August 2021), 'Toxic "forever chemicals" contaminate indoor air at worrying levels, study finds', *Guardian.*

xvii   I.T. Cousins, J.H. Johansson et al. (2022), 'Outside the safe operating space of a new planetary boundary for per– and polyfluoralkyl substances (PFAS)', *Environmental Science & Technology*, 56:16, 11172–11179.

xviii   L. Persson, B.M. Carney Almroth et al. (2022), 'Outside the Safe Operating Space of the Planetary Boundary for Novel Entities', *Environmental Science & Technology*, 56(3), pp.1510–1521.

xix   H.A. Leslie, M.J.M. van Velzen et al. (2022), 'Discovery and quantification of plastic particle pollution in human blood', *Environment International*, 163:107199.

xx   L.C. Jenner, J.M. Rotchell et al. (2022), 'Detection of microplastics in human lung tissue using μFTIR spectroscopy', *Science of The Total Environment*, 831:154907.

xxi   Damian Carrington (12 January 2021), 'Clothes washing linked to "pervasive" plastic pollution in the Arctic', *Guardian.*

xxii   M. Eriksen, L.C.M. Lebreton et al. (2014), 'Plastic Pollution in the world's oceans: more than 5 trillion plastic pieces weighing over 250,000 tons afloat at sea', *PLOS ONE.*

xxiii   Adam Vaughan (17 December 2014), 'Microplastic deposits found deep in world's oceans and seas', *Guardian.*

xxiv   Ben Chapman (4 February 2021), 'Fashion industry has development "dangerous addiction" to fossil fuels, say campaign groups', *Independent.*

xxv   Damian Carrington (21 January 2022), 'Nanoplastic pollution found at both of Earth's poles for first time', *Guardian.*

xxvi   Nick Lavars (23 November 2021), 'Mouse study shows microplastics infiltrate blood brain barrier', newatlas.com

xxvii   S.B. Fournier, J.N. D'Errico, D.S. Adler et al. (2020), 'Nanopolystyrene translocation and fetal deposition after acute lung exposure during late-stage pregnancy', *Particle and Fibre Toxicology*, 17:55.

xxviii   Environmental Audit Committee of the House of Commons (19 February 2019), 'Fixing fashion: clothing consumption and sustainability'.

xxix   Ellen MacArthur Foundation, 'Design and the circular economy'.

xxx   Kirsten Brodde (2 March 2017), 'What are microfibers and why are our clothes polluting the oceans?', greenpeace.org xxxi Andrew Brooks (2015), 'The ethics of fast fashion', rgs.org

xxxii Elizabeth L. Cline (13 February 2020), 'Ask a sustainability expert: how do I recycle my worn-out shoes?', fashionista.com

xxxiii BBC News (6 February), 'The fast fashion graveyard in Chile's Atacama Desert'.

xxxiv Environmental Audit Committee of the House of Commons (19 February 2019), 'Fixing fashion: clothing consumption and sustainability'.

xxxv Harriet Agerholm (19 June 2019), 'Fast fashion: should we change how we think about clothes?', BBC News.

xxxvi J.A. Roberts & A. Clement (2007), 'Materialism and Satisfaction with Over-All Quality of Life and Eight Life Domains', *Social Indicators Research*, 82, pp.79–92.

xxxvii Christine Ro (11 March 2020), 'Can fashion ever be sustainable?', BBC Future.

xxxviii WRAP (2012), 'Valuing our clothes'.

Chapter 4 Industry illusions

i Danny McLoughlin (6 August 2021), 'All eco sneakers do is kill the planet a little bit slower [study]', RunRepeat.com

ii Tansy E. Hoskins (21 March 2020), '"Some soles last 1,000 years in landfill": the truth about the sneaker mountain', *Guardian*.

iii gov.uk press release (28 January 2021), 'Global sweep finds 40% of firms' green claims could be misleading'.

iv Nike, FY14/15 Sustainable Business Report. Chief Sustainability Officer Hannah Jones commented, 'We've set a moonshot challenge to double our business with half the impact.'

v Billy Saundry (8 July 2020), 'Ethical trainers', EthicalConsumer.org

vi Changing Markets Foundation (March 2022), 'Licence to greenwash'.

vii The Climate Board (2021), 'Friction Points in Fashion & Textiles'.

viii Josie Wexler (20 August 2021), 'The carbon cost of clothing', EthicalConsumer.org

ix 'Why making clothes from plastic bottles is a false solution', citytosea.org.uk

x Changing Markets Foundation (March 2022), 'Fossil Fashion'.

xi L. Geng, X. Cheng et al. (2016), 'Can Previous Pro-Environmental Behaviours Influence Subsequent Environmental Behaviours? The Licensing Effect of Pro-Environmental Behaviours', *Journal of Pacific Rim Psychology*, 10(E9).

xii designlife-cycle.com (13 March 2018), 'Bamboo Rayon: Raw Materials'.

xiii Emma Bryce (6 November 2021), 'Are clothes made from recycled materials really more sustainable?', *Guardian*.

xiv K. Laitala, I.G. Klepp & B. Henry (2018), 'Does Use Matter? Comparison of Environmental Impacts of Clothing Based on Fiber Type', *Sustainability* 10:2524.

xv Environmental Audit Committee of the House of Commons (19 February 2019), 'Fixing fashion: clothing consumption and sustainability'.

xvi Ruth Strange (23 February 2022), 'Ethical sportswear', EthicalConsumer.org

xvii slowfactory.earth, 'Stop fashion-related deforestation in the Amazon'.

xviii Marisa Meltzer (7 March 2017), 'Patagonia and The North Face: saving the world – one puffer jacket at a time', *Guardian*.

xix Vincent Stanley (22 April 2021), 'How Patagonia learned to act on its values', *Yale Insights*.

xx Sina Horsthemke (15 February 2021), 'Climate protection: can the running industry keep up with the outdoor industry?', ispo.com

xxi Heather Higinbotham (29 March 2022), 'You're an eco-hypocrite, but it's not your fault – you've been sold a recycling lie', *Independent*.

Chapter 5   Racing away from net zero

i   A. Collins, C. Jones & M. Munday (2009), 'Assessing the environmental impacts of mega sporting events: two options?', *Tourism Management*, 30(6), pp.828–837.

ii   Kate Carter (3 October 2013), 'Are running events an environmental disaster?', *Guardian*.

iii   Kate Carter (13 February 2020), 'The greenest races in the UK', *Runner's World*.

iv   Council for Responsible Sport, 'Climate impacts & endurance events'.

v   Climate Neutral Group (24 May 2019), 'Carbon tax bill signing into law by Ramaphosa'; and Schneider Electric Marathon de Paris press release (1 March 2018), 'A committed marathon'.

vi   George Monbiot (29 October 2006), 'How sport is killing the planet', *Guardian*.

vii   A. Collins, M. Munday & Run 4 Wales (2019), 'Cardiff half-marathon: the race for sustainability'.

viii   L. Castaignède, F. Veny , J. Edwards & V. Billat (2021), 'The Carbon Footprint of Marathon Runners: Training and Racing', *International Journal of Environmental Research and Public Health*, 18(5): 2769.

ix   David Moulding (2020), 'A critical investigation into the attitudes and behaviours of runners in the UK towards climate change and the environmental impact of their sport'.

Chapter 6   Great training?

i   Rosie Watson (26 June 2020), 'Building a sustainable outdoor community after COVID-19', AdventureUncovered.com

ii   Hannah Ritchie (22 October 2020), 'Climate change and flying: what share of global CO2 emissions come from aviation?', OurWorldinData.org

iii   M. Klower et al. (2021), 'Quantifying aviation's contribution to global warming', *Environmental Research Letters*, 16:10.

iv   Andy Hoskins (8 February 2022), 'Mike Berners-Lee: Business travel's difficult relationship with carbon emissions', *Business Travel News Europe*.

v   S. Gössling, P. Hannah et al. (2019), 'Can we fly less? Evaluating the "necessity" of air travel', *Journal of Air Transport Management*, 81:101722.

vi   Damian Carrington (17 November 2020), '1% of people cause half of global aviation emissions – study', *Guardian*.

vii   Andy Hoskins (8 February 2022), 'Mike Berners-Lee: Business travel's difficult relationship with carbon emissions', *Business Travel News Europe*.

viii   L. Castaignède, F. Veny , J. Edwards & V. Billat (2021), 'The Carbon Footprint of Marathon Runners: Training and Racing', *International Journal of Environmental Research and Public Health*, 18(5): 2769.

ix   Andy Hoskins (8 February 2022), 'Mike Berners-Lee: Business travel's difficult relationship with carbon emissions', *Business Travel News Europe*.

x   'Less stuff, more joy', takethejump.org

xi   Hannah Ritchie (6 October 2020), 'Cars, planes, trains: where do CO2 emissions from transport come from?', OurWorldinData.org

xii   David Moulding (2020), 'A critical investigation into the attitudes and behaviours of runners in the UK towards climate change and the environmental impact of their sport'.

xiii   Mike Berners-Lee (2021), *There Is No Planet B*, Cambridge University Press.

xiv   Andy Hoskins (8 February 2022), 'Mike Berners-Lee: Business travel's difficult relationship with carbon emissions', *Business Travel News Europe*

xv   *Which?* (14 July 2021), 'UK domestic flights nearly 50% cheaper than the train, but six times worse for carbon'.

xvi   Andy Hoskins (8 February 2022), 'Mike Berners-Lee: Business travel's difficult relationship with carbon emissions', *Business Travel News Europe*.

xvii   Rosie Watson (26 June 2020), 'Building a sustainable outdoor community after COVID-19', AdventureUncovered.com

xviii   David Moulding (2020), 'A critical investigation into the attitudes and behaviours of runners in the UK towards climate change and the environmental impact of their sport'.

xix   M.J. Davies, E. Hungenberg & T.J. Aicher (2019), 'The relationship between runner environmental paradigm and their motives to participate in an urban or rural marathon', *International Journal of Event and Festival Management.*

Chapter 7   The planet-based diet

i   A. Reguant-Closa, A. Roesch et al. (2020), 'The Environmental Impact of the Athlete's Plate Nutrition Education Tool', *Nutrients*, 12(8), 2484.

ii   Hannah Ritchie & Max Roser, 'Emissions by sector', OurWorldinData.org

iii   Renee McGregor (2022), *More Fuel You*, Vertebrate Publishing.

iv   Damian Carrington (31 May 2018), 'Avoiding meat and dairy is the "single biggest way" to reduce your impact on Earth', *Guardian.*

v   J. Poore & T. Nemecek (2018), 'Reducing food's environmental impacts through producers and consumers, *Science*, 360, pp.987–992.

vi   Natalie Brown (7 July 2022), '7 reasons why meat is so bad for the environment', greenpeace.org.uk

vii   Greenpeace (5 August 2020), 'How JBS is still slaughtering the Amazon', greenpeace.org.uk

viii   Damian Carrington (7 March 2022), 'Climate crisis: Amazon rainforest tipping point is looming, data shows', *Guardian.*

ix   Damian Carrington (19 June 2020), 'Why you should go animal-free: 18 arguments for eating meat debunked', *Guardian.*

x   United Nations Convention to Combat Desertification, 'Global Land Outlooks: second edition'.

xi   Food and Agriculture Organization of the United Nations LEAD Initiative (2006), 'Livestock's long shadow'.

xii   Damian Carrington (14 September 2021), 'Nearly all global farm subsidies harm people and planet – UN', *Guardian.*

xiii   George Monbiot (11 July 2017), 'The Lake District's world heritage site status is a betrayal of the living world', *Guardian.*

xiv   George Monbiot (19 May 2017), 'Fell Purpose', monbiot.com

xv   Food and Agriculture Organization of the United Nations, 'Towards blue transformation: A vision for transforming aquatic food systems'.

xvi   M. Clark & D. Tilman (2017), 'Comparative analysis of environmental impacts of agricultural production systems, agricultural input efficiency, and food choice', *Environmental Research Letters*, 12:064016.

xvii   Hannah Ritchie (4 February 2020), 'Less meat is nearly always better than sustainable meat, to reduce your carbon footprint', OurWorldinData.org

xviii   Hannah Ritchie (24 January 2020), 'You want to reduce the carbon footprint of your food? Focus on what you eat, not whether your food is local', OurWorldinData.org

xix   Mike Berners-Lee (2021), *There Is No Planet B*, Cambridge University Press.

xx   S. Clune, E. Crossin & K. Verghese (2016), 'Systematic review of greenhouse gas emissions for different fresh food categories, *Journal of Cleaner Production*, 10.1016.

xxi   Rosie Watson (26 June 2020), 'Building a sustainable outdoor community after COVID-19', AdventureUncovered.com

xxii   ScienceDirect (2019), 'Meat Consumption', *Sustainable Meat Production and Processing.*

xxiii   C.Z. Watling, J.A. Schmidt, Y. Dunneram et al. (2022), 'Risk of cancer in regular and low meat-eaters, fish-eaters, and vegetarians: a prospective analysis of UK Biobank participants', *BMC Medicine*, 20(73).

xxiv   M. Springmann, H.C.J. Godfray, M. Rayner & P. Scarborough (2016), 'Analysis and valuation of the health and climate change cobenefits of dietary change', *PNAS*, 113(15).

xxv   Lydia Baxter (9 February 2021), 'What differences does a plant-based diet make to your carbon footprint?', impactnottingham.com

xxvi   Damian Carrington (10 October 2018), 'Huge reduction in meat-eating "essential" to avoid climate breakdown', *Guardian*.

xxvii   Mike Berners-Lee (2021), *There Is No Planet B*, Cambridge University Press.

xxviii   Hannah Ritchie (4 February 2020), 'Less meat is nearly always better than sustainable meat, to reduce your carbon footprint', OurWorldinData.org

xxix   Renee McGregor (2022), *More Fuel You*, Vertebrate Publishing.

xxx   Department of Health and Social Care (6 February 2012), 'Dangers of vitamin D deficiency highlighted', gov.uk

xxxi   IPCC special report on climate and land (2019), 'Food Security', ipcc.ch

Chapter 8 Fossil fuelling

i   R. Geyer, J.R. Jambeck & K.L. Law (2017), 'Production, use, and fate of all plastics ever made', *Science Advances*, 19:3(7):e1700782.

ii   R. Geyer, J.R. Jambeck & K.L. Law (2017), 'Production, use, and fate of all plastics ever made', *Science Advances*, 19:3(7):e1700782.

iii   Ipsos (April 2021), 'Perils of Perception: Environmental Perils', ipsos.com

iv   L. Zimmermann, G. Dierkes et al. (2019), 'Benchmarking the in Vitro Toxicity and Chemical Composition of Plastic Consumer Products', *Environmental Science & Technology*, 53:(19), pp.11467–11477.

v   Damian Carrington (7 December 2021), '"Disastrous" plastic use in farming threatens food safety – UN', *Guardian*.

vi   Oceana (11 March 2020), 'Recycling myth of the month: those numbered symbols on single-use plastics do not mean "you can recycle me"', oceana.com

vii   John Hocevar (18 February 2020), 'Report: circular claims fall flat', greenpeace.org

viii   Oceana (11 March 2020), 'Recycling myth of the month: those numbered symbols on single-use plastics do not mean "you can recycle me"', oceana.com

ix   Oceana (1 July 2021), 'Recycling myth of the month: that plastic bottle you thought you recycled may have been "downcycled" instead', oceana.com

x   George Bowden (25 October 2021), 'Recycling plastics does not work, says Boris Johnson', BBC News.

xi   Oceana (21 July 2020), 'Recycling myth of the month: plant-based bioplastics are not as "green" as some think', oceana.com

xii   Oceana press release (10 February 2022), 'Coca-Cola pledges to increase refillable bottles, but commitment lacks transparency', oceana.com

xiii   Michael E. Mann (2021), *The New Climate War*, Scribe UK.

Chapter 9 Well stuffed

i   L. Castaignède, F. Veny, J. Edwards & V. Billat (2021), 'The Carbon Footprint of Marathon Runners: Training and Racing', *International Journal of Environmental Research and Public Health*, 18(5), 2769.

ii   Jane Shaw (16 July 2021), 'Enough is enough', ethicalbusinessmarketing.com

iii   Ipsos (April 2021), 'Perils of perception: environmental perils – GB findings', ipsos.com

iv   Victoria Masterson (4 May 2021), 'Which climate action really reduces carbon emissions?', weforum.org

Chapter 10   Little bit activism

i   BBC News (14 April), 'What is Extinction Rebellion and what does it want?'

ii   Drilled News (19 April 2022), 'On climate, the public holds two sticks: activism and litigation (IPCC mitigation report, part 3)', drilledpodcast.com

iii   J. Gabbatiss, S. Hayes, J. Goodman & T. Prater, 'Analysis: how UK newspapers changed their minds about climate change', carbonbrief.org

iv   Lucas Chancel (7 December 2021), 'The richest 10% produce about half of greenhouse gas emissions. They should pay to fix the climate', *Guardian.*

v   Emma Pattee (10 December 2021), 'Forget your carbon footprint. Let's talk about your climate shadow', mic.com

vi   *dontlookup.count-us-in.com*

vii   Rebecca Solnit (23 August 2021), 'Big Oil coined "carbon footprints" to blame us for their greed. Keep them on the hook', *Guardian.*

viii Heather Higinbotham (29 March 2022), 'You're an eco-hypocrite, but it's not your fault – you've been sold a recycling lie', *Independent.*

ix   Zoë Rom (7 February 2021), 'Climate heroes and hypocrites', trailrunnermag.com

x   Mike Berners-Lee (2020), *How Bad Are Bananas?*, Profile Books.

xi   Leor Hackel & Gregg Sparkman (26 October 2018), 'Reducing your carbon footprint still matters', slate.com

       The cited study is B. Latane & J.M. Darley (1968), 'Group inhibition of bystander intervention in emergencies', *Journal of Personality and Social Psychology*, 10(3), pp.215–221.

xii   Jocelyn Timperley (10 September 2019), 'Why "flight shame" is making people swap planes for trains', BBC Future.

xiii Diego Arguedas Ortiz (5 November 2018), 'Ten simple ways to act on climate change', BBC Future.

xiv Christine Macaulay-Turner (14 January 2022), 'A conversation with Isabel Losada, Author of The Joyful Environmentalist', thefutureforestcompany.com

xv   Thomas S. Bateman (10 November 2021), '7 ways to get proactive about climate change instead of feeling helpless: lessons from a leadership expert', theconversation.com

xvi Mike Berners-Lee (2020), *How Bad Are Bananas?*, Profile Books.

xvii Zoë Rom (7 April 2021), 'Do my actions matter?', trailrunnermag.com

xviii Green Alliance (2018), 'Building the political mandate for climate action', green-alliance.org.uk

xix Jen Gale (2020), *The Sustainable(ish) Living Guide*, Green Tree.

xx   Leor Hackel & Gregg Sparkman (26 October 2018), 'Reducing your carbon footprint still matters', slate.com

xxi The Grantham Institute, '9 things you can do about climate change', imperial.ac.uk

xxii Mike Berners-Lee (2021), *There Is No Planet B*, Cambridge University Press.

© Stuart March

ABOUT THE AUTHOR

Damian Hall is a parent, accidental activist and record-breaking ultrarunner who has represented Great Britain and competed in some of the world's toughest races. His attempt to break into the top ten at the 105-mile Ultra-Trail du Mont Blanc was made into an award-winning film, *Underdog*; and the documentary *Totally FKT* followed him and John Kelly as they raced to break the Pennine Way record in 2020. Damian has also set records on the Paddy Buckley Round, the South West Coast Path, the Cape Wrath Trail, and Wainwright's Coast to Coast. He is a UK Athletics running coach and a widely published journalist who has made regular contributions to *Runner's World*, *Women's Running* and *Trail Running*. His previous books include *In It for the Long Run*, *A Year on the Run* and the official National Trail guide to the Pennine Way. He is a founding member of The Green Runners (*thegreenrunners.com*), a community of runners working towards a fitter planet. He is a big fan of midlife-crisis haircuts and tea.